T0277439

FIRST LOVE

FIRST LOVE

Guiding Teens through Relationships and Heartbreak

LISA A. PHILLIPS

ROWMAN & LITTLEFIELD
Lanham • Boulder • New York • London

Published by Rowman & Littlefield
An imprint of The Rowman & Littlefield Publishing Group, Inc.
4501 Forbes Boulevard, Suite 200, Lanham, Maryland 20706
www.rowman.com
86-90 Paul Street, London EC2A 4NE, United Kingdom

Distributed by NATIONAL BOOK NETWORK

British Library Cataloguing in Publication Information Available

Library of Congress Cataloging-in-Publication Data
Names: Phillips, Lisa A., author.
Title: First love : guiding teens through relationships and heartbreak / Lisa A. Phillips.
Description: Lanham : Rowman & Littlefield, [2025] | Includes bibliographical
    references and index. | Summary: "First Love is about teens' experiences in the
    maelstrom of crushes, relationships, and breakups. It offers parents the information
    they need to navigate the complexities and challenges of their child's first love and
    guidance on how best to support them on their journey through all of love's stages"—
    Provided by publisher.
Identifiers: LCCN 2024025471 (print) | LCCN 2024025472 (ebook) | ISBN
    9781538161685 (cloth) | ISBN 9781538161692 (epub)
Subjects: LCSH: Interpersonal relations. | Teenagers. | Love. | Parent and teenager
Classification: LCC HM1106 .P53 2025 (print) | LCC HM1106 (ebook) | DDC
    302—dc23/eng/20240712
LC record available at https://lccn.loc.gov/2024025471
LC ebook record available at https://lccn.loc.gov/2024025472

For my daughter

Contents

INTRODUCTION

Teen Relationships Matter

WHEN MY DAUGHTER WAS 13, SHE FELL IN LOVE WITH A NEIGH-bor boy. They went for walks in the woods, snuggled, watched movies, and texted each other as much as house iPhone rules would allow. My daughter had, certainly by middle school stan-dards, a healthy, sweet relationship with a nice boy who adored her.

I wanted to be ready for this, the beginning of her love life. I'd done what I could to help her be ready. When she was a toddler, I read to her *The Paper Bag Princess*, whose royal protagonist saved her beloved prince from a dragon, only to have him chastise her for wearing a paper bag after the dragon burned her gown. She dumps the prince and dances off on her own. My daughter mem-orized the princess's kiss-off line, gleefully shouting along as I read, "You look like a real prince, but you are a bum!" The message was clear: Be devoted and brave in love, but if your sweetheart isn't deserving, get out of the relationship.

Later, films and her own reading kept the conversation going. She disdained Bella of the *Twilight* series as too emo and self-subjugating. She favored Katniss of *The Hunger Games* and the open-hearted Hazel of *The Fault in Our Stars*—both as heroic and forthright as the Paper Bag Princess *and* with partners who shared these qualities. I struck up discussions about puberty and sex as often as she would let me and gave her books to supplement the meager information she was getting in health class.

I made getting ready for romantic love a priority because I knew it mattered. I am a journalist who specializes in writing about mental health and relationships and a professor who teaches a seminar of my own creation called Love and Heartbreak. I wanted her to recognize the signs of an unhealthy relationship. I also emphasized the ways healthy intimacy can be richly rewarding, expanding her perspectives, giving her the sense of feeling connected and understood, and supporting her well-being.

I knew that, for adults, having a committed partner in a healthy, long-term relationship is associated with all kinds of advantages: decreased risk for heart disease and other serious health problems, improved mental health, and longer life. Conversely, when relationships are unhappy or even, as science writer Florence Williams calls it, just "so-so," our health may suffer. Close relationships of all kinds can also do a lot to boost our health, though platonic ties don't often achieve the same level of constancy and commitment, nor unfortunately, do they enjoy the same level of social and economic privilege.[1]

None of this means my daughter needed to start dating as a teen. She didn't. No teen does, and teens shouldn't feel pressured—by peers, parents, community, or their social media feeds—to date before they're ready. But she would likely experience at least the desire for a relationship. I wanted her to value wherever she was along the wide spectrum of romantic feelings and experiences, not only so that she could enjoy healthy relationships later, but also because these feelings mattered in the moment. They would likely take up more space in her brain than anything else.

Before the neighbor boy came into her life, she seemed to have zero interest in dating, so her romantic future was purely theoretical. I imagined semichaperoned pizza outings, my husband and I sitting on one side of the restaurant, she and her date on the other. If she turned out to be attracted to boys, I would one day take her to the gynecologist for birth control, the way I knew a good mother should. I saw myself taking on these responsibilities with an attitude of wise maternal cool. I would be open-minded and informed, with the bonus of my professional insights. This stage, I thought, would be *so interesting to watch.*

But when it finally happened, I was a mess.

I worried about whether my daughter and her boyfriend were spending too much time together. Then, if I didn't see her boyfriend for a while, I wondered whether they were on the rocks. I checked in with my daughter about how the relationship was going, but not too often, because I didn't want her to think the boyfriend was now the only important thing in her life. My husband travels frequently. When he was out of town, I rushed out of work early, the way I used to when she was too young to be home alone, knowing I'd have to make up the hours somehow at night. I needed to be there, a sentry guarding against the temptation of long hours of fooling around in an empty house.

I didn't know the boyfriend's parents that well, even though we were neighbors. I did know that his mother ran a small business out of her home doing facials and body hair removal. Making a connection felt so urgent that I scheduled an appointment. She greeted me at the door with a conspiratorial smile. She knew exactly why I was there.

We talked about ground rules for the kids. Thankfully, we were on the same page: no closed doors, no being in the house without a parent present. We joked about becoming each other's "in-laws," the expression in our small town for the parents of the kid your kid is dating. We agreed that our children seemed well-matched. "It's like they're two wide-eyed deer who wandered into each other in the woods and were smitten," she said.

What we didn't dwell on but both knew: This wasn't going to last. It was a middle school relationship.

I could enforce the "bedroom door stays open" policy we'd set, but I couldn't control what was going on emotionally between my daughter and her boyfriend. He had so much power to delight her, thrill her, distract her, frustrate her, and hurt her. That frightened me. I wanted to shield her from the inevitability of rejection, blows to her self-esteem, the temptation to dim herself or neglect her needs for the sake of a relationship, and going too far sexually before she was ready.

One evening after she came home from her boyfriend's house, she plopped down on the couch, grinned, and shook her head in dreamy disbelief. "I'm just so gone," she said.

I knew what she meant. *So gone* was teen slang for feelings so deep they're impossible to explain.

"I'm happy for you," I said. I genuinely was. This was her first romance, a life event extolled from ancient poetry to K-pop, and it was going well.

But the words she used—*so gone*—hit home, taking on a different meaning. She felt so gone from *me*. She turned away from my hugs and answered my questions with pithy, dead-end answers that made clear she wasn't interested in talking. This change began before her relationship started—she was 13, after all—but the boyfriend's presence catalyzed it. He was a new and far more exciting attachment figure. I knew this was normal, but I had no idea how much it would affect me. Watching her be affectionate with her boyfriend was a startling preview of a future I'd never before considered: that from now on she would love others just as much or more than she loved me.

I felt gone, too, cast back in time to my own first love, which changed my life in ways I'm still grateful for. Yet the experience was, much of the time, more painful than gratifying, a description I'd use often for relationships in my teens and twenties. Before I met, at age 30, the man who would become my husband, I led a messy love life, characterized by boom-bust cycles of passionate beginnings followed by disappointments that left me, as I wrote about in my book *Unrequited*, obsessed and desperate. The strife of dating took a significant toll on my well-being and my life choices. I wanted my daughter to have a better love life than I had, but I also envied her for having the chance to try.

Even though this was my daughter's rite of passage, I also was going through something momentous: a renegotiation of my relationship with my increasingly independent child, a challenge to my identity as a mother and a woman, and a reexamination of my past. I felt, in the words of writer and friend Elizabeth Lesser, "broken open," grieving what had been yet receptive to meaningful change. My daughter's first relationship was a pointed shove, forcing me to see that I was losing my central place in her life—and that my presence on the sidelines was still crucial to the woman she was becoming. As my daughter distanced herself from me, my role seemed even more crucial. I was keenly aware of my emotional legacy as a parent: How I raised my daughter would shape how she would navigate intimacy. Was I doing a good enough job?

This was the beginning of my daughter's love life, her entry into the world of romantic relationships, an inevitable developmental shift. This is what we *do* as a species. Romantic love, attachment, and lust form the triad of mating drives that evolved to sustain the human race. Relationships are fundamental to what makes us human. But nothing about what was happening felt simple. A love life changes the dimensions of existence. Feelings become huge and hard to shake, demanding enormous amounts of time and energy. The line between self and other may blur, at times euphorically, at times confusingly. Entwined with these emotions are the moral questions of love and attraction. First relationships are mini-labs in ethics and responsibility: What do we owe our fellow human beings when we express desire; draw close; fall in love; disagree; lose interest; and cope with anger, sadness, and disappointment? And what do they owe us? How do privilege and power—matters my daughter's generation is highly attuned to—come into play?

Friendship can and does pose similar challenges, particularly in adolescence, but the acute vulnerability of romantic longing and love raises the stakes. The rewards are grander, and the risks are greater. Relationships can wreak havoc in young people's lives. Teens can get too enmeshed and dependent or feel overly responsible for the well-being of a partner. A partner may be a bad influence, affecting school performance, friendships, and other interests. Young people may struggle to express their needs and heed their partners' needs. They may be dealing with the strain of forging a connection in a world where their very existence is marginalized or threatened because of gender identity, sexual orientation, race, or other aspects of who they are. They may be among the growing number of teens who wake up each day feeling sad, hopeless, or contemplating suicide, in what CDC officials have called a mental health crisis that disproportionately affects girls and LGBTQ+ youth.[2] Dating abuse is shockingly common. One in three teens say they've experienced it, and about the same number admit to perpetrating it.[3] Even in the most fulfilling relationships, breakups are nearly inevitable, which for many teens is their first experience of real, wrenching loss.

My daughter belongs to a generation of young people wary about relationships and sex. Young people are dating later than in prior generations and doing less of it.[4] They're even having sex later in life than their parents did. In 1991, the majority of high schoolers—54 percent—said they'd had sex. By 2019, that figure was at 38 percent, and the pandemic drove the numbers in 2021 still lower, to 30 percent.[5] Generation Z (born after 1996) and Generation Alpha (born after 2010) will likely follow in the footsteps of their millennial forerunners, who put off marriage and even living together to unprecedentedly late ages. There are many potential causes for what seems like young people's tentative stance toward closeness, including social media, rising rates of anxiety and depression, and porn. Dating apps convey the message that there's always someone better out there, reducing attraction to a binary: swipe right, swipe left, move on. As young people become adults, growing economic inequality and student loan debt may delay their ability to live on their own, affecting their readiness to commit to a future with someone else.

The pandemic exacerbated all of this. Lockdowns and remote school jacked up the already-immense amount of time young people spent online. Dating was difficult and scary (if allowed at all), save for the few enviably solid teen partners allowed in each other's household bubbles. In the aftermath, many young people say they're still not the same.[6] Even if we might be tempted to celebrate the delay in sex and dating because of fewer worries about unwanted pregnancy, STIs, and other problems, there's not much to cheer about the conditions young people are reacting to, which continue to complicate their lives when they do start to date and become sexually active.

My college students tell me all the time how empowering it is to gain a better understanding of love and how intimacy influences people's lives. Learning about healthy relationships and what makes relationships unhealthy is liberatory. The whole endeavor becomes less daunting and more hopeful as their romantic selves grow wiser. This awareness—what we might call love-life literacy—can start much sooner. The adults in their lives should be a part of the process.

First Love is a book about young people's early forays into the maelstrom of crushes, dating, relationships, love, and the various forms of quasi relationships—friends with benefits, hookups, "situationships"—they're likely to face in their teen and college-aged years. In these pages, you'll read about how these experiences enliven and test young people emotionally, ethically, and socially; why the quality of their relationships matters to their well-being, now and in the future; and how they contend with the influence of their parents, peers, and communities. Sex is part of the story, of course, but this is pointedly not a book that focuses on sex. There's already a great body of resources out there on teens and sex; I recommend several in the bibliography. Sex tends to take up all the air in the room, putting a distant second the emotional dimensions of adolescent relationships. Here, I'm putting feelings first. I view the beginning of a young person's love life—a term that has a sexual connotation, but I'm reclaiming it as a phrase that applies whether sex is in the picture or not—as a meaningful rite of passage. Afterward, young people won't be the same.

Neither will their parents, and you'll also hear from them. This rite of passage, I've found, is a dual-generation one. Once a child's love life begins, parents won't be the same, either. Relationships transport an adolescent out of childhood and into the vulnerability and risks of intimacy. First loves illustrate the impossibility of protecting your child from loss and the inevitability of letting go. The beginning of a love life gives parents a glimpse into their emotional legacy and may lead them to reckon with time and age and life choices. In the bloom of youth, their children are living out all their romantic "firsts": first crush, first rushes of desire, first love, first sexual experiences. Parents, meanwhile, can't live these firsts all over again, as much as they might want to.

Many parents go through profound changes of their own when their teens start to date. A study by psychologist Laurence Steinberg's Families at Adolescence Project shows parents can feel envy and a longing for youth. Mothers may grapple with increased self-doubt, regret over past decisions, and a yearning to transform their lives. Fathers may become less satisfied with their marriages. When sons start to date, a significant percentage of fathers get more anxious and depressed. Some experience a rise in self-esteem, as if their sons' appeal is somehow a reflection of their own. I was struck in particular by the project's finding that parental angst in the teen years was more a factor in the popular notion of the midlife crisis than midlife itself. Forty percent of parents suffer a decline in mental health when their children enter adolescence, no matter what age they are.[7] That means a 36-year-old dad is just as susceptible to a so-called midlife crisis as a 50-year-old one, if both have a teen.

Being the parent of an adolescent, I've found, stirs up unresolved feelings from when we were teens. We're wired to remember our adolescence and young adulthood more vividly than any other period in our past. The strong emotions and developmental brain changes of these years heighten our memory, in what researchers call a "reminiscence bump."[8] This period, for many of us, is rife with unanswered questions and unresolved conflicts: why certain friendships imploded and others lasted long after they should have faded; whether your peers found you ugly or attractive, pretentious or interesting; why your parents couldn't truly see you for who you were; why the girlfriend who said she loved you suddenly didn't. The painful experiences of our youth shadow the adults we've become. As one parent friend sagely told me, "We are all still recovering from being teens."

As parents manage these heightened emotions, they have to figure out their role in what's happening. Gauging what is healthy and right and what is hazardous about adolescent relationships is the frontline challenge for parents. They must stay aware of a dynamic that they can only partially see. A romantic relationship, by nature, is largely private and independent, something young people do on their own. We can insist on open bedroom doors and curfews or even forbid relationships entirely, but teens—armed with phones and laptops, then driver's licenses—will find ways to get close anyway. Whether the household rules are strict or permissive, what develops between two adolescents can be beautiful and sustaining or unhealthy and abusive or a perplexing wilderness of feeling that challenges their sense of self. Parents may feel cast aside, as if they have no place in what's happening.

But they do.

Young people are hungry for information from their parents about love. A report from Making Caring Common, a Harvard-based organization dedicated to fostering young people's capacity to care about others and the common good, found that many teens and young adults feel unprepared for healthy, lasting romantic relationships. A remarkable 70 percent of 18- to 25-year-olds wished they had more information from their parents about the emotional aspects of dating.[9] My cohort of Generation X parents—one of the "least parented, least nurtured generations in U.S. history," as one study put it—knows well the drawbacks of the laissez-faire parenting we grew up with.[10] Many of us didn't hear much from our parents about dating and sex. Yet overly protective and invasive parenting—so-called helicopter parenting—isn't the answer either. Younger parents are millennials who grew up under its influence and don't want to raise their children that way. Children need to succeed and fail on their own in life and in love to develop resilience and character. We can't protect them from making mistakes and experiencing disappointment in relationships. But we can still be there for young people as engaged, knowledgeable, tuned-in, and caring adults who openly and explicitly value healthy relationships and the skills and insight they entail. And we can gain a deeper understanding of what young people go through when they begin their love lives.

The best way to do that is to listen to them. I've interviewed or corresponded with more than 100 young people and parents to explore the complexity and diversity of ways adolescents go through their first romantic experiences and how parents react as eros swoops into the house. The stories I've curated are in turn romantic, cautionary, sad, hopeful, and disturbing. They are portraits of how young love plays out in city streets, suburban neighborhoods, and rural outposts; school hallways and college campuses; tightly knit immigrant communities; households under economic strain and McMansions; and families of faith and secular families. I've sought out a wide variety of backgrounds, identities, and perspectives. To put my reporting in context, I delved into the peer-reviewed research on adolescence and romantic relationships, and I spoke with experts whose research and advocacy focus on teens and young adults.

While the book provides guidance on how parents and other adults can support young people, its most profound insights come from young people themselves. From them, I learned that, though it's worthwhile for the adults in their lives to remember what it was like to be young and in love, those reminiscences won't be enough if we want to fully support today's teens. We need to know what teens are going through now.

Young people are growing up in a world vastly different from the one in which their parents came of age. They have nowhere to hide, emotionally speaking, when they're grappling with the urgent emotions of attraction and love. Smartphones constantly within reach convey the impression that there's always something they can *do* to strike up a connection, fix (or cause) a problem, express an emotion, or distract themselves from an uncomfortable feeling. They can rarely truly separate from their peers, crushes, and partners. They may shut themselves away, alone in their bedrooms, but if they have a phone or a laptop, whoever or whatever was preoccupying them during the school day will still be there, wriggling in a TikTok video or smiling in "golden hour" light on Instagram.

Whenever I imagine growing up that way, I wither inside. The prospect strikes me not just as trying but also frankly *impossible* to endure. Yet this is the water teens now swim in. They routinely experience the most significant moments of their love lives on tiny screens. I think of the 13-year-old girl weeping with joy in the aisle of Walgreens because the girl she loved messaged her to ask her to be her girlfriend. Then there's the 16-year-old boy who told me he knew he shouldn't have ended his relationship over text, but he *didn't know how else to do it*. We can blame the ubiquity of technology, but just as telling is the boy's genuine bafflement. He had no idea how to cope with the moral dilemma of the rejector: You cause harm if you're honest, and you cause harm if you try to hide that you're no longer feeling the same way. His smartphone was the tool he used to dodge the larger problem: that young people, especially boys, need more support for their emotional lives and the skills to respectfully communicate what they feel.

Technology is also seen as the culprit for teens' declining mental health, though the science isn't settled on this question; many researchers feel it's a too simple explanation for a vastly complicated problem.[11] I'm not going to be the one to resolve this debate, but one of the most crucial takeaways from my years of talking to young people is this: *Every teen relationship story is also a mental health story.* I was struck by how many of my subjects either went through significant mental health problems while in relationships or tried to take care of partners in crisis. I think of Aaron, who realized too late that he'd overwhelmed his girlfriend with panicked texts about how badly he wanted to hurt himself, and Bethany, who confronted school administrators over their failure to help her boyfriend, only to have him turn on her after he spent time in a residential treatment program.

Even relationships without anyone in crisis can test young people in ways that make them feel temporarily out of their minds: the inherent obsessiveness of new love or a crush, the all-consuming grief of an unwanted breakup. Teens are remarkably literate when it comes to mental health. They care about it tremendously, and they'll go to great lengths to support each other. But I'm also troubled by the ways this sense of responsibility tries to compensate for adults who can't or won't see the struggles troubled young people and their partners undergo. Teen relationships can't make up for that. Relationships themselves can become part of the problem. They can be ruinous to mental health or worse. I think of Kiki, who endured emotional and sexual abuse by an older man who'd been in her life since she was 14. The abuse destroyed her self-esteem and isolated her from her parents, who didn't learn what was happening until years after the relationship was over.

Then there are the young people who can't turn to their parents at all to talk about relationships because they aren't allowed to have them. While plenty of parents have rules about dating, they likely more or less accept Western ideals about love: The heart wants what it wants. Parents can't do much to influence a young person's choice of partner, even if it means they have to stew in private feelings of disapproval and worry. For immigrants and others from more traditional cultures and religions, though, relationships are an extension of family and community. Parents exert considerable control over their children's dating lives, often posing a dilemma to their more assimilated children. I think of John and Athira, an Indian couple who kept their relationship secret for seven years, terrified of what would happen if her parents found out. Queer young people growing up in homophobic households bear a not-dissimilar burden. They have to hide their love. An underground relationship creates stress in every area of young people's lives. They can't be themselves or seek advice when they're living in fear.

This brings up another key finding of my project: Young people's lives and loves are increasingly, unabashedly queer, even as our political landscape becomes increasingly hostile toward LGBTQ+ identities. From conversations I've had with young people from Utah to Texas to North Carolina to New Jersey, I'm certain this phenomenon is not just a blue-state thing or a social media–fueled fad. Research confirms that fewer and fewer young people identify as straight.[12]

Even when being queer is hard, young people tell me, it's the ideal way to be. They question the rigid male/female binary of prior generations. They're less likely to assume their next partner will be the same gender as their last one. Transgender youth no longer see the gender they were assigned at birth as a life sentence, though they're terrified about the spread of state laws restricting access to gender-affirming care. Teen relationships have always raised questions of identity formation: how to become the person you want to be and whether you *can* become the person you want to be while staying loyal to someone else. Gender expansiveness and sexual fluidity complicate and, I believe, ultimately enliven these questions. I think of Chase, who identified as a lesbian when he fell in love with his girlfriend, then came out as trans. While he coped with how to go about his transition in a transphobic world, his girlfriend grappled with her own identity confusion: What did it mean that the girl she loved was becoming a boy?

How Chase and his girlfriend worked through these questions, challenging for any couple at any age, impressed me. What surprised me the most in my reporting was how often I was *inspired*. I was struck by young people's willingness to tackle problems, overcome obstacles, and tend to their individual growth while being part of a couple. They worked through excruciatingly painful breakups and emerged with new wisdom and strength. Parents, too, strived to stay connected and supportive. Nobody was perfect. Plenty of my sources made mistakes they're still trying to rectify. Several suffered wounds that are not yet healed.

If anything unified all of the people I interviewed, it was their willingness to take love seriously. As I wrote this book, I worked closely with Kay, a student who did her senior thesis on what she wanted out of love in the aftermath of an abusive high school relationship. In her final presentation, she spoke movingly about realizing a loving relationship would inevitably entail taking risks and being vulnerable, even though she still had a lot of fears about trust. "The risk in love will not be my physical, mental, or emotional well-being," she said. "You should never have to sacrifice yourself for a relationship." Afterward, a middle-aged woman in the audience, herself an abuse survivor, echoed what I felt in my own heart: "If I had done a project like this when I was in college, my life would have been entirely different." My student is one of many people I've come to know who see *love* as a verb, a project to nurture, figure out, and get better at. I hope they are a harbinger of things to come.

A few words on my approach to this book: I've written this book as a journalist and a parent, seeking to reach other parents and anyone invested in the emotional well-being of young people—educators, mental health professionals, the many unsung informal mentors and sages who make it a priority to matter to the teens in their lives, and teens and young adults themselves. I focus on experiences in adolescence, defined as the phase of life between childhood and adulthood. I often use the term *teen* as a rough synonym for the more clinical *adolescent*. The age range of adolescence, once considered 10 through 19, now extends to 24 to consider later transitions into the markers of adult life, such as a career, living independently, marriage, and family; adolescent brain maturation also continues well into the 20s, significantly affecting decision-making. Though most of the situations I describe occurred or began in the teen years, I also include accounts of relationships during the college years, a time when dating can be particularly fraught.

Though all the stories I recount are true, many of my sources requested that I use a pseudonym to protect their privacy. Occasionally other minor details are changed. I gathered the accounts in this book through in-depth interviews and, in several cases, by spending time in person with young people and their parents to get a richer view of their lives and communities. Over and over, I've been gratified by the trust my sources placed in me to write about them, given the sensitivity of the subject matter. They've also expressed gratitude to me for my attention and interest. As one person told me, "You're the first person who asked, 'What happened?' instead of 'What's wrong with you?'" From my subjects, I've learned that, while we may romanticize first love and sing along to countless angst-filled songs about heartbreak, it's rare in our culture to truly honor love and heartbreak as the meaningful, life-changing events that they are.

Speaking of which, you may be wondering what happened to my daughter and the neighbor boy. The relationship lasted a respectable six months before he broke up with her on the school bus. It was rough. What she said that night again and again: "There was so much I wanted to do with him. I had so many plans."

I held her and thought, *This is heartbreak.* The end of a narrative of hope. That essential truth doesn't change, whether a relationship ends at 13 or at 83. What did change is that she now knew what that felt like, and I knew what it was like to be the mother of a girl who'd faced her first significant loss. Her subsequent relationships would pose plenty of challenges to her and to me. But I no longer felt that she was gone from me or that I was gone from myself. She was doing the human thing of seeking love, and I had the great privilege of being her parent as she did so.

Chapter 1

Crush

Becoming a Romantic Being

GIA BARELY REMEMBERS ANYTHING FROM HER SOPHOMORE TO senior year high school classes. "All I did was sit there and think about Melanie," she said.

Melanie used to hate Gia. They went back a long way, taking tap and jazz dance classes together in their rural Pennsylvania town since they were, as Gia put it, "in the single digits." Two strong personalities, they jockeyed for friends and attention. Melanie was tall and blond, with a jocular, friendly air that drew people to her. Gia was moodier and edgier, favoring platform boots and multicolored hair dye; her warmth emerged slowly once she trusted you.

When Gia was 15 and Melanie was 14, their dance troupe went on tour. The trip started badly. On the plane, a mutual friend told Gia that Melanie thought she was bossy and couldn't stand her. Gia tried to shrug it off. The trip improved. She grew closer to the other dancers. By the end, they walked around in easily shifting pairs or trios, arms linked together—except Gia and Melanie, who carefully avoided touching each other.

After they returned, Gia felt more confident about her place in the social world of the dance center. She decided to try to defuse the tension with Melanie, so she invited her to hang out.

Being alone together for an afternoon was a revelation. They got along much better than she could have imagined. They listened to each other and laughed. The old tensions quickly felt meaningless, something they shed as easily as a pair of dance tights with a run at the calf. Soon they were spending as much time together as they could. The years of haughtily steering around each other at the dance center were over. They became a tightly bonded pair. During the long breaks in between dance classes, they huddled together on the scuffed carpeting in the corner of the center's lounge, talking and ignoring the homework splayed out in front of them.

Melanie moved Gia. She wrote poems of longing and illustrated them with paintings of nude women who looked nothing like Melanie yet had everything to do with her—so much so that Gia couldn't bear to show Melanie her work. Gia had been attracted to girls before; she'd identified as bisexual since middle school. What was new was the tenderness she felt, what she described as wanting to "fix what was broken" in Melanie, who was getting into drugs and drinking. Melanie drunk-called Gia late one night in an incoherent state of distress. Gia talked to her until she calmed down. Melanie showered her with inebriated gratitude. "You're the best thing that's happened to me," she told Gia. "I love you so much. I couldn't live without you."

The next day, Gia mentioned the call. Melanie said she didn't remember a thing about it. Gia didn't offer a recap. There was no use. Gia knew the rule: She was not to fall in love with Melanie. When another girl at the dance center developed a huge crush on Melanie, Melanie fiercely exiled her, warning the girl not to talk to her or her friends—basically, all the other kids in their dance classes. The girl became too distraught to attend class and dropped out. "I hate it when my friends fall for me," Melanie told Gia. "It's my biggest fear in friendships with girls."

Gia tried to be content with the limits. Melanie became her closest confidante, the first phone call she made when she was feeling down. Melanie was good at cheering her up but only to a point. A certain sadness always lingered because Gia wanted more. The longer she respected Melanie's boundaries, the more Melanie seemed to blur them. She sang love songs to Gia over the phone. She approached Gia from behind, wrapped her arms around her waist, and kissed the side of her neck. She watched Gia primping in the mirror and said slowly, as if astonished, "You're so beautiful."

Gia flailed in confusion, hope, and the terrifying prospect of one day risking their friendship to confess her love. She lived for Saturdays when they had dance class together. When Melanie didn't show up, which happened often, Gia would be left distressed over the prospect of another week of pining. She felt guilty over all the time she spent fixated on Melanie, all the real life she wasn't living because she was lost in daydreams about her crush.

THE URGE TO MINIMIZE TEEN CRUSHES (AND WHY WE SHOULDN'T)

It's just a crush. I've heard this phrase many times. We all have. That belittling *just* that insists that crushes don't count. They're not a real relationship. They're certainly not real love. They're cute. They're sweet. They'll go away. Yes, they hurt. Who doesn't remember how much crushes can hurt? But that will pass, like other seemingly unbearable sensations, a poison ivy of the soul in need of the salve of reality.

I am a longstanding defender of the crush, the feeling of intense infatuation for another person, often someone unattainable or inappropriate. Though crushes are most strongly associated with adolescence, they can be experienced at any age. Crushes are, at least at first, delicious, a reason to put on lip gloss. Your life is a story full of suspense, the driving question of *Do you like me back?* propelling you forward in anticipation. You become a detective, looking for clues that your feelings might be returned. Your confidantes rally around you, willing spies in the quest. That's the fun part, the stage that feels good. If only crushes could stay there in that sweet spot, but they usually don't.

Wanting someone you can't have may get lonely and frustrating. The fun is over, and no one knows what to do anymore, except to dismiss the whole sorrowful situation by telling you *It's going nowhere. Move on.* Which is very hard to do. Instead of dismissing crushes or feeling ashamed of them or letting them get out of hand with behavior we may regret, we are better off considering what our feelings might mean. If they can't take us into a relationship, where might they lead us instead? What can this attraction tell us about our world, about who we are, what we want to become, and how we want to love?

When I notice the tendency to minimize teen crushes, I think, "We want to make crushes small because we don't want to acknowledge how big they really are." Emotionally, they are the most real thing in the world, particularly for young people new to romantic feelings. Watching the teens in our lives endure their first crushes is scary, a reminder of the long-ago (or not-so-long-ago) times when we felt that irrefutable magnetic pull toward another, a pull that seemed both destined to lead to a miraculous love story and totally doomed.

Crushes, though, are not small matters in popular culture. They are the subject of countless pop songs; films; television shows; YA novels; TikTok videos; and confessional Finstas, the fake Instagram accounts teens try to hide from their parents. Children learn early on that we are supposed to have crushes and that they will be both glorious and sad, a song we'll want to sing over and over.

Starting from the time her daughter was in preschool, Donna, a New Jersey mother, played old *Partridge Family* episodes for her and reminisced about David Cassidy, Donna's first celebrity crush. She and her daughter mooned together over Hanson, a popular boy band at the time. When her daughter started having crushes on boys at school, Donna would ask her for the daily blow-by-blow: Did you talk with him today? What did he say? "It was fun to talk to her about boys," Donna said. It all seemed part of the joys of girlhood. Donna and her sister had grown up giggling over celebrity crushes and talking for hours about real-life ones.

When her daughter entered adolescence, Donna became self-conscious about these moments. "Did I encourage crushes and boys too early?" she worried. "Kids learn from us—the things we stress and make important become important to them."

It's a common concern. Without question, parents can over-emphasize romance, particularly if they have girls. We live in a culture that makes it easy to do so. But I'll play devil's advocate for a moment. Parents can easily pivot from celebrating crushes to meaningful conversations about romantic feelings, which is what Donna eventually did. When her daughter's little girl crushes turned into teen crushes and then into relationships, her daughter could turn to Donna because they were used to talking about love.

When young people have their first big crush, the predominant script for how it's supposed to go is the one with the happy ending: Person A crushes on Person B in tortured secrecy. Person B, it turns out, has been crushing back all along. Somehow, they suss each other out, *et voila!* They ride off into the sunset together. A crush that doesn't end in reciprocation seems a failure, a nothing, something to move beyond quickly and forget about, at least after you console yourself by rewatching *Riverdale* and playing Olivia Rodrigo songs on repeat on your Spotify queue.

Crushes do pass. But while they're happening, they are not nothing. A crush seizes the brain and body in the same way that falling in love with the person you may end up spending the rest of your life with does. Crushes are a young person's first experience of what in my Love and Heartbreak seminar I call "the symptoms," the traits of romantic love that anthropologists have identified in societies across the globe: Obsessive thinking. Possessiveness. Mood swings that revolve around whether the object of your crush offers a kind word or ignores you. Stomach butterflies, a pounding heart, high energy, sexual desire, and a longing for emotional union.[1] These symptoms are precisely what gives a crush the potential, at 15 or 84, to spark a relationship. They're also what creates the frustration of an attraction that isn't returned. As biological anthropologist Helen Fisher told an online magazine for teen girls, "A crush is basically romantic love. The same brain system and neural pathways are triggered."[2]

Romantic love, as research by Fisher and her colleagues has illuminated, is a drive, like thirst and hunger, propelling us toward the reward of a desired mating partner.[3] We don't need a partner the way we need water and food, but securing one does help us survive and thrive in fundamental ways. In the primitive beginnings of humankind, the drive of romantic love likely evolved as a trait through natural selection, because two people who are crazy about each other are more likely to protect each other from threats, reproduce, and stay together long enough to provide the shared resources that help their young survive.

Even though teen crushes probably won't lead to this future, that doesn't diminish their force. As Gia described it, you feel like there's no room in your brain for anything else. Whether a crush is met with rejection or crashes against an immovable boundary or goes nowhere because you can barely put together a sentence in the presence of your crush, the letdown can trigger shame, guilt, and self-castigation. The way Gia described herself—as having an "addictive personality"—is something I hear often from young people. They're coming of age in a culture where people under 25 check their phone an average of about 200 times a day, binge-watching has replaced appointment television, and jump-drive-style vapes make it easy to sneak hits of—and get hooked on—nicotine or weed.[4]

Romantic attraction can feel like yet another form of addiction because it *is*. The feelings engage the pathways of the brain's reward system, including the dopamine-rich regions associated with addiction.[5] As Fisher told me in an interview, "It's a wonderful addiction when it's going well, and a perfectly terrible one when it's going poorly."[6]

Inasmuch as Gia wished she could control her yearning, she was also in awe of it. "I had never experienced that feeling before, and even though it was so unrequited, I still didn't want to let go of it," Gia said. "I had the capacity to love somebody. That felt really good. So I hung onto the hope that she would turn around and love me back."

While plenty of young people emerge from adolescence without having had a romantic relationship or their sexual debut, very few will do so without having had a hefty crush. Crushes can start well before adolescence, as young as the preschool years, and they can strike at any age.[7] That said, crushes are a quintessential experience—perhaps *the* quintessential experience—of being a teen.

Adolescents are in a time of rapid change. They're driven to take risks and explore, think creatively, and gain independence from their parents. A new capacity for abstract thinking leads them to reflect on who they are and their place in the world. They hunger to engage deeply with peers. They're given to intense emotions and operatic mood swings. They become more sensitive to what people think of them and more judgmental as they hone their abilities to interpret social situations independently of their parents. Increased levels of sex hormones bring on feelings of attraction and arousal, potent new sensations that can be overwhelming, uncomfortable, and frightening. The prefrontal cortex, the region most involved with decision making, reflection, thinking, planning, and moral behavior, is still developing, making them susceptible to peer pressure, risk taking, and emotional outbursts. Brain activity increases in the neural circuitry involving dopamine, a neurotransmitter associated with reward-seeking behavior and integral to romantic love.[8] All of these changes prime young people for the euphoria and the angst of a mind-seizing crush.

The irony is that, with all that is transforming in the brains, bodies, and lives of young people, crushes are fantasies of permanence, of undying commitment and affection. Not in a delusional way. Somewhere inside, teens are fully aware that they won't feel this way always, and they won't really want to be with their teen crush until the end of time. But when a crush is most vivid, that knowledge is just a whisper compared to the loud volume of the dream. And there's something to this, given the value of love and close relationships in adult life. It makes sense that young people spend so much time dreaming of lasting love, given how vital relationships are to the well-being of the adults they will become.

THE IDENTITY CRUSH

Some crushes, though, are more about the possibilities of the self than the possibilities of intimate love. Jolene has had crushes ever since she can remember. When she was six, she started liking her brother's best friend, who was five years older than she was, because he stuck up for her when her brother picked on her. The boy came along on a family trip. From the back seat of her parents' minivan, she scratched out a love note. "He crumpled it up and threw it back to me," she said. "My dad makes fun of me to this day." In fifth grade, she offered her email to a substitute teacher she adored in hopes they would stay in touch over Google Plus. He laughed, told her she was sweet, and politely declined to take it.

When Jolene was a high school junior, she struck up a Snapchat conversation with Peyton, a classmate she described as athletic, smart, and totally out of her league. She was amazed when he readily responded to her and how easily their correspondence flowed. They discovered they'd had the same knee injury and the same doctor. She expressed her cynicism about their large, competitive suburban North Carolina high school and how preoccupied the students were with checking off all the right boxes so they could get into good colleges. He seemed to understand, even though he was thriving there. He earned good grades in challenging AP classes and had plenty of friends.

Jolene wasn't thriving. She had trouble focusing on schoolwork, and her grades weren't good. Her injury kept her from playing soccer, which had always been an important outlet for her. Her older sister, who went to the same school, had a developmental disability. Jolene was her sister's main source of support and protection, a fact that made Jolene both proud and acutely self-conscious. No one else she knew carried such a burden. The Snapchat conversations with Peyton made her feel that, if circumstances were different, *she* could be different, more at ease socially and more accomplished. She imagined how surprised her peers would be if they knew how often she and Peyton were talking online.

In person, they were nearly strangers. They had class together first period and last period, his presence bookending each trying day, but they acted as if their exchanges never happened. "It was really easy to Snapchat him, but I couldn't talk to him in person," she said.

She transferred to a small, private school to get more academic and social support. The Snaps ended. "I don't think it was ever really him," she said. "It was the idea of him." Their connection online, she told me, made her feel like she was a part of what she felt excluded from: the inner circle of high-achieving students who also enjoyed life, or so it seemed from the Instagram photos they posted. Peyton, she believed, was free in a way she wished she could be. "I associated him with having a pretty easy life and succeeding," she said.

Carl Pickhardt, an Austin psychotherapist and author of several books about adolescence, coined the term *identity crush* to describe infatuations adolescents have for people they admire: kids they perceive as cooler or more talented or edgier than they are; authority figures; mentors. This is where the teacher/camp counselor crush fits in, along with crushes on enviable peers. The person with the crush gives a lot of power to the crushee, wanting approval, affection, and attention. Identity crushes can be sexual or romantic, though they aren't always so. The feelings are a blend of veneration, envy, and imitation. Though the crush seems to be about the beloved other—what the person does, wears, says, and is—it's more about the person who's smitten.

Parasocial relationships—one-sided, imagined social ties with celebrities—can fall into this category, as well. Research has found that celebrity crushes, characterized by the near impossibility of reciprocation, can help adolescents in identity formation by providing a safe outlet for them to experiment with different ways of being.[9]

"Understand that an identity crush is all about self," Pickhardt said. "One projects personal ideals on someone else who seems to possess ultimately desirable traits and characteristics. Most identity crushes are distortions. The hope is that from association, similarity may grow." This idea goes back to the Jungian notion of the anima and the animus: Men repress the anima, the emotional, nurturing, female side of their psyches, while women repress the animus, the authoritative, creative side. Men and women fall passionately in love with each other, Jung theorized, in an unconscious effort to access this forbidden, dangerous other side of the self. However gendered and heterocentric these notions seem today, the core idea still resonates: We may fall for the people we want to become.

We need to watch for red flags in this dynamic. The very authority and privilege that makes idealized figures so desired can leave their admirers susceptible to manipulation or worse. An authority figure may try to turn a teen crush into a sexual relationship. Even seemingly remote crushes may take advantage of a teen's adoration. Several prominent YouTube personalities have been accused of grooming underage fans. "The idealization makes teens willing to operate on the admired person's terms," Pickhardt said.

It's the dangerous side of the feeling of "I'll do whatever it takes to be liked by such a wonderful person and make me more like them." More typically, Pickhardt said, the message of identity crushes is "what attracts you to this other person is partly how you wish to be yourself," a dream of becoming that has little to do with forming a real relationship. Parents and other supportive people, he advises, can use the dream as a starting point. They can ask young people about what qualities they admire in the other person and what their desires might signal about who they want to become. They can encourage young people to become their own version of those qualities in a way that remains authentic to who they are.

This kind of conversation can move into complicated territory. Teen crushes are transgressive, refusing to heed rigid high school hierarchies and social divides. There are reasons Jolene wasn't as free as she imagined Peyton to be (and Peyton himself may not have been as free as the Peyton she idealized), reasons that had to do with the limited ways our society contends with mental health challenges, different learning styles and intellectual abilities, and the bonds of family and community. While Hollywood crush plots thrive on romances that leap over social and cultural boundaries (think the poor girl/rich guy plot of *Pretty in Pink*), real-life crushes may dead-end at them. Unpacking the reasons why a Peyton is so alluring may help young people—and their parents, who may feel uneasy when their child has a crush on someone unobtainable—see these divides with more clarity.

A DRESS REHEARSAL FOR RELATIONSHIPS

Adolescent crushes, then, are wake-up calls: to existential questions of the self, to sexuality and desire, to the possibilities of romantic closeness, to the vulnerability of caring for someone else. The term originated in the 19th century, when *crush* was slang for a dance or social gathering so crowded that young men and women might accidentally-on-purpose brush up against each other and meet. The term eventually evolved to describe what we know it to be today: a strong romantic attraction to another person who either doesn't reciprocate or whose feelings are unknown.

While historically crushes incubated in physical proximity—think of the attractions that spark in Jane Austen's ballroom dance scenes—today their drama often plays out at a distance. It's not unusual for teens to become infatuated with someone they only know through social media. They'll notice someone on an Instagram comment thread, exchange a witty quip or two, then check out the person's photos and stories and try a DM (direct message). They may never meet face-to-face because they're too far away or, as in the case of young people coming of age in a pandemic, forced to isolate at home. They may "talk" (the term young people use for romantic or sexually tinged messaging and texting, not actual talking) with crushes for hours, hoping the situation turns into something more. These kinds of experiences are near-universal rites of passage for young people. Something huge builds in an online exchange that can't transition into real life, no matter how real it feels as they hunch over their phones, tapping furiously into tiny bubbles on their screens.

Whether crushes are nurtured remotely or by being shoulder to shoulder in the same carpool, the experience can be brutal. The literal meaning of the word *crush*—forceful compression that breaks, damages, distorts—underscores its emotional impact. The word, as noun and verb, seems unavoidable in describing the occurrence, both for lovelorn adolescents and parent witnesses. A father I know told me in an email that his 14-year-old son finally confessed his feelings to his two-year crush, only to be "friend-zoned"—told he couldn't be considered as anything but a friend. "He was crushed," he wrote, "and so was I."

Crushes, like teenagers, can be rebellious, defying social norms and divides of age, social status, and culture. Early 20th-century books on adolescent development cast first crushes on the opposite sex as a proper harbinger of normal adolescent development, while warily noting the ferocity of same-sex crushes, particularly among girls. Writing in the 1930s, psychologist Mary Chadwick likened the jealousy, affection, and constant companionship characteristic of girl-on-girl crushes to opposite-sex adult couples newly in love: "Everything else fades out, or is pushed into the background until the blaze of this fierce passion has burnt itself out."[10] She and her contemporaries maintained that same-sex attractions were only a stage. Once they were old enough, their desire would find the appropriate heterosexual outlet—or, in rare cases, persist into adult homosexuality, then seen as an uncommon psychiatric disorder in need of correction.[11]

Now, we know better. Crushes are early clues to sexual orientation, though not always reliable ones. An 18-year-old gay high school senior told me his first huge crush, in middle school, was on a girl he admired. A 17-year-old girl who described herself as "boy-crazy straight" began to think otherwise when she became infatuated with a female classmate. Crushes aren't destiny. Rather, they're part of the long exploration process young people may go through to figure out their sexual orientation. Though most of Gia's sexual experiences have been with males, she considers her crush on Melanie to be not only the most significant romantic experience of her life but also one of the most significant life experiences, period—a description I heard again and again from young people about their crushes.

What Gia's crush indicated about her sexual orientation was much less important to her than the role it played in her emotional growth. Before she and Melanie became close, she didn't see herself as a likable person. She attended the same small school since kindergarten. By high school, she was convinced that everyone hated her. When she developed breasts in 10th grade, she became, for a while, a "shiny new thing" to the boys her age, who until then had excluded her from parties and cut her down when she spoke in class. Hungry for "attention, any attention, it didn't matter if it was negative attention," she fooled around with several. The encounters made her briefly feel superior to the boys. Then she got sad. "It was like, I literally gave you everything I had, and that wasn't good enough," she said. "Deep down, I wanted more. I wanted approval. I wanted acceptance. I wanted love. But the sexual was all I could get."

Gia, who was 19 when we spoke, looked back at her crush as a relatively safe outlet for her intensity. All her life, she'd been told she was too sensitive and emotional. Her peers, especially the boys, would mock her when they saw her crying over a slight and gossiped skeptically about her bouts with depression. Melanie, in contrast, gave her loving support. Gia believed that getting what she wanted—a romantic relationship with Melanie or someone else—"would have just destroyed me," she said. "Knowing myself, I would have given them my all. I was so fragile in high school. If it didn't work out, that would have crushed me, and usually high school relationships don't work out."

Crushes can be a way to experience many of the emotions of romantic relationships without the very real responsibilities of reciprocated love. One of the baseline conditions for a healthy relationship is self-awareness, or the ability to perceive and understand what makes you who you are: your personality, actions, values, beliefs, emotions, and thoughts. Adolescence is a time when young people are gaining new levels of self-awareness, particularly when it comes to their emotions, but it's a messy and erratic work in progress.[12] They may feel confident and happy in platonic relationships with classmates yet know little about what they believe and feel about how a romantic relationship should go or what they want from it. They may not yet be ready for the hard work of being close to someone else—the times when love entails a level of honesty, intimacy, or generosity beyond their abilities. Crushes are a way to experience some of the challenges and emotions of dating before you're ready to take the risk of getting close to someone else. Crushes can also be simply what happens en route to a relationship, that time when attraction builds and you gradually figure out that the other person is feeling the same way. Earlier on—a.k.a. the middle school years—the odds of a crush evolving into something mutual aren't good. If you've ever seen a couple of sixth graders on a date, the reason is immediately apparent: The kids hardly know what to say to each other, the chasm vast between inner fantasy and the reality of their social skills and maturity level. From a parent's point of view, early adolescent crushes are familiar—we've all been there—yet surreal because they function with a logic all their own. A case in point from my daughter's peer group, circa age 12: A girl secretly crushes on a boy. By the time she learned, just a few months later, that the boy was crushing back on her, she'd lost interest and got a little freaked out by his attention. "It's sad that she couldn't somehow summon back what she used to feel," a parent friend sighed wistfully to me, as if what happened was a missed moment in a rom-com. But the missed moment is, at that age, what's supposed to happen. In early adolescence—ages 10 through 14—young people are more interested in popularity and social status than in dating. Fewer than 20 percent of middle schoolers have reciprocated romantic relationships. The majority experience at least one crush.[13] Developmental psychologists call this the "infatuation" stage, when feelings of attraction don't include much actual interaction.[14]

The all-imagination, no-contact nature of crushes is, in early adolescence, a very good thing. Having a crush doesn't entail the same risks as being in a couple, particularly for younger teens, whose relationships tend to be fragile and don't last long. Researchers call extensive dating at an early age "pseudomature behavior," which is what it sounds like—acting older than you're emotionally ready for, which is stressful. As teens get older, greater maturity and self-awareness helps them reap the benefits of relationships and avoid the risks.[15] There's no question adolescent relationships can be fun, healthy, supportive, and safe, even when they start young. It's just that they have a much greater chance of being all these things at 16 than at 12.

Even with minimal real contact, early crushes can still feel enormously risky, an unfamiliar eruption of vulnerability, sadness, and loneliness.[16] The summer when he was 11, Dominic became infatuated with Alice, a girl at his YMCA day camp in Hartford, Connecticut. "It was the first time I thought about how pretty girls look," he recalled on a Zoom call from his college dorm room in Maine. "She had a really gentle voice, and it was nice to talk to her." He had no idea what came next after the thrill of their brief daily conversations. On a field trip bus ride, he confided in a friend that he liked Alice. The friend stood up in the aisle and yelled, "Dominic has a crush on Alice!" The bus erupted in laughter. Dominic froze, stunned by his friend's betrayal and the shame of exposure. When they got back to the YMCA, he ducked behind the gymnasium bleachers and wept as quietly as he could. The unsettling realizations piled up: Girls were starting to flock around and flirt with other boys but not him. He was always the one to strike up the conversations with Alice. He didn't think he was attractive. She couldn't possibly find him so. He was infatuated with her anyway.

From his perch beneath the bleachers, he watched her walk toward him. She ducked her head and crawled under to join him. She patted his back. "Are you okay?" she asked. The tears kept coming. She rested her hand on his shoulder. He knew Alice consoled him out of pity, not genuine affection. Her touch amazed and embarrassed him at once. He rarely cried. His mother, a chemical engineer, and his father, a machine operator at a lumber company, were Peruvian immigrants who'd come to the United States to better their lives. They pushed him to do well in school. When his uncles teased him about girls, his mother countered with the insistence that he stay focused on his studies. His father wouldn't talk to him about relationships or sex until years later, when Dominic was 17 and had his first girlfriend. In his interview with me, when he was a college sophomore, Dominic was struck by not only the intensity of his shame and grief but also by the power of his distress. His tears allowed him to win attention and make his inner world known, a strange relief mixed with the awareness that "a boy, a man, is not supposed to cry. That's how I grew up my whole life."

What stood out to me about Dominic's story was the opportunity of a crush to foster emotional literacy: how to identify, understand, and respond to strong feelings. We send different messages about this to boys and girls. Starting from preschool age, boys are told, explicitly and implicitly, that they must hide their emotions to be accepted by their peers. They don't stop wanting to reveal what's inside of them, but there aren't many social situations where it's safe to do so.[17] The moment Dominic confided in a friend, he was mocked. At home, matters of the heart were a non-topic, leaving him without a way to process what had happened, even though it felt momentous.

Girls seem to have it better. Crushes and anything else having to do with romance are an acceptable—indeed, a highly valued—topic of conversation among girls, who relish and dissect each microdevelopment of an infatuation.[18] Girl code would condemn outing a friend's crush so publicly and so derisively, though girls often take it upon themselves to investigate the viability of each other's crushes. None of this inoculates girls against rejection, shame, judgment, and disappointment—the unique sting of mourning a relationship that never was.

First crushes yank boys' submerged emotional vulnerability to the surface, presenting an opportunity for parents and other trusted adults in their lives to provide a safe outlet for expressing feelings. Even though girls typically (though not always) have more social permission to be emotionally expressive, they need this space, too, as they sort through the difficult questions a crush raises about attractiveness, desire, and self-worth. All genders need to be heard without derision. Parents may feel that treating a crush as no big deal will help convince their child that it isn't, lessening the pain. More likely, young people will feel that you don't get them and no one understands how they feel.

Supporting a child who has a crush sends the message that what they are going through is important. Because crushes are such irresistible news items in early adolescence—everyone's always talking about who likes whom—the discretion of adult confidantes matters. The new and potent social radar young people develop in adolescence means they'll find out when parents are discussing their business, and they don't like it. This had me in a bind. From the time I became a mother, I relied on my local parent friends to work through the challenges of child raising. Suddenly (and reasonably), my daughter let me know that wasn't okay. I remembered all too well the vulnerability of my first crushes, a vulnerability I wanted to shield my daughter from—and knew I likely couldn't. I wanted support, as any parent would when what's happening with their child stirs them up. But I had to respect my daughter's privacy.

THE CRUSH IS A MILESTONE, TOO

Romantic and sexual rites of passage are defined by reciprocation: the first date, the first relationship, and the sexual debut (a more inclusive phrase for *losing your virginity*, a term that centralizes the first heterosexual intercourse). A first big crush, I believe, is an equally significant milestone. Crushes draw young people into their futures as romantic beings, previewing both the pleasure and the pain of love. First crushes send young people through the proverbial looking glass. In one instant they are children who know nothing of romantic yearning, and the next they feel its force. The self-possession they never realized they had is replaced with daydreams that career from the delight of possibility to the anguish of uncertainty.

I remember from my own first crush a distinct feeling of loss: I could no longer immerse myself in a book in the pure way

I used to. The boy in my head competed with the words on the page, and I was disappointed in myself for letting that happen. What I would now tell my younger self: It can suck to moon over someone who doesn't know you're alive. But what you are going through is fundamental to what it means to be alive. Your crush ties you to an essential force in life, a form of human connection that has the potential to be sustaining and gratifying, even if the particular connection you're longing for isn't meant to be. You can honor what you're going through for what it has to teach you about understanding love and its inherent risks.

Crushes are love-life learning experiences. Sometimes the lessons are concrete. As her daughter Mallorie approached adolescence, Serena's main concern was teaching her that what she wanted mattered. Serena was sexually assaulted when she was a teen. She assured Mallorie that she would always come to get her if she found herself in an uncomfortable situation. "She should know she has a voice and that it's expected that she be heard and that she be treated with kindness and respect and that she can have whatever boundaries are important for her," Serena told me.

When Mallorie was 12, she started flirting with a boy over text and FaceTime. Serena sensed the crush was getting "a little obsessive" and warned her daughter to ease up, to no avail. Then the boy's mother called.

"Please tell Mallorie to chill out," she asked Serena. The mother said that Mallorie was messaging her son too often. Even when he didn't respond to her, Mallorie would press on, asking him pointedly, "Do you like me?" He told her he wasn't interested. She kept asking him anyway, in hopes of getting a different answer.

Serena's first thought was "Have I not taught her any self-worth?" She was a single mother. Mallorie's father was no longer in their lives. Was this the inevitable price—Mallorie scrambling to win over a withholding male? "I was mortified," Serena said. "I put it on myself that she was putting herself in that position." It's one of the many confessions of guilt I've heard from parents: that their family situation or personal shortcomings are to blame for their kids' missteps in love. Serena pushed past these feelings to reinforce the point: the importance of boundaries works both ways. "I said, 'Hey, put yourself in his position. How do you think that feels? You are making this boy feel uncomfortable. I don't think you'd appreciate being treated that way.'" Mallorie got the message and stopped reaching out.

The workshops I've led on healthy relationships, developed by Stony Brook University psychology professor Joanne Davila, emphasize that one of the foundational conditions for romantic closeness is emotion regulation: the ability to cope with your own feelings and moods. Crushes are the first proving ground. The emotions are intense and nearly constant. Crushes have the potential to help young people learn to distinguish between the risk of expressing interest—a risk anyone trying to start a relationship takes—and making someone else responsible for soothing their outsize feelings.

Parents' first impulses are often to shield their child from harm. We want to beg the universe for the crushee to answer that text, smile back, invite our child to the junior high dance. But it's not up to the crushee to fix the mess of feelings—some of them stubbornly painful—that romantic yearning entails. Asking for a relationship is just that—asking—and it means being prepared to cope with rejection. Consent is typically framed in terms of physical touch, but it should also be used to assess emotional willingness, even before sexual desire enters the picture.

A mother told me about her seven-year-old son's crush on a classmate. He excitedly detailed his daily interactions with the girl, whom he proudly called "my crush." Every morning, he gifted her with a drawing. An adorable gesture, his mother thought— as long as it's wanted. "I told him, 'It's important to make sure the attention is welcome and wanted when you have a crush on someone. You need to ask her if it's okay to keep giving her your artwork,'" she said. "He did, and she said yes."

Crushes raise the question, When is it worth it to move from crushing to courting, and what is the right way to do so? If you're the crushee, how do you let someone down with kindness and dignity? None of these questions have ready answers. Crushes open the door for parents and children to become "romantic philosophers," approaching love as a subject of study and reflection. It's an idea from the Harvard Graduate School of Education's Making Caring Common, a project with the vision of a "world in which children learn to care about each other and the common good."[19] Adolescents enter their love lives with ideas and expectations about what romantic relationships entail. They're influenced by experiences with family and friends and portrayals of idealized relationships in television, movies, and social media. A crush is an early opportunity to unpack these impressions. What makes someone attractive? What social forces shape our desires? Why does a crush stir up so much feeling, even when you barely know the person?

Young people's willingness to share what they're going through varies widely. Some are eager to confide. I know of young people who ask their parents to rehearse scenarios as they figure out what they should say to let crushees know they care. Plenty of adolescents, though, won't want to go there. Privacy isn't just a big deal to teens; it's also inherent to their quest to individuate. They may be reluctant to answer questions about crushes or anything else that develops in their love lives. But in my conversations with young people about what they would have wanted from their parents during middle school and high school, it's abundantly clear that the degree of interest parents show matters a lot. Even if adolescents don't want to talk, parents can still send the message that love and relationships are subjects worthy of curiosity, discussion, and debate. Parents can also keep trying. A 13-year-old who clams up may be more open in a month or even the next day.

When parents don't ask or are dismissive or treat relationships and sex as shameful, teens get the message that they're on their own.

Films and television shows are often effective entry points with young people who don't want to talk about their own situation. This can start with the gender dynamics of Disney princess movies; then *Twilight*; then the workplace flirtations in *The Office* or the ironic plot twists of *Sex Education*, a series featuring a mother and teen son gifted in their ability to fix the love lives of others yet clueless when it comes to their own.

Being reflective about love, I've come to believe, isn't just something good for children. It supports parents' well-being, too. Many of the parents I've interviewed spoke of their efforts to raise their children in a healthier way than they were raised. How their children cope with crushes feels like an early hint of whether the strategy is working and whether their children will be able to make better choices in life and love as a result. Sari, a 55-year-old middle school teacher with two adolescent sons, grew up with an abusive father who "had a lot of anger against females" and a mother who routinely dismissed Sari's emotions. "She would say I was pretending, that I can't really be in love," she said. "So whatever feelings I had for boys, I never felt like I could share that with my mom." Her love life was rocky from the start: Her first boyfriend, in eighth grade, cheated on her with her best friend. "It reinforced all the messages I had from my parents: You're not worthy. You're not good enough. I would go over to his house and sit on the steps and cry and beg for him to come back to me."

From the time her oldest was very young, Sari was intent on being a different kind of parent. "I did a lot of talking. Like if we were checking out at the supermarket and he wanted gum, I would have a conversation about it! I felt it was important that he felt like he was respected. I didn't ever push away his feelings." Later, when he confessed his feelings for girls, Sari took him at his word. She emphasized that what he was going through wasn't just about his own desires; the girls he liked also needed to be respected for who they were. "I did everything I could to be accepting and talk to him about what was good," she said. "I told him, 'When you do have a partner, that should be the person you're nice to. You shouldn't be nicer to strangers than you are to your loved ones.'"

None of this, of course, protected her son from being hurt. In his sophomore year of high school, he had a rough breakup with his first serious girlfriend. "But he didn't kowtow," Sari said. "I saw his determination to take good care of himself. He took a stand and told her what he needed. And when that wasn't going to be, the relationship was over. He has better self-esteem than I did. I was happy when I saw him do teenagerhood better than I did."

CHAPTER 2

Catching Feelings

Relationship Wariness

IN MY LOVE AND HEARTBREAK SEMINAR, WE DISCUSSED AN excerpt from Plato's *Symposium* on the nature of true love. In the beginning of time, humans were round creatures with two sets of arms and legs and a great ambition: They wanted to overthrow the gods. To thwart the plan, Zeus split them in half, creating humans as we know them today. Each half longed for the missing other. When they found each other, they fell madly in love, their reunion curing the original "wound of human nature."[1]

I'd found the myth romantic since a long-ago beau first described it to me. I thought my students would feel the same.

They didn't.

My students didn't like the idea of all that yearning and the notion that they were meant to be with one particular person. They resisted the notion that love would complete them. They were intent on completing themselves. Love, one student asserted, was an inappropriate preoccupation at their stage of life: college and the period after, when you figured out what you wanted to do, pursued your degree, and proved yourself in internships and first jobs. "I want to feel like a whole soul inside myself first," she said, "and then I'll feel ready to let someone else in."

This generation of young people calls romantic attraction "catching feelings," an expression that likens falling for someone to a head cold—and speaks volumes about their wariness of relationships. Most of the class was single. To some extent, I admired my students' priorities. When I was their age, I was always catching feelings and letting relationships influence my decisions. I can't claim that living this way made me happy. Often I was miserable. The euphoria of a passionate romantic connection would fade, giving way to desperate grief. If my students had known me then, I would have been exhibit A for the kind of person they didn't want to be.

But I worried that my students were invested in a rigid way of thinking: that self-actualization was a separate process from finding love, one thing the prerequisite to the other. I didn't feel settled in my career until I'd worked in seven cities in six states, gotten a master's degree, had five major relationships and several minor ones, married, and had a kid. Even in my late middle age, I'm often reminded that the process of becoming is not a finite one; there are plenty of days when I don't feel whole. More importantly, the idea that the completed, independent self is the self most ready to love ignores the ways that love shapes, challenges, and enriches us. However long my students delayed romantic love, when it came into their lives, it would influence their identities and life paths.

This isn't simply because, as my students often argue, we live in a society that uses love and romantic fantasies to make money and brainwash us. While we can and should critique how the mass media and social media sell us overglorified messages about love, we should acknowledge that anthropologists have observed that the feelings of being in love are quite similar around the world, even in remote societies where children are raised without Disney movies or any media at all. Love is inherently a state of emotional dependency. Even if you're happy before you fall in love, once you do, your happiness will greatly hinge on how your beloved responds to you. Love also changes your priorities—what anthropologists call "reordering motivational hierarchies" to nurture and sustain the relationship.[2]

"Not that you throw everything you want out the window for the other person," I explained to my students. "But what the person you love wants or needs to do and what it takes for you to be that person's partner—these things affect your personal goals. You might start to want new things because the person you love wants them or figure out that something you used to think was important isn't that important anymore. You might even decide to make genuine sacrifices, like delaying a career goal because of the other person. You might need to ask your partner to do the same for you."

The challenge of getting my students to question a vision of love as self-sufficient-being-plus-one felt personal. My students expected any worthwhile relationship to accommodate all that they wanted to become. My reference was the myriad compromises and negotiations of a long marriage, which has influenced where I live and what I do. Being coupled (and a parent) mattered in countless daily decisions about how long my workday is, what I eat, how much emotional support I give and get, what I tolerate, and what I protest.

I couldn't get a read on whether the message reached them. I had to accept that this was one of those teaching moments that professors talk about all the time: Students may not get it now. But we had to trust that, sometime later—likely years later—they probably would.

Delaying Love, Embracing Friendship

The idea of emotional dependency and the prospect that someone else could influence your priorities are not easy for young people to accept. Generationally, as I've mentioned, today's teens are less experienced. Only about a third of teens ages 13 to 17 say they've had some kind of romantic relationship.[3] The percentage of high school seniors who say they've ever gone on a date is 63 percent, down from 84 percent in their parents' generation. Young people are waiting longer to have sex.[4] There's plenty of good in these trends. Prior generations overemphasized relationships. My mother felt left out because she was one of the few girls to graduate college without getting "pinned" or engaged. When I went to high school in the 1980s, you had to have an opposite-sex date to go to the prom, a policy that unnecessarily and cruelly excluded many students. Teachers observe that high schoolers who don't date have better social skills and leadership abilities than peers who do. Nondaters reported fewer symptoms of depression and had positive relationships at school and home, refuting the notion that not dating means you're maladjusted.[5]

Indeed, though teen dating offers important learning experiences, you don't have to have them to be happy in adult relationships. When researchers at the University of Virginia followed a group of people from age 13 to age 30, they found that the skills teens learn in same-sex friendships mattered more than teen relationships for having a good adult love life. How much dating experience teens had and how satisfied they were in their relationships, meanwhile, didn't have much of an impact.[6] Strong friendships give young people stability, a chance to be assertive about their needs and stay close to someone else over time without the risk (well, with *less* risk) of getting dumped. The skills gained from a friendship "correspond most closely to the skills needed for success in adult romantic relationships," said Joseph P. Allen, the UVA psychology professor who led the 2019 study.[7] Close friendships matter because they tend to be the higher-quality relationships in a young person's life and better models for adult commitment. In contrast, what it takes to have a satisfying romantic relationship in your teens may have little to do with what it takes to have one at 27.

Friendships have always been a kind of antidote to the poison of romantic uncertainty. As the ancient Roman philosopher

Seneca the Younger put it, "Friendship always benefits. Love sometimes injures." Friendship is a gut check on dignity and respect. Hence my daughter's description of a short-lived relationship: "I knew it was over when I watched him treat his friends better than he treated me. I want someone who treats me as well as they treat their friends." As romantic uncertainty, demographically speaking, lingers well beyond adolescence and the college years, the age of first marriage steadily inching past 30, the bonds of friendship take on increasing importance.

My students love friendship. They tell me they'd rather celebrate "Galentine's Day" by going out with a posse of friends than follow the lockstep commercialist script of a date on Valentine's Day. They question whether, aside from sex, friendship love was really that much different than romantic love. Their idol, Taylor Swift, lauds the glories of female friendship, and her fans enthusiastically make and exchange bracelets with fellow Swifties. A UCLA study found that adolescents want to see less sex and romance in TV shows and movies and more of a focus on friendships.[8]

Maybe we would be better off if we did put friendship at the center of life. But I'm not sure we can. It's rare for close friendships to have the fealty of a long-term committed relationship, at least beyond young adulthood. You might move across the country with your bestie at 23, when you're both up for an adventure, but doing the same at 40 is far less likely. The intensity of friendships fades and resurges, with fewer expectations and more freedom. Admittedly, our society values friendship less than romance. When a friendship falters, no one talks about seeking couples counseling or makes you soup, the way they would if you'd been dumped.

But even though friends can be as intimate as romantic partners, making each other feel known and understood, the connection is fundamentally different. No matter how wonderful friendships are, our brains and bodies are designed to be preoccupied with romantic relationships, sex, and love and to prioritize these experiences when they enter our lives. Whether young people are in a relationship or not, concerns about love, sex, and attraction will probably take up more mental real estate and emotional energy than anything else, at least until (or unless) they have children.

Delaying dating and sex may have benefits, but it's also a part of a trend of putting off other aspects of growing up: going out unsupervised, driving, getting a job, drinking alcohol, getting your own place, getting married. Researcher Jean Twenge has found that this "slow life strategy" is becoming more common, persisting through economic good times and bad, which suggests that young people are putting off these markers of "adulting" even when they're better able to afford them. She points out that one result may be that delayers feel less capable when they finally do take on these freedoms and responsibilities, to the point where employers are noting some young hires are still leaning on their parents to help them get their work done.[9] What's even more concerning is that the trend of delaying sex and dating coexists with the increasing isolation of adult life. Just over half of 18- to 34-year-olds in the United States say they do not have a steady romantic partner, up from a third in 2004.[10] Even before COVID, people ages 15 to 24 spent 70 percent less time together in any capacity—platonic, romantic, or otherwise—than they did in 2003, part of what a recent surgeon general's report called an "epidemic of loneliness and isolation."[11]

DEFINING THE RELATIONSHIP. OR NOT.

When young people do start to date and have sex, they may find themselves in a confusing, precarious arena that places little value on interrelatedness: the idea that how you act in any form of human connection has an impact on the other person and vice versa. Though hookups—the term for no-strings-attached, often alcohol-fueled sex—are a feature of this landscape, they're not as widespread as they may seem; the average college student hooks up about eight times over four years, or one hookup a semester.[12] What young people face is actually much more complicated. They're reluctant to even use the term *dating* for what they do: fits and starts of "talking" in chat bubbles on their phones; hanging out; having sex; feeling some kind of connection to someone else; then pulling away or sensing the other person do so, often without explanation. I'll add here that this is by no means just a young person's world. A fifty-something divorcée I know likes to hang out with her best friend's teen daughter and compare text chains with dodgy suitors, a bit of intergenerational fun they find cathartic and empowering.

Even when relationships seem fairly steady, young people may hold back on labels or create new ones. Parents puzzle over why their daughter insists that the boy she's cuddling with in the living room every weekend is "*not* my boyfriend" or why their son won't say he's "in a relationship" with the camp friend he FaceTimes nightly and busses hours to see every month. Young people may act like a couple, but a couple they are not, until or unless they decide to become "official." Instead, they're in a "situationship": a romantic attachment without a clear definition or commitment.

Their reluctance to "define the relationship" (a phrase so common young people use the social media-ready acronym *DTR*) can come across as a denial of what's really going on, and sometimes it is. If teens define a romantic connection as a relationship or say they'd like to do so, then they risk rejection in a period of their lives when they are particularly sensitive to it. Not defining a relationship might be a strategy to avoid losing a relationship.

But it also might not be. In adolescence and emerging adulthood in particular, other priorities may take precedence over the intimacy of a clearly defined relationship.[13] Young people may want to ease loneliness or horniness, have a no-strings-attached good time, boost their self-esteem, explore and experiment, or prioritize schoolwork and other commitments. They might be feeling too stung by a past relationship to get into another just yet. They might need time to heal wounds from a troubled childhood. While I'm concerned about the tendency of young people to place too much emphasis on readiness, there is nothing wrong and plenty right with putting other priorities ahead of partnering up and being able to say, "I'm not up for the responsibility of a relationship right now." Young people who feel this way are not misguided or avoidant. They're valuing where they are.

Young people are also embracing ways of relating that their parents may not recognize. Some may be polyamorous, meaning that they openly have or desire to have relationships with more than one person at once. Once thought of as dysfunctional and rare, asexuality, a term that describes people who don't experience sexual attraction, is also becoming more visible. Asexual people can still have relationships and have a wide range of reactions to sex: If they have it, they may enjoy it, or they're repulsed by it and want nothing to do with it. They may be demisexual, which means they feel sexual attraction only when they feel very close to someone, or aromantic, which means they don't experience romantic attraction.[14] Life and relationships on the "ace" (asexual) spectrum may entail coming up with a new language to describe relationships. A trans girl who describes herself as a "gray ace"—meaning that she experiences sexual attraction only occasionally—told me that she and her close friend, who is nonbinary, embrace the blurriness and fluidity of what they share. Their connection falls outside the boundaries of traditional friendships and romantic relationships. "We call it 'our thing,'" she said. "It's the most committed either of us has been to another person, even if the label isn't defined."

Eli Sheff, a sociologist and relationship consultant, urges parents to be "curious in a respectful way" if their child is exploring a less familiar path. "Let them know that you want them to tell you who they are, in a way that makes it safe for them to tell you the truth," Sheff said. The emotions involved won't be that different. Polyamorous or aromantic teens still feel the joy of connection.

They still get worried and insecure. They still suffer when they're rejected. They still need their parents' support, particularly given that they'll face the added strain of a world that doesn't get what they're doing. But they'll quickly lose faith in their parents' ability to help if their parents are judging them, too freaked out to deal, or disgruntled about yet another new and baffling label.

Blurry Lines and Gray Areas

Remember Harry's much-quoted insistence in the late-'80s rom-com *When Harry Met Sally* that "men and women can't be friends because the sex part gets in the way"? Today, little in that line speaks to young people: not the assumption of heterosexuality and certainly not the binary idea that you can either be friends or lovers. Teens live and love with a lot of blurry lines.

Jessie, an 18-year-old college student, went to a small high school in Los Angeles, the kind of place where all the kids know each other. Her friends, sensing the chemistry between Jessie and her close friend Amos, urged the two to get together. They didn't become a couple. But from freshman year to the beginning of senior year, they fooled around when they got drunk at parties. "This would have never happened if we were sober," they would tell their friends.

"It was our defense mechanism," Jessie explained. "We didn't want to feel judgment from others." They hooked up sober a few times, their physical connection growing more intimate. She started to hope each encounter would be the start of something more. Rumors swirled around as their friends speculated about whether they'd lost their virginity to each other, which they hadn't. The chatter made Amos uneasy. He grew distant. "I want to stop," he told her.

The next thing she knew, he was dating someone else. "I hated the idea of him talking to another girl," Jessie said. "I would do everything not to see them." She thought back to the beginning of their long friends-with-benefits saga. She'd sensed back then that he wanted more, but she'd kept him at bay. "That's something I regret," she said. "I think we were both afraid of rejection."

After Amos and his girlfriend broke up, Jessie hooked up with him again, an encounter she described as restorative. The old fondness returned, and they texted each other daily even after they went their separate ways for college. "What's the label for what you have?" I asked her.

"Before, he was my hookup buddy. Now, I just consider him one of my closest friends. A lot of people say, 'I see you two ending up together.' If we do, great. If we don't, I'll just go with the flow."

"It sounds incredibly stressful to keep switching the identity of the relationship," I said.

Jessie agreed that, yes, sometimes it was. "I used to think, in middle school, that relationships were like, you kiss a guy and then you're a couple and you're sending flowers and being romantic," she said. "Now I realize it's not that black-and-white. There are a lot of gray areas. The gray areas are fine as long as you talk about them and see what's going on with the other person. You need to know what the other person is thinking to make sure they're okay, and they need to know what you're thinking to make sure you're okay."

Jessie isn't alone in her faith that good communication and negotiation were key to getting all parties to a place where they felt "okay" in hookups and situationships. My students bring this up all the time. Missing from this ideal, though, was the reality of how sexual desire functions. Sexual stimulation triggers the dopamine system in the brain, which can lead to romantic attraction. Orgasm brings on a rush of oxytocin and vasopressin, hormones associated with feelings of trust and attachment. In as much as we may want to believe that sex can be just sex, it's not siloed off from our capacity for deeper connection—in fact, quite the opposite. "Casual sex is really never casual," biological anthropologist Helen Fisher often says.[15] Though plenty of people part ways after a sexual encounter without wanting an emotional connection, catching feelings is one of the most natural reactions in the world. It entails wanting more—a lot more: more go-arounds in bed, more time together. We might even dream of merging our lost half-soul with the other. Figuring out what to do with these feelings is an unsettling process, full of uncertainty and risk, especially when the expectation is to keep everything casual.

Technology doesn't help. Young people grew up with peer relationships that played out just as much online as in person or more. They're accustomed to the pace and abundance of digital contact, what scholars call "cheap" communication: tapping a heart, commenting, posting, watching. The speed-oriented names of all the apps assure us of effortlessness: Insta, Snap, TikTok. But with all this easy contact comes a myriad of unspoken rules—such as being a good friend means liking and commenting on all the posts of all your friends, all the time—and regular, piercing social pain. Anyone who's felt the sting of watching an Instagram video of a sleepover they weren't invited to or a crush who stops opening their Snaps learns early the real costs of cheap communication. But these lessons don't inoculate you from feeling like shit when you're older and see posts of the person you've been exchanging flirty text messages with for weeks—with their arms wrapped around someone else. If you've hooked up with the person, it can be even worse. What makes people want Instagramable closeness with someone else when they didn't want it with you?

Dating apps are the inevitable next step of a social media–soaked youth, offering abundant possibilities for connection, only now with more overt erotic possibility and less humanity, every left swipe a tiny, routine banishment. Even though minors aren't supposed to be on adult dating apps, many are. They fib about their age the way they did when they were 11 to get on Instagram. The party line about dating apps, young people tell me, is that they're just for kicks. It's fun to swipe and see who's on the app. Sure, maybe sometimes they do end up on dates, but they don't expect them to go anywhere.

There are, obviously, some huge holes in this narrative. For queer youth, apps can be a way to find other queer people that may seem safer than, say, hitting on a classmate who could turn out to be rabidly homophobic and rally classmates to ostracize and bully you. But LGBTQ+ youth are also more likely to experience unwanted and risky interactions online.[16] For both queer and straight young people, apps open the door to encounters with older people, who could use their age and authority to gain their trust and manipulate them, grooming them for an abusive relationship.

What this means, on a practical level, is that the adults in young people's lives need to engage in conversations about safety, reminding them that the people they meet online may not have the right intentions. They shouldn't meet up alone with a stranger for the first time, and they should choose public meeting places, such as a coffee shop, where they can easily leave. They should also have a safety plan in place, essentially agreements with parents, trusted adults, siblings, or friends who know when they're meeting someone new and can help them if they're in a situation they need to get out of.[17]

But the conversation shouldn't end there. Parents should investigate what teens might be seeking when they join apps or talk to older people. What in their lives has left young people open to this kind of connection? In what ways are they vulnerable? Are they feeling safe, loved, and valued at home? Do they value themselves?

What can get lost in fears about whether minor teens are on dating apps and what they are using them for are the broader questions of how technology shapes young people's views about their romantic and sexual selves. They're engaging in a business enterprise that functions on (and makes billions from) the profoundly cynical notion of potential partners as fungible, one prospect easily replaced by another. And the first step in the process is to lie. I think of the girl who told me she first downloaded

Tinder at 16, using a fake birthday because the minimum age is 18. She never told the guys she met on the app her real age. She told herself it didn't matter because she wasn't that interested in them. Then, her first year in college, she started seeing a match who lived a couple of towns away. After they had been spending time with each other for a couple of months, he confessed he was only 16. The lie bothered her because she actually liked him. Yet how could she criticize the deception, given that she'd done the same herself at his age?

IF YOU CARE, YOU LOSE

Andrea told me she spent her college years "swiping all the time." The Long Island–raised daughter of Colombian immigrants, Andrea is one of the most self-assured young women I've ever met. She's openly polyamorous and an evangelist for affordable, adventurous international travel. Her dark curls, riveting gaze, and curves attract a steady stream of heart-eye emojis from the men and women she matched with on Tinder. She'd pick one or two at a time to respond to. If that went well, she would start messaging on another app, each one with its own connotation: Snapchat was silly. Instagram suggested you were okay with having the person show up in your feed—a risk given the ambient permanence of the app, which means you could for years be watching the stories of someone you might never meet in person. Texting was a more distinct sign of interest. "If you pass the Tinder part and have my number, you've leveled up," Andrea said.

Through messaging, she got a better sense of what she wanted and what the other person wanted: Netflix and chill: code for a hookup. A fuck buddy: ongoing casual sex with no commitment. A date: setting aside time to genuinely get to know each other. An ardent suitor might offer the "girlfriend experience," a well-planned evening—dinner at a decent restaurant, watching a movie in an actual theater. When I looked the term up, I was taken aback to find out it comes from escort services to describe more romantic activity than sex workers traditionally provide, such as kissing and handholding. A few dates, strung together with bouts of messaging, shifted the connection into the "talking" phase, when you're open to possibilities but not officially in a relationship. A relationship was a distinct romantic commitment. For monogamous people, it meant not seeing other people. For Andrea, it meant putting the other person in the center, with the agreement that they could have other lovers. She'd only had one, short-lived relationship, her second year of college, with someone at another school a couple of hours away.

Andrea had her rules: Don't message with someone for more than a week without meeting in person or moving on. If she just wanted a casual hookup, she kept the conversation minimal to make it clear the relationship wasn't going anywhere. But the rules didn't always work. After a night of dancing to trap rap with a boy she'd been flirting with over Instagram, he asked her to come home with him. The vibe between them felt real, but he'd told her in a DM that he wasn't interested in a relationship. She liked him too much for a mere hookup.

"I'm not having sex with you," she said bluntly.

"That's not what I asked," he said.

He explained he simply wanted her company. They spent the night at his apartment, talking until 5 a.m. Lying next to each other, they discussed how they felt about their bodies. He had a chronic skin condition. She had recently gained weight, which made her uncomfortable yet conflicted. As a feminist, she felt she had to display a fake confidence anyway, proving she valued her body at any size. "There are things you learn when you're laughing together at three in the morning," she said. "It was refreshing to be so open and honest. It was the opposite of what I was expecting."

They continued to message each other. Then he went silent. Weeks went by. Finally, she got a late-night text. She could tell he was drunk and sad. He was worried about his younger sister back at home, living with their emotionally abusive stepfather. He felt guilty that he wasn't there to protect her. "It's not your burden to carry," she reassured him, using the training she received as a resident assistant in her dormitory. "It's your choice to get an education, and it's better for both of you in the long run that you're here." She told him his sister was lucky to have a brother like him.

There were, she realized, ulterior motives to her compassion. "I remember thinking, 'I'm just trying to get him to fall in love with me by being an emotional support,'" she said. "I can be that someone who's always there and gets him and listens to him."

It seemed like he wanted to be close. In the days to come, she consoled him through a few more sad-boy jags. One night, she asked him if he saw anything developing between them.

He said he didn't know.

Reeling, she thanked him for the information and told him she didn't want to talk to him anymore. She castigated herself for wanting more from him, falling prey to what she called "dumb-bitch hours," the blurry, lonely stretches of night in her dorm room when her guard was down. "I hurt myself," she said. "He told me before he didn't want anything with me. When you have that kind of clarity, you can't put the blame on the other person."

Listening to her tale, I couldn't help thinking both that she was right and that her vulnerability and disappointment were entirely justified. What was unfolding between them had distinct elements of intimacy: emotional disclosure and unmistakable sexual chemistry. Just as people once in love fall out of love, people who say they don't want a relationship may change their minds. Andrea was hard on herself about catching feelings, her emotions not heeding the stated limits. No one wants to be Tom in *500 Days of Summer*, whose not-girlfriend has shower sex with him and likes to cuddle in IKEA showroom bedrooms yet insists she doesn't want a relationship. After trying to play it cool, he explodes, "Well, you're not the only one that gets a say in this! I do, too! And I say we're a couple, goddamn it!"

However disconcerting this moment is for its aggression, it also strikes a chord, speaking to an all-too-familiar frustration with dating as a game of, as one student described, "who gives less of a shit." If you're the one who cares, you lose. Though girls are traditionally assumed to be the ones at a disadvantage, no gender, sexual identity, or sexual orientation goes unscathed. Young people may know the terms, agree to them, and play it cool yet also feel, somehow, that they had no real choice in the matter and no way to express romantic desires and vulnerability. After I gave a talk at a small liberal arts college, a young woman with worry in her dark eyes pulled me aside to tell me about the boy in her life. By nature, he told her, he wasn't monogamous and was too restless to be in a relationship. Even though she wished for more, she consented to sleep with him when he wanted to because she was in love with him. "I take what I can get," she said.

I've also talked to young people on the other side of this dilemma, who unabashedly maintained they did not want to be in a relationship, even though they enjoyed the sex and company of a vaguely defined situationship. I interviewed Maximo on the recommendation of one of my former students, who assured me that he was the "king of undefined relationships." He fit the picture: handsome in a scruffy way, his beard somewhere between intentional and "I lost my razor," poke-and-stick tattoos on every finger, black nail polish. He had gotten into plenty of friends-with-benefits liaisons, and he believed in them. He'd started his love life with back-to-back serious relationships, each lasting several years. Both ended with his infidelity, which he explained as a reaction to the pressure he felt to be a good boyfriend. "I wasn't getting time to myself or working on what I wanted," he said. After the second breakup, he didn't think he had the capacity to get serious with anyone. When he met girls he was attracted to, he laid his cards on the table, letting them know at the outset that he was not on the boyfriend track. At its best, what developed was liberating and intimate. "If you open up to a person you're not dating, it's nice, because you're both just people, and you listen, and you talk, whether it's traumatic stuff or not, you feel safe opening up to a person you don't know super well," he said.

From a brain-systems perspective, this is playing with two lit fires: sex and a feeling of connection, with the third—romantic attraction—right nearby, waiting for a spark to jump its way. Maximo has had to tell girls who wanted more, "I can't be that person." Which usually means the end of the situationship. At times, he's been the one to end up wanting more. When a girl he'd developed feelings for stopped texting him back with the pithy explanation that she was "too busy," he did his due diligence and unfollowed her on Instagram. He knew any reminder of her would disturb him. "Then her profile kept getting suggested to me, and I was like, I don't want to see this! This is crazy," he said. The reality of our vulnerability to falling for people we hook up with and hang out with has to coexist with the fact that they, in the words of psychology researcher Joanne Davila, "don't want what you have to offer," part of the inherent risks of desire.

Grieving the Relationship That Never Was

As with letting go of a crush, mourning a situationship that you wanted something more from can be just as intense as mourning a long-term relationship—and sometimes more so because of all the unrealized possibilities. Not to mention all the pressure to be okay, because you were warned, weren't you? Young people who get tossed around in situationships may hasten to tell themselves what happened shouldn't matter. The adults in their lives may go along with that, in the hope that making the experience seem like no big deal will make the pain go away faster.

"The more parents attempt to shrink the pain by shrinking the experience, the more the teen stays stuck and confused," said clinical psychologist and Northwestern University professor Alexandra Solomon, who teaches a course called Marriage 101 about love and relationships. "The path forward is to validate the hell out of the length, width, and height of your young person's pain. Even though it feels paradoxical, you shrink the pain by giving space for it." Validation becomes particularly important when young people struggle to call what they went through a breakup—because how can something be broken when it wasn't a thing in the first place? Emotions, Solomon emphasizes, aren't going to heed labels or the lack of them. "Because there was ambiguity in the relationship, there's ambiguity in the loss, and it can be hard to feel like you're getting the support you need," she said.

It's also important to emphasize to young people that no one should weaponize the lack of official relationship status. If you're friends with benefits, you're still friends and should treat each other that way. What I tell the young people in my life: A connection with someone else that includes emotional disclosure, desire, and sex *is* a relationship, no matter what you decide to call it. It may not be exclusive and committed. It may not have a future. It may have looser routines and expectations. But we are still supposed to be concerned for each other on a basic human level. While, as sociologist Lisa Wade sagely points out, young people may believe hookups should be carefree, in practice they are often care*less*.[18] We aren't supposed to treat friends or even acquaintances callously by cutting off communication without an explanation—what's known as ghosting—or stringing people along with hints of interest, so why would we treat people we're attracted to this way? Nor should we accept disrespectful behavior, even when it seems like the person who cares less holds more power.

This dynamic, which starts in adolescence and plagues the adult dating arena, fuels a kind of "collective attachment disorder," as Solomon described in a popular Instagram post.[19] Ambiguously defined relationships create uncertainty and anxiety, which by design drives us to resort to coping strategies, such as taking whatever attention we can get or obsessing over what to do. Young people in particular may be reluctant to ask for clarification about where they stand with someone else. "They think it will be awkward. They're afraid they'll seem desperate. There's such pressure to seem chill and low drama and not needy or clingy," Solomon said. "Trusted adults who talk with teens can ask them about their fears of getting clarification and tell them that it's not the same thing as neediness. Clarification is just clarification. It's not asking for a promise or making a demand."

Providing support to young people troubled by situationships is challenging precisely because of their lack of definition. Young people may silence themselves—again for the reason that what they're doing isn't a thing or because they're worried they'll be judged for being sexually active, particularly without exclusivity or commitment. You may pick up on hints and fragments—"this guy I've been talking to," "this friend I'm hanging out with"—and convey interest on the same terms: "Are you still hanging out with ___? How's she doing?"

If a situationship seems to be troubling the young person in your life, Solomon suggests asking what happens before, during, and after they spend time together. A healthy situationship is one in which partners look forward to their encounters, enjoy being together, and part ways feeling glad. An unhealthy one: At least one of the partners is anxious before an encounter, stressed during it, and empty or sad afterward. Young people can also consider: How does this situation feel *in your body?* Does it feel aligned and comfortable—or does it feel like abandonment? "You're inviting the young person to be a scientist of sorts, collecting data on their own experience, which is important, because they've got so many voices all around them—friends telling them what to do and not to do, TikTok videos about what they should and shouldn't do, which becomes noise that crowd out their own internal signals," Solomon said.

During COVID, I wondered if situationship culture was going to change. The impact of the shutdown on teen relationships reminded me of musical chairs. The music stopped, and you either had a chair to sit in or you didn't. If you had a chair—a steady girlfriend or a boyfriend—you were lucky. The music wouldn't resume for more than a year. Several high school couples, including the relationship my daughter was in, stayed together, partners eventually getting permission to become part of each other's family pods. One mother told me that her son's best friends all had girlfriends, which compounded his isolation. "There's no room in the pods for him," she said.

Was the long-term lesson going to be that young people would value relationships more? Single people in their late teens and twenties are more likely than older adults to say the pandemic made them more interested in serious relationships. But finding one doesn't seem to be any easier. The majority say they're dissatisfied with their dating lives and believe the pandemic made dating harder.[20]

One of the issues may be that young people don't feel they have a "social script" for dating, as Boston College philosophy professor Kerry Cronin told the *Washington Post*. Throughout her teaching career, she's watched norms around relationships and sex transform to the degree that she realized many of her graduating seniors had never been on a date. So she came up with an assignment: Ask someone out on a date. You have to ask in person. If someone puts you off with claims of being busy or not up to it, move on to ask someone else. When you're on the date, don't drink or take drugs. Don't get physical. The person who asks should be the person who pays for the date. The outing should cost less than $10 and not last longer than 90 minutes.

The dates don't necessarily lead to anything more. That's not really the point. It's more about practicing clarity of intention and getting used to *trying* to connect and all that entails: the potential reward of connection, the possibility of being turned down, the process of getting to know someone. Cronin's argument is compelling: Taking risks in small doses is one way to prepare for greater risks, when there's more at stake.

"LET'S GROW": BEYOND THE WHOLE-SOUL / RELATIONSHIP BINARY

There's another crucial factor behind young people's emphasis on feeling complete before they find love: fear of rejection. When they catch feelings, they experience a new dimension of their heart—how much they can feel for someone else—and if it doesn't go as they'd hoped, they feel incomplete, anxious, sad, and unwell. Even though the distress may be an inevitable part of mourning what happened, it can become fodder for the argument in their heads that they have a long way to go before they are "whole souls" deserving of love.

When Nat, who is pansexual, nonbinary, and uses *they* pronouns, was a freshman at Bellingham High School, they met Luna, an out lesbian with a girlfriend. Luna wore a binder under crisp button-down shirts, her blond hair cut androgynously short, a style foreign to the Christian private school Nat attended through eighth grade. Right away, Nat was drawn to Luna. "I'm like, I might actually burst into flames if I talk to this person," they said. "But at the same time, I felt so comfortable with her. I could talk to her."

Luna and her girlfriend broke up. For the next year and a half, Nat and Luna spent most of their time together. They sat next to each other in class at school and spent afternoons at each other's houses. They held hands. They snuck cigarettes on Nat's balcony while their mother worked late nights as an intake nurse at a detox center. Luna's mother took them out to dinner and to get their nails done. When Luna's relationship with her mother got rocky, she confided in Nat. "I was very much a person that she would come to, to feel safe," they said. "It was like we were in a relationship, but we didn't talk about it."

On the balcony one evening, Nat and Luna kissed. After Luna left, Nat Snapchatted her to confess their crush. "Where do we stand?" they asked.

Luna messaged back to say she loved being with Nat. She treasured their friendship. But she didn't want a relationship with them. "Then she was like, 'But would you be down to be friends with benefits?'" Nat said.

Nat had assumed they were courting each other, with a building, shared love. "It felt really real, as real as you could get in high school," they said. Suddenly their bond felt like a house of cards that Luna knocked down with an unthinking wave of her hand. Nat was stunned that all the support and love they'd given had culminated in an insultingly nonchalant response. "I can't be your friend anymore," Nat told Luna. "I can't put myself in the position of constantly being hurt."

Nat wished they'd been brave enough to define the relationship sooner. They were used to keeping their feelings inside. They had a complicated childhood. Their father grew up in an observant Mormon household and ignored their gender identity and sexual orientation. Their mother battled drug addiction and abusive boyfriends. "Instances would happen where we'd have to call the cops in the middle of the night. I would be up until 4 a.m.," they said. "I'd have to get up two hours later to go to school, where no one was supposed to know about what had happened. I felt like I couldn't talk to anyone about it, and I had to put on a happy face."

In the wake of Luna's rejection, Nat joined a local sexual health awareness program and trained as a peer educator. They started facilitating conversations with other teens about sex, boundaries, and consent. "Young people can get into the mindset of, 'We should only think about our partners,'" they said. "For so long, I went through my life not really listening to myself. If I'd had better knowledge and a better grasp of my boundaries and how to communicate them, I could have had that conversation with Luna earlier, and maybe we could still be friends."

Five years later, Nat is a high school graduate and a peer advocate with a local domestic violence and sexual assault services organization. They have yet to be in a romantic relationship. They admitted they're still mourning the relationship that never was with Luna. "I'm working on being okay letting myself get to that point with other people, because if I gave all my love to this person and I didn't get it, how am I supposed to do that again?" Nat said. "Point blank period, I don't know that's not going to happen again. I need to be okay with the fact that it could happen again. I have to be opened up to the good and the bad."

In my interviews with older teens and emerging adults, I'm struck by how often I hear versions of Nat's resolve: to work hard to be ready for relationships before letting yourself have one. This is distinctly different from what I earlier described as developmental not-readiness, when the interpersonal skills, self-awareness, and responsibilities emotional intimacy entails may demand far more than a young person is prepared to give. Young people imagine a future state of mental well-being that will make catching feelings less fraught and mutual love, once it comes around the bend, go smoothly. In many ways, it's a beautiful goal. We want to be able to approach relationships with a healthy sense of self. But none of this will protect us from the pain of what Nat called "the bad": getting hurt, which can send us into dark places and make us feel, for a time, broken. Nat, at 20, had a plan for their love life, with a prerequisite they hadn't yet passed.

I shared Nat's story with Esther Perel, the renowned couples therapist, author, and podcast host. She's written about sociologist Andrew Cherlin's idea of the "capstone marriage"—couples that marry later in life, after they've formed fuller personal identities, gained economic security, and proven themselves as devoted partners.[21] I told her my impression that young people like Nat perceived relationships themselves as capstone experiences: Romantic love is the reward you get for mastering yourself. In this light, stories like Nat's, of situationships and crushes that failed to flower, intensified into enduring cautionary tales. "They make young people gun-shy," I explained. "They feel like they have to do all this inner work before they're ready for a relationship—sometimes years of work."

"They should not separate growth and relationships," Esther said. "Growth occurs *in* relationships."

She was stating a simple but profound truth: We are relational beings. Our ability to thrive and have meaningful lives and even our capacity to act independently are rooted in our connections to other people. The people we're close to transform who we are, particularly in romantic relationships. In a follow-up Zoom call, I described the conversation to Nat. "What do you think?" I asked.

"It's easier said than done," Nat sighed. "Even when you know growth happens in relationships, it still can be hard to enter a relationship and admit to yourself you have to grow. I just need to feel more comfortable with myself, and that will allow me to be more comfortable with another person. Then I can be better prepared when I'm in a situation that I don't enjoy."

I got the sense Nat was digging into their position—and that the goal of being prepared was sounding ever more elusive and unrealistic, a fantasized ta-da moment of being comfortable enough. So I pressed, "What do you do to get more comfortable with yourself?"

Nat's answer surprised me. "I really like looking in the mirror," they said. "It's not a vain thing. I like analyzing the fact that I'm alive, and I'm a human, and I have skin. And that lets me know myself more. It makes everything more real. Because I get in my head sometimes, and I tell myself everything's fine. But if I look in the mirror, I can think about things for how they actually are."

Because Nat was looking at me over Zoom, I could easily imagine them searching for answers in the reflection of their pale, oval face, their high forehead exaggerated by hair pulled back in a bun, the generous flesh of their cheeks and chin, the silver horseshoe rings through their nose and left eyebrow. I was stirred by the idea of this direct, visual confrontation of the self and the pleasure Nat took in it. "What if you started to get feelings for someone again, and you weren't sure whether to go forward with it?" I asked. "What would the mirror be able to tell you?"

"I'd ask my reflection, 'Did you enjoy that? Was that fun?'" they said. "Do you look happier than you did before? I would have a conversation of looking in the mirror and being like, 'Can you see yourself looking in this mirror with that person? Can you see yourself being able to just be with that person and not feel like you have to perform in a certain way? Can you be with that person the way you are right now, looking in the mirror? Because right now you're comfortable with yourself. Would you be like that with this person?'"

"What would you say if the other person was in the mirror with you?"

"I would ask them, 'Could you see yourself with me as I am? Is this comfortable for you?'"

Later in the conversation, Nat told me the idea that growth occurred in relationships and wasn't just work you did on your own was new and liberatory. Maybe the process of feeling ready for their first romantic relationship could work differently than they'd envisioned. Even just thinking about it made them want to go on a date. "Like right now! Like, let's go. Let's grow! Let's grow right now!" Nat said. They tittered bashfully and looked off to the side. "I think I'm getting to that spot where I'm ready to do that stuff. Which is nice. Really nice."

CHAPTER 3

So Gone

It's Serious

WHEN ELISE WAS A 15-YEAR-OLD HIGH SCHOOL SOPHOMORE IN Morgantown, West Virginia, she attended an open house for a theater program. There Luka was, with blond curls and an appealing smirk of a smile. He captivated the audience with his performance of Edgar Allan Poe's "The Tell-Tale Heart." His delivery was "like classical music, with the crescendos and the decrescendos," she remembered.

She joined the theater class, which was taught by Luka's stepfather. He wrote skits about bullying prevention and sexual health for his students to perform at local schools. He cast Elise and Luka as a couple in a bit about the dangers of unprotected sex. They were supposed to kiss at the end. For weeks, at every rehearsal, the teacher would yell, "Cut!" right before the moment arrived. Finally, at the dress rehearsal, the kiss happened. Soon after, Elise and Luka became a couple.

Elise was raised in a devout Christian household. Luka came from a different world. His parents were spiritual seekers, averse to strict doctrine. His stepfather was Buddhist. His mother was a Reiki healer and yoga instructor. Lavishly attentive, Luka drew a cartoon strip he called *Favorite Moments with Elise*. He wrote her mash notes: "My dearest love. It's been two days since I've seen you. I can't breathe!" "My love burns for you with the intensity of a thousand suns." They dreamed aloud about the vacations they would take together and mused over what their children would look like. Would they be fair, like Luka, or have Elise's dark hair and petite frame? "You have to be the mother of my child because you're perfect in every way, and I have to pass on your genes," he gushed.

In her generation's words, Elise was "so gone." As the phrase suggests, she'd embarked on a kind of journey: away from her childhood, away from her parents, and away from the life she'd known before Luka swept into it. She was deeply, utterly in love.

Contradicting mythologies surround the idea of first love. We fantasize that it's something pure and innocent, two enraptured young people entering each other's lives as blank slates, unmarked from past disappointments. Yet we also worry about the impact of young love on the process of growing up. We wonder if romantic closeness interferes with the process of gaining a sense of self distinct from parents and peers. Famed psychoanalyst Erik Erikson called adolescence a time when young people grapple with identity confusion. They're figuring out what they believe, what they value, where they fit it, who they are, and who they want to become. He maintained that the uncertainty of this stage may mean that young people won't feel ready for relationships or be good at them. Once they achieve a strong sense of self, they'll be ready to seek out lasting, loving relationships.[1]

These clashing ideas about young love mean that, while we fawn over the sweetness of an adolescence romance, we maintain a vigilant watch on its influence. Peers complain about a once-loyal friend who's disappeared into the arms of another, listening to different music, hanging out with a new crowd, dressing in styles they hadn't worn before. When couples seem too close or are together too long, we may become uneasy. Parents fret over what a friend of mine deemed the "pseudo-marriage," cozy high school couples that last for years. On one hand, we're happy for them. We might even be impressed with their steadiness or way of relating, if it seems kinder, more open, more romantic, or more egalitarian than the relationships we had—or have. On the other hand, we ask ourselves if these pseudo-marriages are too much, too soon, preventing young people from getting the most out of their youth.

Elise told me she "missed being more carefree" while she was with Luka. "I'd think, 'This is too good to be true, it's going to end, and it's going to be the worst day ever,'" she said. "There was always this anxiety."

A child's first love also may lead parents to reckon with their own sense of loss. Signs of this future mount throughout adolescence, whether a child has a serious relationship or not. Young people push back against parental authority and even parental attention. Witnessing a child grow close to a romantic partner takes this one step further with a potent message: You are being replaced as the main focus of your child's love.

What happens between teens and their partners can weigh heavily on parents because they consider first relationships as a kind of evidence: What kind of person did I raise? Are they unwittingly absorbing household troubles, old family patterns? Are they going to make the same mistakes I did? Are they selfish or big-hearted? Needy or confident? Did I say enough about what's right and what's wrong, and did they listen?

What stands out for me in the interviews I've done with parents is their concern that whatever has been amiss in their own lives might rub off on their children. I think of one mother in an empty marriage who closely watched her son with his girlfriend, wondering whether he was affectionate enough. A father who got married in his early twenties worried that his son would end up spending his life with his first love and miss out on other relationships. A mother who never got over her high school boyfriend's betrayals was dismayed to learn that her "sweet, sensitive" son habitually cheated on his girlfriend. A woman who had taken pains to shield her daughter from the contentious end of her marriage told me, "I can't tell you how much it means to me to see my child in a healthy relationship with someone I like."

No matter where you're coming from, the beginning of a young person's love life hits deep. Elise's mother, Marie, remembered the afternoon when, as she waited in her car in front of the high school, she spotted Elise kissing Luka goodbye. "It was a big kiss," she said. "It was the first time I'd seen any of my children be physically affectionate. It sucked the air out of my lungs. It was like, wow, she's crossing a threshold, and she's not coming back."

WILL THEY LOSE THEMSELVES TO LOVE?

Elise's father, Allen, a bald, burly ex-athlete, is a college football official who runs a beer distributorship. After two-decades-plus as a stay-at-home mom, Elise's mother re-entered the workforce as a freelance writer. She looked the part, with dark red lipstick and huge, black-framed glasses.

Marie had grown up going to church every Sunday. Allen came from a close-knit Catholic family. When they met in college, both had drifted away from religion. "We drank and partied," Allen said, smiling bashfully. "We lived together. We had our own sin long before we had children." After they married, they decided to raise their children with a Christian worldview. They didn't hide their past, but they made it clear they wanted their kids to make different choices than they had. Elise and her two siblings weren't allowed to date until they turned 16. Allen and Marie urged them to wait until they were married to have sex.

Elise is their middle child, but she was the first to get romantically involved. On her 16th birthday, Luka swept into their lives, fully in character as their daughter's eager suitor. "May I date your daughter?" he asked earnestly.

At first, Marie and Allen were more amused than worried. Yet as the relationship progressed, they became concerned that Elise's identity was taking a back seat to Luka's. Elise's senior year, Allen was alarmed when she chose to attend college in Staten Island, a short commute from where Luka would be living in Manhattan. Elise adamantly denied that proximity to him influenced her decision. Once she started college, her parents worried about all the time she spent with him and the impact it was having on her finances. "I think she ended up spending every penny that she got for high school graduation money on him because he was a poor, starving actor," Marie said. "She would help him furnish his apartment with IKEA stuff and buy their meals on Grubhub."

On Instagram, Marie saw a photograph of Elise's bare thighs, a cup of coffee balanced in her lap. Marie could tell the shot was taken in Luka's bedroom. "It was probably meant for her friends and not meant for me," she said. "But I thought maybe this is her way of telling me, 'I've grown up. I'm doing this whether you like it or not.'"

Along with its suggestion of sexual intimacy, the post underscored for Marie all that her daughter was missing out on. Elise wasn't spending her first year in college making friends and joining clubs. Her heart was in Luka's apartment, not on campus.

Meanwhile, Marie and Allen were concerned that Luka was becoming increasingly uncertain about the relationship. He would break up with Elise, throwing her into turmoil, and then they'd get back together again.

"I didn't see her growing," Allen said. "I felt she was declining. Or whatever the opposite of growing is. Wilting!" He grew so frustrated watching his daughter go through cycles of devastation and relief that he called Luka to reprimand him.

During Elise's three years with Luka, she and her parents contended with some of the most fundamental questions of first love: When is young love too absorbing, fostering dependency, undermining confidence, and interfering with an adolescent's ability to make life choices? When is it healthy, providing growth experiences and fostering emotional intelligence? How can we tell one from the other during the ego-fragile, independence-seeking teen years, when young people will use both good and not-so-good relationships to grow up and gain distance from their families?

The couple broke up for the last time the summer after her first year of college. Elise went back to college, made friends, and thrived. After she graduated, she spent a year traveling and teaching English. She returned to West Virginia and joined the family beer distributorship, a job she loves. She lived an earthier life than she did when she was with Luka, when she put on makeup every day, as if preparing for the theater of their sweeping love story. Her post-Luka, post-college life was about hiking and camping with her face bare and her dog by her side. She looked back on the relationship with a combination of nostalgia, pride, and the wisdom of hindsight. Luka was, she'd come to realize, over-the-top adoring in a way she would never trust now. His charms made it hard to see how stubbornly self-centered he was. The agenda of their relationship usually revolved around him.

But the romance also widened her world in indelible ways. The time in New York that her parents feared was taking her away from college life was, to her, a "total blast—playing house in New York and eating fancy food we couldn't afford, then cooking for weeks until we could save up even more money for fancy food."

More importantly, Luka helped her shake off the mental shackles of her religious upbringing. When Elise was 12, the family had joined a church known for its large Sunday school program and youth group. The youth pastor and his wife told the members that, if they had premarital sex, they'd burn in hell. The girls, he and his wife counseled, should think of themselves like a piece of tape: "The more boys you try to stick to, the less sticky you'll be."

The dogma haunted her. When Elise and Luka started to go further than kissing, she would hyperventilate. She was terrified that touching him and being touched would be her ruin.

Luka turned what was happening into an intellectual project. "How do you know you're going to burn in hell?" he'd ask. "What about all the people who do have sex before marriage—were they *all* in hell? Wouldn't hell be getting really crowded? And why wouldn't God pay attention to all the good things people did—wouldn't that outweigh the relatively minor transgression of having sex with someone you love?" Elise's own parents had lived together before they found Jesus. Surely *they* weren't headed for hell? Together, through hours of conversation, they dismantled her fears. It would be more than a year before she had sex with him. "He wasn't trying to get me into bed," Elise said. "He just wanted me to stop being so stressed and scared. As a 16-year-old boy, he handled really difficult things that not many people know how to."

Elise quit the youth group. To her relief, her parents supported her. They hadn't realized how extreme the youth pastor and his wife were. The courage to leave the church was "one of the greatest gifts Luka gave me," she said.

What Elise's account suggests is that there are no easy answers to the question of whether a first love interferes with a young person's coming of age. The same relationship that her parents saw as posing a real obstacle to her emerging sense of self was, in her eyes, utterly essential for her to become the person she wanted to be.

A Capacity for Deep Connection

The fear that young people will lose themselves to love is at the core of the arguments I hear against adolescents getting involved in serious relationships: They're too young, immature, and self-centered to sensitively negotiate the boundaries between self and other. They should be focusing on other priorities. Relationships will lead to sex, which entails the risk of pregnancy and disease and forever regrets. Adolescents aren't ready for the emotional anguish of a breakup. But these protests don't just come from parents. They come from young people themselves, who watch peers becoming overly dependent on their partners and distancing themselves from their friends—at least until the relationship goes bust. All of these things can and do happen to young people in serious relationships. But that doesn't mean young love is just some potent elixir that, with the lure of sex and attention, takes young people away from their real lives instead of enlivening them.

Teen relationships don't have to be a pro-or-con kind of thing. Relationships happen in adolescence. As I've mentioned, around one in three teens have had some kind of romantic involvement, with 14 percent indicating they were in a relationship they considered serious.[2] About half of college students have at least one serious relationship while they're in school.[3] Romantic relationships happen because it feels wonderful to adore and be adored, to explore the world with someone else, and to share each other's private lives and feelings. Relationships are exhilarating. They take young people to a new planet, far from the routines and hang-ups of the homes they were raised in. Relationships happen whether young people feel ready and whether parents think their children are ready. And, for that matter, whether *parents* feel ready.

There is nothing inherently wrong with getting serious and no evidence showing teens in committed relationships are fundamentally less self-reliant or miss out on essential aspects of growing up. Being in a loving, healthy relationship can be a fruitful part of the process, fostering generosity of spirit, big-picture thinking, and confidence in resolving disagreements and understanding needs.[4] Wanting and having romantic relationships are part of what approaching adulthood is all about.[5] Young people are exploring the possibilities of adult attachment—the capacity of a close bond with a partner to do a grown-up version of what their parents hopefully have been doing for them since they were born: helping them feel safe, seen, and secure.

We are better off focusing on the quality of relationships and their impact than on whether young people should or shouldn't be having them. Frequent, short-lived relationships in early adolescence aren't good news. They're linked to later troubled friendships and romantic relationships, along with mental health and behavioral issues.[6] Teen relationships with a lot of conflict and hostility aren't beneficial either, as they're more likely to make young people withdrawn and anxious.[7]

But even less obviously problematic relationships aren't easy. This truism endures into adult life, but young people may take relationship ups and downs harder because they're susceptible to moodiness, particularly in response to interpersonal conflict, and less experienced at dealing with emotional challenges.[8] Relationships are one of the most significant sources of stress for young people and one of the most common reasons for them to seek counseling.[9]

All this means the ability of young people to gauge the quality of a serious relationship and how well they're dealing with it is key. The idea of mutuality can be a powerful starting point for a generation that values gender equality. It gives them and the adults in their lives a language for figuring out whether one person's identity is being subsumed to the other's: Is one partner usually the one to set the agenda and the subject of conversation? Or is the relationship, over time, a balanced exchange? Are both partners just as willing to meet the other's needs?

Another, related issue is that of overenmeshment. If young people are ignoring friends, losing interest in school and activities, and are unable to do anything without the boyfriend or the girlfriend, they need to pull back—and parents need to help them do so, just as they would if video games or smoking weed were having the same impact.

This level of awareness will be a challenge for young people as they figure out what they need as opposed to what's rewarding in the moment—which, when they're passionately in love, can seem like anything and everything that involves the person they adore. Hence the challenge: What are the right limits on the seeming limitlessness of teen desire?

Setting Relationship Policy

We live in a time when what I'm calling relationship policy—the rules and expectations families set for dating—varies widely. Some families set a minimum age when children can start to date. Others enforce religious restrictions that limit physical contact before marriage. Some cultures forbid anything resembling dating until the time comes to be introduced to marriage prospects. Some parents won't let a young couple be alone together. Others allow their children's partners to sleep over. One 18-year-old girl told me that her parents are so open and affirming about sex and pleasure that when she wants to be alone with her boyfriend, she asks her parents to go out to dinner so they can have privacy, and her parents oblige.

Sex educators emphasize that parental policies about sex and dating are rooted in values: parents' fundamental beliefs about what's important. A first serious relationship almost always entails sexual feelings, exploration, and potentially a young person's sexual debut. The majority of young people have sex for the first time in a serious relationship, and they are more likely to view the experience as positive than people whose first experience is in a casual hookup.[10] You have to hand it to the going-out-to-dinner parents for walking their talk. They're conveying to their daughter that they value her having the space she needs to enjoy sex unselfconsciously—and that they're chill enough about the matter to have a nice meal in the meantime.

Hearing about them challenged me. I've discussed with my daughter the fact that teen girls commonly experience what's known as pleasure inequality—difficulties feeling pleasure and expressing what they want, particularly in straight relationships. They still receive strong messages to prioritize male desire.[11] I knew that having to sneak around, with sex limited to the back seat of a car or a rushed few minutes in an empty house, probably doesn't help girls feel relaxed enough to explore what makes them feel good. At the same time, the going-out-to-dinner family's degree of openness is daunting. But there's a middle ground. Parents could express support for pleasure equality and that they value sex as a private act, something they'd rather not know was going on as they tucked into their appetizers.

Relationship policy is also complicated because it's a moving target. Setting an "open door when the partner is in the house" policy may work well when a child is 13. But when the child is 16 and in a serious relationship, parents may find themselves reconsidering.

Policy for the oldest child sets a precedent for younger ones, who will cry foul if they sense a double standard. "I have to think about what I tell my son, because I know it has to be the same for my daughter, and my impulse is to be more protective with my daughter," a father told me. Then there's the matter of to what degree you can coordinate relationship policy with another household. You might be vigilant about being in the house to supervise when your kid's partner is over, but the partner's parents might not care as much or simply be unable to play relationship cop. Making the effort to connect with the other parents is still worth it. "I made sure to walk into my daughter's boyfriend's house, meet his parents, and let them know what my rules were," a mother told me. "I knew things were probably going to be looser over there, but I wanted them to know where I was coming from."

Contemporary experts say the best parenting style is authoritative, the sweet spot between being rigidly authoritarian and overly permissive. One of the tenets of authoritative parenting is explaining the rules. Values give parents a language for this. So does bringing to bear past experiences. My own first intense sexual encounter was unsettling and confusing, in a relationship that was more longing than substance. All this came back to me vividly when my daughter started to date. I felt an acute vigilance. I did not want my daughter to be alone behind closed doors with a boy until she was in a trusting, loving relationship. I told her about my past in broad brush—young people don't like knowing the details, either—so she knew where these values came from. When she was 15, she got into a relationship that would last for the next two and a half years. As I watched them grow closer, I realized that they had a trusting bond, nothing like the relationship I had. My protectiveness gradually faded. After they'd been together a year, we started letting him sleep over on the weekends.

Sexual health advocates love the sleepover for the ways it encourages an open dialogue about adolescent sexuality and relationships, at least the way it's practiced in Holland. There, according to research by sociologist Amy Schalet, two-thirds of teens ages 15 to 17 in serious relationships say their partner is allowed to spend the night. The practice grew out of a culture where parents and teens openly discuss sex and love. Body awareness, an early form of sex education, starts in preschool. The outcomes are impressive: Dutch teens are more likely to use birth control. They have fewer sexual partners and are more likely to have their sexual debut in loving relationships where they're comfortable talking about what they want and what feels good.[12] Most compellingly, Dutch teens didn't feel that they had to "split their burgeoning sexual selves from their family roles" the way American teens do, as Schalet wrote. "When children feel safe enough to tell parents what they are doing and feeling, presumably it's that much easier for them to ask for help. This allows parents to have more influence, to control through connection."[13]

If you buy the argument—not an easy thing to do, given the raised eyebrows you'll get, even in my relatively progressive community—the next step is figuring out when sleepovers are appropriate. The concept of age of consent—the legal notion that, once you reach a certain age, you are mature enough to agree to sex—gave my husband and me a kind of conceptual guide. We assumed the age was 16 in New York State, so that's what we told our daughter (we would eventually find out that it's 17, but the point wasn't really what the state thought—it was what we did). We had other rules, too. During the school year, we limited sleepovers to once a week. Sleepovers for any new relationship in the future would have to pass a similar test to this one: It had to be a relationship with some history and with a person we felt right having in our home. And it had to *be* a relationship. If the relationship was too emotionally precarious to be defined, then it was too emotionally precarious for sleepovers.

Several of my teen subjects emphasized to me what they saw as the irony of the sleepover debate: that to them, it isn't really about sex. "Parents are always like, 'Oh, if this kid sleeps over, they're going to have sex,' and I'm like, 'They probably already had sex in the back of a car like an hour before,'" one teen told me. "When I want to be able to sleep over with a partner, it was so I can sleep next to someone I care about. As cheesy as that sounds, that's what we want."

The sleepover may play a somewhat different role in the narrative of same-sex couples. Several of my LGBTQ+ sources told me that their first relationships began on the sly *during* sleepovers. They would hide what was happening from their parents so they could continue spending nights together. Once they confessed, their parents scrambled to backward-engineer a relationship policy. This can be awkward. Some parents will end all sleepovers, even with same-sex friends. They may reason that, if they wouldn't let a straight child have sleepovers with the opposite sex, then a same-sex-attracted child shouldn't have sleepovers with same-sex peers. Bi- or pansexual kids, under that rationale, are totally out of luck. This kind of dictate ostracizes young people from normal teen rituals, and it oversexualizes them by imagining every same-sex friend as a sexual prospect. A better option is encouraging young people to be honest about the nature of their relationships and letting them know why you're concerned. You can say that you don't want sleepovers to be a fast track to sex or overenmeshment. You can put a halt to sleepovers at the beginning of a relationship, or you can have your child's partner sleep in a separate room after curfew.

Same-Sex and Serious

For parents of LGBTQ+ young people, particularly in conservative communities, relationship policy can seem inseparable from their efforts to shield their children from homophobia and discrimination. Greg, a 52-year-old parole officer and father of three in Arlington, Texas, grew up in a Southern Baptist household. When his older sister came out as a lesbian in college, his mother lived in denial for years, then arrived at an ambivalent acceptance. He explained, "My mom would say it's not what God wants, but she tolerates it."

Greg's oldest son, Ian, came out, as Greg described it, "with a bang" the summer before his junior year in high school. He called his close friends to tell them he was gay and made plans to deliver the news to his extended family. Greg alerted his mother in advance. "I want nothing but support," he insisted.

"I'll be supportive," she said. "I love Ian. But I don't want him to have a hard life."

Greg and his wife, Laura, a social worker who started her career with an AIDS advocacy organization, didn't either. The couple stood their ground with neighbors and community members who believed homosexuality was wrong. "I tell them, 'I kind of know how you've grown up and what you've been taught, but there are certain lines you're not going to cross when you're around me,'" he said.

Soon after Ian came out, he started dating Jason, a relationship that would last for two years. Greg and Laura made rules for Ian that would set a fair precedent for Ian's younger brother and sister, who are both straight. Some were uncomplicated: The boys had to keep doors open and weren't allowed to lie down on the bed together. When Ian was out with Jason, he had to text his parents to tell them where he was. But Greg and Laura were also challenged by the ways the boys' relationship *was* different from a straight relationship. Ian was a new driver, not yet allowed to take the highway into Dallas and Fort Worth. But the couple was more likely to be harassed in less gay-friendly Arlington. "Greg and I were out to dinner in Dallas one night and saw gay couples holding hands. I just wanted to say, 'Let's let them go there,'" Laura said. "It was a constant negotiation."

Greg was the stricter parent. He was troubled by what-ifs: Were the boys presenting as guy friends when they were at Jason's house, which meant they could spend time behind closed doors with impunity? Would the couple seek out parks and other public places to fool around? "It's much different to be a straight couple caught making out versus a gay couple making out," he said. "It's the safety issue."

The irony of the effort parents put into crafting the right relationship policy is that young people inevitably find their way around them. Ian was no exception. "I got really good at timing things," Ian said. "I would tell my parents I was going to Starbucks, and then we would leave Starbucks early and go to Jason's house." Jason came from a conservative Hispanic working-class family. His parents were less accepting of Jason's sexual orientation than Ian's parents were. But they weren't as strict. It was a "don't ask, don't tell" situation. "I don't think they wanted us to have sex when they were home, but otherwise they didn't care," Ian said.

Ian wanted to be in love the way he'd come out: without reservations or secrets. His parents wanted that, too. But they worried about the consequences. They cautioned him not to hold hands with Jason in the high school parking lot. They argued over whether Ian should bring Jason as his date to the debate club banquet. Ian knew his father had watched his sister white-knuckle it through her own coming out. His mother had witnessed the pain of her gay clients in the 1980s and '90s facing the double scourge of AIDS and antigay violence. They didn't want their son to get hurt. Ian simply wanted to be free to do what all the other couples around him were doing. "They accused me of trying to be a warrior," Ian said. "I just wanted to be treated like I was in any other teenage relationship. I was like, 'All the straight couples are holding hands. And I just want my boyfriend at the debate banquet. Why do I have to be different?'"

"It *is* different," Greg would say, though he wished it wasn't.

Michael Newcomb, a Northwestern University clinical psychologist whose research focuses on mental health and health disparities in LGBTQ+ youth, points out that queer teens, to some extent, likely share their parents' worries about safety and visibility. He advises parents to ask their children where they feel safe being visible and where they don't and work from there. "Help them think through it," he said. "When you start by telling them where they can't go, you're reinforcing the idea that you should hide yourself rather than fostering critical thinking about where should I be more visible? And where should I not be?" This doesn't mean that any place a teen deems safe is automatically okay. But working through the problem together will help them develop the capacity to eventually make these judgment calls on their own.

Prioritizing What You Are Becoming

Their senior year, Ian and Jason both decided to attend the same state university. In college, Ian knew, he would finally be free of his parents' rules and live in a more accepting environment. But he realized he wanted to start his freshman year single. He broke up with Jason a few weeks before their first semester started. "It was one of the hardest things I've ever done," Ian said. "It made it even harder that we were going to the same college. I couldn't do the whole 'I don't want to do long-distance' thing. I had to be up-front and tell him I didn't want to be in a relationship going into college."

Psychologist and author Daniel J. Siegel emphasizes that adolescents should, when it comes to relationships, be self-centered. The priority should be on growing into "what you are becoming" over loyalty to a relationship. From early adolescence through the college years, young people, even if they're very much in love, should be able to nurture friendships and pursue goals on their own. If the relationship is supposed to work out, it will.[14]

That's likely one of the reasons transitions—summers away, going to college—are frequently breaking points for serious relationships. Transitions are gut checks on whether the commitment is still worthwhile when being together becomes more challenging and individual growth needs to take center stage. When teen relationships end at such turning points, parents often feel a private relief—after all, this was never *supposed* to last—along with the hope that their child's sadness over the breakup will be mitigated by the possibilities of newfound autonomy.

But transitions can also be excruciatingly painful ruptures, especially when they don't fit neatly into this narrative. Neither Juli nor Vinnie had easy lives before they became a couple. Juli has congenital myasthenia, an inherited muscular disorder that often leaves her fatigued and too weak to walk. She wasn't expected to live past childhood. At 12, a change in medications gave her a new lease on life. Vinnie came from an impoverished, troubled family. His mother, emotionally unstable and addicted to opioids, was incarcerated in Pennsylvania. His father was raising Vinnie and his two brothers in Upstate New York while working low-wage jobs.

Even though Juli and Vinnie were young—she was 14, and he was 13—they grew serious quickly. He took refuge at her home to escape the chaos in his, a trailer so dilapidated that "it probably could have gotten blown down by the wind," Juli said. Though Vinnie was a trying boyfriend at times—his chronic flirting with other girls irked her—he never hesitated to help Juli, whose strength could wane suddenly, leaving her unable to cross a room or fix herself a snack. His devotion quieted a doubt she'd grappled with for years: Given her disability, who would want to be with her? Who would take care of her? "Vinnie showed me it wasn't a big deal," she said. "It's just natural. It happens. When you're with someone, you help them."

Then, Vinnie's mother was released from prison. Her probation terms required her to live in Pennsylvania. She summoned her family. With only a few hours' notice, Vinnie was gone. Beth, Juli's mother, saw how bereft her daughter was. "The love of her life, the person she thinks is going to be the father of her children, is moving to Pennsylvania, and how's she going to see him?" she said. When Juli asked her mother to take her to the shabby coal-region town where Vinnie's family landed, she did. Once a month, Beth and Juli made the three-hour trek and stayed over in a hotel room so Juli and Vinnie could spend time together.

It was beyond the call for Beth, a reading specialist who worked two jobs. I asked her if her efforts to support the couple were related to her daughter's disability, to not wanting her daughter to suffer again. Beth said that wasn't it. She wanted Juli to have a normal life, which meant dealing with disappointments in love just like any other teen. But she felt her daughter deserved closure. When Beth was 12, her own mother, an alcoholic who'd left the family after her parents divorced, died of liver disease. No one told her for days, and her mother never had a funeral. "My bottom line is that I have an issue with closure. I just feel like it's necessary," Beth said. "That's why I kept bringing her down there. I wanted her to see it through until she realized she wasn't in love anymore." Gradually, the trips became less frequent, and the couple broke up.

Young people who stay with their partners as they undergo major life changes may end up torn between holding onto their partners and being present in their day-to-day lives, particularly when distance is involved. When Christine, who grew up in Ashland, Oregon, started college in the Midwest, she was determined to sustain her relationship with her high school boyfriend. But being long-distance wasn't easy. "You can't be in two places at once," she said. "I would have to make choices to not hang out with my friends so I could go and do a video call with him."

They tried to break up, a messy, back-and-forth process complicated by technology—they always had a window into each other's lives on social media, even though they were 2,400 miles apart. The sight of her boyfriend with another girl on Instagram more than once drove Christine to resuscitate the floundering relationship. They didn't break up for good until her senior year.

It's never been easy to see someone you've loved move on. But it's particularly trying now, given all of the life we live online. If you're trying to break up, you must contend with the sting of photos, videos, and comments illustrating that your partner is moving on without you. Every moment of the day, we carry in our pockets and purses the near entirety of our social lives, our friends, acquaintances, and lovers, near and far, past and present, always on our phone screens. Not letting go is the default setting.

Christine regretted hanging on too long to her first love. I've listened to many stories of young people who tried to keep their relationships going during college and other transitions. The effort can drag down their well-being.[15] Later, with the wisdom of hindsight, most were unhappy with the ways their relationship kept them from being fully present in their lives. In a time when everyone around them was prioritizing the freedom and opportunity of starting over in a new environment, they were outliers, much of their head space dedicated to someone somewhere else.

While the question of how long-lasting and how central a serious relationship should be in a young person's life seems like a purely personal dilemma, the question is also entwined with the workings of American meritocracy. Young people intent on prioritizing "what they are becoming" over serious relationships will be more available to deal with the "intense economic demands of late capitalism," DePaul University communication professor Kendra Knight told me. Emerging adults, her research has found, want partnerships that don't impede their education and careers and may delay commitment out of concern that a relationship will break their stride.[16] In this light, keeping a first love going beyond high school isn't just about missing out on what we like to imagine young adulthood to be: free, fun, a time of sexual and social exploration. It also poses a challenge to young people's ability to access the American dream. With a partner by their side, will they be able to chase their own goals—especially if that partner wants to be doing the same thing?

WILL MY CHILD MAKE THE SAME MISTAKES I DID?

On the wall of the master bedroom of Michelle and Raul's railroad apartment in the Bronx hangs a photo novelty keepsake from their beginnings as a couple in 1996, when they were 16: Michelle's bangs are curled low over her eyes, a tight bun on top of her head, her smile a little startled. Raul's cheek is pressed close to hers, his eyebrows arched mischievously. On each side of the photo is a list of personality attributes associated with their names. For Raul, one of them is "Hard work will pay off." For Michelle: "A good educational background is key to her success."

Raul's parents were from Puerto Rico. His mother raised him. His father struggled with drug addiction, which would end his life at 41. Michelle's mother, who was also Puerto Rican, was an administrative assistant, and her father, a Guyanese immigrant, worked days in a factory and overnights as a delivery driver. When the photograph was taken, Michelle had dreams of becoming a first-grade teacher. Raul hadn't even started thinking about what he wanted to be. "I was just hanging out, trying to be cool," he said.

Then, Michelle got pregnant. Having a baby so young was tough. After their daughter Dynahlee was born, they managed to get their high school degrees, but there would be no teaching career for Michelle. She became a medical secretary. Raul found work in the printing industry. They moved into an apartment on the infamous "last floor" of the Weston projects. Neighbors and strangers passed through the hallway to party on the roof. Dynahlee and her younger sister learned from an early age to stand up straight in the elevator without leaning against the walls to avoid touching urine and feces. They were forbidden to play in the project playground. The other tenants recognized Raul and Michelle as "young parents with old-school values," a description Raul still cites with pride.

By the time Dynahlee entered adolescence, they were a family of five. Through a city program that transitioned families from the projects into home ownership, Raul and Michelle bought a three-bedroom apartment in a co-op in a quieter neighborhood on the east side of the Bronx. Dynahlee was a model firstborn sibling. She loved school and spent hours reading. She helped her cousins with their homework, earning her the nickname "the Genius." Dynahlee started eighth grade with the highest GPA in her class, on track to become the valedictorian of her small public middle school. She hummed with ambition, intent on seizing opportunities her parents never had. She wanted to go to college. She wanted to see the world. She wanted to become a journalist.

Unbeknownst to her parents, she was also enjoying a budding AOL Instant Messenger flirtation with Joseph. He was the class clown. He spent most afternoons in detention and got by with Bs and Cs. After a week of gathering his nerve, he tapped her on the shoulder in history class. "Want to go out with me?" he whispered.

When Dynahlee confessed to her parents she was in a relationship, they told her she was too young. It would be months before Joseph was allowed to visit. He had to stay in the narrow front living room. They would sit next to each other without touching on the plush navy-blue couch, in easy view as the rest of the family circulated through the adjacent kitchen. At school, the rules were also firm: no kissing, holding hands, or hugging.

The teachers noticed Dynahlee whispering and giggling with Joseph. They told Joseph that he wasn't smart enough for her. Everyone seemed to want to divide the students into camps. There were the ones who had promise, a shot at attending college and escaping the neighborhood, with its high rates of poverty, single-parent families, teen pregnancy, and drug addiction. And then there were the students the teachers didn't think could make it because they were disruptive, skipped class, cracked too many jokes, or wore lipstick. Years later, Dynahlee was still indignant at how readily the teachers dismissed Joseph's potential. "They should have been trying to empower him to become better," she said.

After a teacher warned her that Joseph was going nowhere in life, she told him flatly, "You need to have some goals, because I have goals, and I need to be with someone who has goals. You have to have a plan and do something with it. You can't spend your life making jokes."

One evening, her parents got a call from the principal. Their daughter still had the highest academic GPA in the class, the principal reported, but her behavior grades had slipped. The eighth-grade teachers decided she no longer qualified to be valedictorian. It was barely concealed code for "You have a boy-friend who is leading you down the wrong path." "I was pissed," Dynahlee said. "It was the one time I had something that needed improvement out of my entire tenure as a star student."

She was accepted at the Beacon School, one of the most selective public high schools in New York City. She and Joseph planned to break up before high school, but when the time came, they couldn't do it. They were too in love. Joseph also had gotten attached to Dynahlee's family. Her parents provided guidance and structure. His parents were preoccupied with their own troubles. His father was an alcoholic, and his parents' marriage was falling apart.

"He was just a young kid trying to find his way and do the best he can without his parents," Raul said. But as the relationship grew more serious, Raul and Michelle became concerned about where it might lead. Joseph adored their daughter. He wanted to be by her side as much as possible. Was he clinging too tightly? "I worried he wasn't going to give her room to make her own decisions," Michelle said.

Above all, they worried that Dynahlee and Joseph would follow in their footsteps. They knew they were good role models. They had a healthy, loving relationship. They did well in their jobs. But they did not want their children to start out the way they had. "I told Dynahlee that it might not work out as long as me and Mommy," Raul said. "If you have a kid and don't finish school and he leaves, it's going to be harder to go back with a kid. And you're always going to be the mother of that child. The father's got legs and can walk away."

Dynahlee and Joseph felt at times like their relationship was the projection of everyone's fears: middle school teachers who had seen good kids get derailed by drugs and sex, a family history on both sides of people who became parents too young. Dynahlee and Joseph didn't want to become teen parents, either. But they did want to be in each other's future. They both got into SUNY New Paltz, the college where I teach and where Dynahlee would become my student. It was Dynahlee's first choice and the school that gave Joseph the financial aid and academic support he wanted. Raul and Michelle weren't entirely comfortable with the idea that they were going to the same college, but they didn't object.

One Sunday morning during their freshman year, Raul and Michelle got a call from their daughter. "Joseph proposed!" she told them excitedly. They were engaged.

Raul and Michelle were stunned. She and Raul showed up in front of Dynahlee's residence hall the next morning. They took her to breakfast and peppered her with questions: "Are you going to get married tomorrow?" "Are you going to have kids right away?" "If that happens, you're not going to finish college," Raul warned.

Dynahlee was indignant. She reminded them that everything she'd ever said about her future still held true. It would be a long time before they got married and even longer before they had children. Excited by the challenge and depth of college course-work, Joseph was turning into an excellent student, with grades that rivaled Dynahlee's. Dynahlee was as motivated as ever. "You know me," Dynahlee shot back at her parents. "I'm not going to do anything that gets in the way of my career and my life and what I want to do."

Raul and Michelle held her to it. Ever since she started college, Dynahlee had been talking about spending a semester abroad in Madrid to improve her Spanish. But when the time came to commit to the program, she hesitated. Raul told her he didn't want her to miss an opportunity he and Michelle had never had. "Why don't you both do study abroad?" he suggested.

Joseph liked the idea. "Can we go together?" he asked Dynahlee.

Dynahlee wanted to go to Spain alone so she could completely immerse herself in the culture and become fluent in Spanish. Going without Joseph, she realized, was about more than learning a language. It was about her identity: as a student, as a young woman, as a Latina who wanted to be able to converse with her Puerto Rican great-grandmother. She was keenly aware of the example she set for her younger sister. "There's pressure for me to make sure that I stay true to myself," she said. "I couldn't lose myself to the relationship. Because if I did, that trickles down." She told Joseph she didn't want him to come with her.

They argued for days. Then, in a combination of whimsy and, as Joseph would later admit, a little pettiness, he told her that he would study in Australia. "I literally just Googled, 'Hey, what's the farthest place from here?'" Joseph said. Raul was thrilled. He told Joseph that going to Australia would make him the coolest Dominican kid in the Bronx.

As they prepared for their time away, friends echoed the same things people had been saying to them since middle school: Your relationship isn't going to last. "Oh, people had a field day," Joseph said. "They're like, 'You guys are going to be apart for a few months. You might find someone else.'"

Dynahlee and Joseph thrived on different continents. When they returned, they sensed a newfound respect from their friends and their parents. The time away had clarified that they weren't together just because they couldn't deal with being apart.

At the end of their senior year, they were chosen as outstanding graduates, an honor given to the students with the highest GPAs in each major. It was a lovely corrective from their beginnings as a couple, when their teachers decided their relationship made Dynahlee unworthy of being named valedictorian—and deemed Joseph unworthy, period.

After the awards ceremony, Dynahlee and Joseph stood next to each other proudly, holding their certificates, as friends took their picture. They made a striking couple: Dynahlee in towering heels, Joseph in white shirt sleeves and a tie. "Those two," another student of mine said admiringly. "What a power couple."

What Dynahlee and Joseph have is rare. Few young people in the Western world today meet their life partner in middle school. Few would want to—and few parents would wish this fate for their child. At every turn, Dynahlee's parents had to grapple with the question, Is something this long-lasting and serious so young going to get in our child's way? I wouldn't want to deal with this question so soon in my daughter's life, nor would I wish for her to spend her entire adolescence with the same person. But after following Dynahlee and Joseph's story, I considered that, if my daughter found a relationship that valued mutual thriving as much as theirs did, I might be convinced.

Healthy relationships at any age are what husband-and-wife psychology researchers Arthur Aron and Elaine Aron call "self-expanding." Simply put, when we become close to someone else, we incorporate the person's identity into our own, enlarging our capabilities and expanding our perspective. Through intimacy, we have more resources to navigate life. We have new experiences we wouldn't have had otherwise. Real intimacy, then, is the opposite of losing yourself to someone else. It is becoming a *larger* self because you're close to someone else.[17]

While we may be more inclined to watch for what a relationship is taking away from young people as they come of age, we also should consider intimacy's capacity to add to their sense of themselves and their impact on the world. Is the relationship enlivening, helping young people explore new dimensions of themselves and the world? Is it two-way, with both partners benefiting? In short, does the relationship leave you feeling like you are more than you used to be—more capable, more informed, more supported, more able to give your best? There's little question a serious relationship will transform a young person's life in a time already characterized by rapid change. It's how that matters.

CHAPTER 4

Are They Right for Each Other?

Communicating Concerns

MY DAUGHTER AND I PULLED INTO THE DRIVEWAY OF HER BOY-friend's house. His mother's car wasn't in there.

"You said his mother was going to be home," I said.

"His sister is there," my daughter said. "She's like his mother. She bosses him around."

"You didn't say sister. You said mother. It's not the same. The rule is a parent has to be home."

This was boyfriend number 2, in our lives for a couple of months. She was 14; he was 15.

"I told you *someone* would be there."

"We're going home," I said. I started to back up the car.

"Wait," she pleaded.

I stopped backing up, because I remembered what it felt like to be 14 and want badly to see a boyfriend, though at the same time, I hated that this memory might have any influence on my actions. I told her, "If you want to see him, he'll have to come to our house."

She texted him to let him know. No answer. She went in to search for him. It took a long time. I imagined him in a basement bedroom, at one in the afternoon, still asleep in a teen-boy-dank tangle of blankets, reluctant to be roused or peeved that the unsupervised afternoon he had in mind wasn't going to happen.

The boyfriend, who was very tall, emerged and folded himself into the back seat of my car. My daughter climbed in and buckled herself into the middle seat. On the way back, I glanced at them in my rearview mirror. The boyfriend's arm was wrapped around my daughter. His eyes and hers were vacant with disappointment.

Hoping to change the air, I took a stab at making conversation. Football. I knew he played football. In our music- and arts-oriented household, football was exotic. Maybe I could learn something? When I asked him what position he played, he told me he'd been out with a shoulder injury most of the season. He was better, but he wasn't sure if he wanted to keep playing.

"Why?" I asked, hopeful of engaging him on the stresses of playing high school sports or getting gossip on a shitty coach or something.

"I don't know," he said.

He also didn't know the name of his shoulder injury, and he was vague about how he got hurt: "Something in the weight room, I guess." He answered most of my questions this way, with dead-end phrases that suggested he would rather not continue the exchange.

"He's shy," my daughter had explained. She was animated and talkative around him. She cracked jokes. She insisted he talk to *her*. But seeing her with him was like watching a novice camper try to light a fire by striking flint against steel. A lot of work for an elusive reward. His shyness was so extreme I couldn't help but feel it was somehow—hostile. And hostile is not what you want your child to be dating.

My husband and I talked about the situation a lot. My husband, an introvert, was sympathetic to the pressure on a teen boy to be social with his girlfriend's parents. But we both couldn't help being somewhat peeved that he made so little effort as we carted the couple from house to house and hosted him for family dinners.

Being uncomfortable with the boyfriend or the girlfriend is a peculiar dilemma for parents. They grapple with the instinct to protect and the urge to judge and control. Expressing disapproval, the general wisdom goes, will only alienate young people, making them even more determined to be together. The notion is also grounded in basic psychological principles. When you have a goal, the frustration of obstacles heightens the quest and makes it more desirable. When your freedom is threatened, you'll want even more to restore it by acting out—an idea called reactance, as old as Eve's hunger for the forbidden fruit in the Garden of Eden.

Telling young people they can't see a "bad boy" (or girl) makes them more likely to do so and more likely to be influenced by the person.[1] As adolescents strive for independence and an identity separate from their parents, they see the freedom to choose a romantic partner as integral to their autonomy. Limits on that choice feel intrusive and personal. Teens are being told not only not to see someone but also, implicitly, *not to be who they are.*

Outlawing an adolescent relationship, then, is unlikely to work. Two young people who want to be together will find a way to do it. Sneaking around leaves them vulnerable. A couple who must go underground functions in isolation from caring adults. This happens a lot to young people in same-sex relationships who live in homophobic households and young people whose family's strict beliefs don't allow dating. They're more likely to put up with problems and to feel that they don't really have choice or control over their relationships.[2] If the relationship turns unhealthy, abusive, or sexually exploitative—the subject of chapter 6—then teens will be less likely to reach out for help.

Yet it's hard on parents *not* to outlaw a relationship that worries them. They must watch and wait, doing their best to keep the lines of communication open as their child grows close to someone they're uneasy with. Parents must gauge how much to say or not say about how they feel. It's part purgatory, part detective story. Is that whiff of hostility from a partner a foreshadowing of worse to come or just a fleeting sour mood? Will my child get trapped being the fixer to someone who's broken? Will this person somehow transform into someone who, with time and trust, I'll like having around? Or not? Sometimes, the problem is as simple as that. Parents won't always like the people their children do.

Sometimes, parents do like the person but not the circumstances of the relationship. While my daughter was seeing the boy I didn't like, I interviewed Samuel, a Minnesota rabbi beloved in his community for his progressive interpretations of scripture. When his daughter Ruthi was 14, he grew concerned at the attention she was getting from Greta, a girl who was four years older. The age difference was too great. He looked up state law on the age of consent. He and his wife sat the two down and explained why they couldn't be a couple yet. "I told them, 'This is illegal. You can be friends. But you have to wait to have a serious relationship,'" he said.

Beyond that talk, Samuel couldn't do much to stop them from getting close. They went to the same small school. Their phones gave them a 24/7 portal into each other's lives. "If this was another time, when I could sit guard on the front porch and the whole family shared one landline, I could have controlled it," he said. "But I couldn't."

Samuel decided that the only leverage he had was love. He went out of his way to engage Greta and listen to her attentively. After she left the area for college, she regularly called him for advice, seeing him as a kind of father figure. "I wasn't faking it," Samuel said. "I cared about her. I was still fundamentally disturbed by the age difference. But I decided to go with the carrot rather than the stick. The only leverage I had was caring."

The relationship lasted for four years. Listening to Samuel, I wondered, Was I in for *years* of the unknowable boyfriend? If I couldn't even sustain a short conversation with him, how could I show him that I cared? As much as it pained me to admit it, did I genuinely care? It's a distressing and helpless feeling to watch a child be with someone you're concerned about. I worried my husband and I were being too passive, then I worried about what I could possibly say or do to take more control.

Young people's romantic involvements are a separation task, part of the process of shifting their primary support system away from their parents and toward peers and partners.[3] It's not an easy process for parents, even when their children are forming bonds with wonderful partners and friends. When children choose someone we can't feel at ease with, it can feel like a rejection of who we are.

STAY CURIOUS

I never had much success with getting to know the shy boyfriend, though I kept trying. The more important mission was making sure my daughter knew that I was interested in the relationship and how she was faring in it. I observed how different their personalities were. I asked her what drew her to him in the first place. Her response gave me the impression that he was a challenge, a boy other girls were attracted to but didn't know how to talk to. My daughter seemed proud of penetrating his façade. She assured me he did open up with her. "It's good he can talk to you," I said.

I like to believe that, because I was curious, she didn't hide what was happening when he began to disappoint her. He stopped showing up at her music performances. He couldn't get a ride, he would tell her. She tried to be understanding. Sometimes people can't get rides. But they usually can if they plan a little. "Was he even trying?" she pondered. It's never easy to hear someone caught in this kind of thought loop, trying to solve the little puzzles people put forth when they can't be clear.

"I don't know why he couldn't get a ride," I said. "But the fact that he couldn't be there for you—that's information, right? You deserved better."

I wanted to cry out, "Don't you see how wrong he is for you?" But I held back. I kept the focus on the behavior, not the person, and chose my words carefully. The phrase *that's information* is one I use often to underscore that people give you evidence of whether they're able to meet your needs. The evidence often flies in the face of how attracted you are to them.

One of the core skills of a healthy relationship is mutuality: the ability to express needs, get them met, and work it out together when needs conflict.[4] The boyfriend wasn't giving my daughter much evidence that he wanted to meet her needs, and she would have to figure out what to do with that. Telling her that she deserved better appealed to broad principles about how a relationship is supposed to go: Partners should show up for important moments in each other's lives.

Pointing this out could have been a risk. She might have dug in deeper to try to redeem the relationship. But I would have regretted responding in any other way, and I trusted that she would take what I said into account as she considered what to do. She hung on for a few weeks, hoping the relationship would improve. Then he broke up with her.

All she felt was relief. My husband and I felt the same way.

Even with all the hue and cry about how rebellious teens are, they care a lot about what parents think. However mighty peer influence may be, young people still view their parents as the most important moral authority in their lives.[5] They anticipate their parents' reactions before they act.[6] They even consider parents a more accurate source of information on dating than peers.[7] As I've mentioned, they crave more conversations and guidance about romantic relationships.[8]

But they don't want to be lectured or preached at. Nor do they want to hear your criticisms of the person they are dating. "When you get into personal territory, like who they choose to hang out with, kids will reject our involvement," said Ken Ginsburg, the founding director of the Center for Parent and Teen

Communication. "I'm not saying not to discuss a specific partner. I'm saying to be strategic when you do so. If you make it about their having unwise choices or that you don't like the person, they're going to respond by telling you, 'You're not dating them. I'm dating them.'"

Staying curious about adolescent children and their relationships is an art, not a science. Parents may find it helpful to ask their children for the go-ahead to start a discussion about their relationship, as in "You seem sad a lot after you talk to X. Can I ask you a couple of questions about how things are going?" It's possible to ask for conversation consent even before a young person starts dating or is between relationships, as in "If you're ever in a relationship that I'm concerned about, do you want me to tell you?" The advance agreement becomes a kind of touchstone, sending an important message: The business of relationships can be fraught, and I want permission to be a part of your support system.

Young people, as my daughter's situation suggested, will likely be more open in times of uncertainty when they're considering whether they're getting their needs met and whether they can meet their partners' needs. Joanne Davila's relationship workshop teaches that there are three conditions for a healthy relationship: (1) I know and like myself. (2) I know and like my partner. (3) My partner knows and likes me.[9] These are a good starting point to help them take inventory. Strong attraction—love, lust, chemistry—can often make it hard to acknowledge what's really going on in a relationship. The three conditions bring the situation down to earth. They're agonizingly basic, and that's what makes them so powerful. The list helps young people realize they can feel in love with someone they don't actually like or someone who doesn't see them for who they are.

For longer-term, serious relationships, big-picture questions may help children—and their parents—see their situation more clearly. I reached out to Richard Weissbourd, a psychologist and senior lecturer at the Harvard Graduate School of Education who directs Making Caring Common (MCC), a national organization that promotes moral and social development in child raising. MCC's seminal report *The Talk: How Adults Can Promote Young People's Healthy Relationships and Prevent Misogyny and Sexual Harassment* was one of the inspirations for this book, and I see Weissbourd as a kind of rabbi figure in the parenting world. He acknowledged how delicate it can be to get young people to open up about their relationships, then suggested a few questions parents and other trusted adults can ask: Does your partner expand your sense of who you are or contract it? Does your partner make you feel like you have more to give to the world or less? I loved these questions because they guide young people to think of their relationship in terms of the quality of the intimacy and whether their partner is fostering their larger self, with new capabilities and perspectives.

Then, Weissbourd offered another question suggestion: "Would you want your partner as your parent?"

I was a little taken aback because of the Freudian resonance. He explained he was thinking of people old enough and committed enough to consider raising children together. In the coming days, though, I found myself thinking more and more about the question and how it might apply to teens, as well. In some relationships in my youth, I felt desire and need, and I felt desired and needed. But I didn't feel truly *cared for*. In context (and maybe with some nervous laughter), the question "Would you want your partner as your parent?" could be high impact. Even teens not old enough to consider their partner as a future parent benefit from thinking about whether their partner cares for them in a way that makes them feel safe, seen, and secure.

Young people don't always respond right away to curiosity. They'll shrug; stick earbuds in their ears; give the minimal answer; or say, "I just can't go there." Being a curious parent is exhausting, a game with a high ratio of fruitless queries to actual answers. Young people may be particularly defensive when it comes to questions about relationships because they may be at a loss to explain why they're with someone or to admit to ambivalent feelings.

Broaching the subject can feel like microsurgery. Make the wrong move, and the conversation is over. But when a parent or another trusted adult poses calm, thoughtful questions from time to time, they underscore to adolescents that what is going on is worthy of discussion and reflection. Even when teens aren't up to talking or they reprimand you for probing into their private lives, they also know the door to your support is open.

Adolescents clam up very fast when they sense that door isn't open. When Belle, a New York City teen, was 12, she told her parents that she had a girlfriend. Her parents responded by saying she was too young to know she would never like boys. "Although they didn't have a problem with me liking girls, I was looking for more explicit support," she said. They didn't discuss the relationship again until many months later, when her mother casually queried about her "special friend." They'd long since broken up.

At 16, Belle started seeing a 20-year-old man. Her parents disapproved of the age difference. Her father accused her of dating him just to piss off her mother. "I was like, 'Screw you, I wouldn't do that,'" she said. Her boyfriend became controlling. He criticized what she wore. Sometimes he'd rage at her on the street or shove her in frustration, warning signs of an abusive relationship. She didn't tell her parents about any of it. She'd gotten the clear signal, more than once, that they cared more about judging her relationships than finding out what was going on in them.

HISTORY VERSUS IMAGINATION: THE POWER OF SELF-DISCLOSURE

Parents may not think they have much to offer on the matter of partner choice. They may have lingering regrets about the mistakes they made during their own adolescence. They may fret over how their adult relationships influence their children, particularly if they've experienced divorce, remarriage, and other big shifts in family life. Even intact marriages are still, well, marriages, susceptible to entrenched resentments, unmet needs, betrayals, and other conflicts that may affect children just as much as parents who aren't together. All this means that parents may feel the least qualified to provide insight into relationships at a time when that insight feels the most urgent.

Yet these life struggles may be one of parents' greatest sources of strength and authority when it comes to talking to children about love. One of the fundamental differences between how young people regard their relationships and how their parents do comes down to this: Parents see their relationships from the vantage point of history. They take into account all that is entailed in sharing a life and raising children with another person, whether the union has endured or not. They also consider past lessons learned from other experiences of romantic love and dating. Adolescents see relationships from the vantage point of imagination. They don't yet have the insights of experience and time.

This difference is exactly why parents should consider mining their own romantic experiences for insight when talking to their children. "A lot of parents think they don't have wisdom about love," Weissbourd said. "But you can go through a divorce, and you can be in a marriage that's not happy and still have wisdom to transmit to your kids. It's important that history talks to imagination, that parents and other adults find ways to share the wisdom they have accrued with younger adults."

Parents can speak, for example, about reckoning with long-standing patterns of behavior: giving too much in past relationships to people who didn't reciprocate or being too self-absorbed to appreciate partners' needs. Parents coping with past abuse can say, "We have a history of trauma in this family, and trauma is intergenerational. There are some things I need to say because I really want you to be able to avoid this."

Weissbourd cautioned that, though self-disclosure can be potent, it's crucial to avoid disparaging a child's other parent. Parents should also avoid shifting the focus of the conversation to solving their own relationship problems—a responsibility teens shouldn't have to take on. In short: Don't make it about you.

I've found in my conversations with young people that their parents' cautionary tales resonate powerfully. The bad boyfriend, the controlling ex, the too-needy partner in their parents' past take residence in their heads. The parent's story becomes part of their own, with young people consciously trying to avoid the scenarios their parents have shared.

Meanwhile, young people who perceive their parents' relationship history as problem-free may feel self-conscious when their own love lives turn out to be less than ideal. Kayla, a 19-year-old college student, grew up with her parents' "beautiful and picturesque" love story entrenched in family lore. Her mother, who was raised poor in a southern Florida trailer park, fell in love at 18 with her father. He built a lucrative career in finance, allowing them to raise their children in privilege and comfort. When Kayla's first high school boyfriend broke up with her to pursue another girl, she drowned her feelings in weed and alcohol, straining her relationship with her parents. "I felt there was no way for them to understand what I was going through," she said.

REBEL RELATIONSHIPS, TRADITIONAL CULTURES

One of the reasons parents struggle when they disapprove of their child's partner may be because our forefathers and foremothers had a lot more power over the intimate lives of their children. There was no dating as we know it now, as a practice of personal choice. Parents determined whom their children would marry, a decision integral to the economic and political status of the extended family.[10] Romantic love was considered a "divine madness" that could threaten these carefully laid plans.

Today, Western society, with its emphasis on individuality and autonomy, has largely moved away from parental involvement in dating and marriage. Falling in love is something young people do on their own. This notion, though, is not universal. In many cultures, parents and other relatives still have considerable authority over their children's hearts. Dating is only sanctioned as part of the pipeline to marriage, and parents determine who's acceptable marriage material. The process is often more expansive than in prior generations, when couples routinely married as strangers. Now, family members—at times with the assistance of a hired matchmaker—make introductions, but the children's opinions also hold sway. The practice is part of a fundamentally different view of not only love but also the place of the self in society. The Western individualist ideals we're familiar with in the United States value independence, pleasure, and the right to privacy. Free will, particularly when it comes to dating and sex, is paramount. Collectivist cultures value group solidarity, sharing, duty, and the good of the group. Loyalty to family takes priority over private preference. In collectivist cultures, adolescent desire, however common, is suspect, a selfish force with the potential to ruin everything.

Athira had always seen herself as a parent pleaser. In high school, she earned straight As. She went to church. She obeyed her parents, who'd moved the family to the Chicago area from India when Athira was two. When it came to dating, she knew the rules: She and her younger siblings would not be allowed to date until their career paths were set. Even then, her parents would have a hand in the process. They would introduce her to young Indian men they thought appropriate husband material until the right match took.

Athira's parents and all the adults in her extended family had arranged marriages. She'd grown up with the story of how her grandfather, a rubber farmer in Kerala, took out a classified ad in the matrimonial pages of the newspaper to find her mother, Regi, a husband. She rejected 20 suitors before Saji, who would become Athira's father, walked through the door. They married two weeks later. "My parents' marriage seemed fine, so for me the concept was never weird," Athira said.

John probably would have eventually become a parent-approved prospective spouse, had Athira not broken the rules first by falling in love with him. Her senior year of high school, John moved from Saudi Arabia to Athira's suburb, Mount Prospect, where neighborhoods of modest, split-level beige-brick ranch homes alternated with strip malls of vape stores, car washes, nail salons, and fast food. It was the kind of place where it's easy to walk to a neighbor's house but somewhat treacherous to get to the drugstore; the main roads were wide and busy, meant for cars and not pedestrians. John fortunately lived only a five-minute stroll away.

They had a lot in common. His parents had also grown up in Kerala. Both their mothers were nurses. John's family joined Athira's church, St. Thomas Syro-Malabar Cathedral, a vast brick building with a neo-baroque façade, built to serve the growing South Indian Catholic community west of Chicago. St. Thomas's on a Sunday morning was a vision of the Kerala diaspora. Mothers in bright saris made their way through the crowded hallways to take their children to catechism class. Then they joined their husbands for Malayalam-language mass in the octagonal main sanctuary, the bell-shaped ceiling reminiscent of Indian architecture.

St. Thomas's was the perfect place to incubate Athira's growing crush on John. She would linger after mass, hoping to run into him. They began to exchange friendly texts. When he was recovering from hernia surgery, she had an excuse to be attentive. One night, they confessed over text that they had feelings for each other.

"Now what?" she wrote. It was a question any girl could ask a guy who said he liked her. But in Athira's case, there was a high-stakes subtext: *Now what, when we're not supposed to date yet?*

"Now we're together," he replied.

Athira had never rebelled before. "I think there was a voice in the back of my head that was like, 'Are you sure you want to keep talking?' But there was a bigger voice that was like, 'Oh my God, I like this kid!'" Her entire life until that moment had been motivated by making her parents happy. Getting together with John would not.

Her parents soon noticed them laughing together at church, and they warned her to stay away from him. Their clandestine courtship thrived anyway. Athira and John would sneak out of their houses in the middle of the night to meet at the neighborhood playground. They'd climb the slide and canoodle under the covered platform. After school, they did their homework together at the public library.

One afternoon, John spotted his mother and father browsing the shelves. "My parents are here, and we need to leave," John whispered. Athira gave him her keys and told him to hide in her car in the parking garage. She had told her parents that she was going to the library to get a book, so she knew she couldn't leave without checking it out. She ran into his parents at the checkout counter. To her dismay, they walked with her to the parking garage.

When John spotted them, he panicked. If his parents saw him, their secret would be out. He backed the Toyota out of the parking space and hit another car.

"His mother was like, 'Oh my God, some crazy drunk guy is driving this car,'" Athira remembered. "Little did she know, the crazy drunk guy was her son."

The damage to the cars was minor. Far worse was her parents' reaction to finding out that she was seeing John. Athira was grounded. Her parents took her phone away. "I had no life," she said. "I had no contact with any of my friends. I was cut off from communication with John. It was just school, home, home, school. It was my worst nightmare." She even had to miss her senior prom. The dress she bought hung in her closet for years, still in the bag, taunting her.

She tried to see John under the pretense of going to the local mall to apply for a summer job. Her mother followed her and caught them together. Desperate to get Athira under control, her parents shipped her off to Kerala for a month-long Catholic retreat. By day, Athira was part of a captive audience of Indian teens, listening to a priest preach about all the awful things that happened to people who had premarital sex: shame, disease, infertility, a future of being alone and unwanted. By night, she huddled over her phone, messaging with John.

Not long after she returned, her parents realized the indoctrination had not worked. John was still in Athira's life.

Saji and Regi charged over to his parent's house.

"You need to keep your boy in line!" Saji shouted at John's father.

"You need to keep your girl in line!" his father retorted.

The moment made Athira feel like property. She was about to leave for college. Her parents told her they wouldn't pay the tuition unless she promised she would have nothing to do with John. If she refused, they would send her to college in India instead.

"Why are you doing this to me?" she pleaded.

"If you see your kid falling into a well, are you going to stand by and watch?" her mother asked.

"Of course not," Athira replied.

"Exactly," her mother said. She unspooled a dire vision of Athira's future: With a boy in her life, Athira would get distracted from her college coursework. Her grades would falter. She wouldn't get into medical school. "You're ruining your life over this," her mother said. "I can't let you fall into a well. You can't be with this person. You can't do this."

Athira pledged she would stop seeing John, even though she knew she wouldn't. She and John had chosen colleges in the same state, a 90-minute bus ride apart. With their parents far away in Illinois, they'd finally be free.

They didn't always feel that way, though. On weekend visits to each other's campuses, sometimes they'd catch sight of a beige Odyssey minivan, the kind of car Athira's mother drove, and shudder. Had Athira's parents, they'd wonder for a panicked moment, caught them once again?

It was always someone else's Odyssey. But Athira could not shake thoughts of her parents' disapproval. On the pre-med track, Athira struggled. She was on the verge of failing organic chemistry. Maybe her mother had been right to think that Athira was throwing her life away over a relationship that cost her too much.

John visited to help her study for her chemistry final. He'd just finished the same course with good grades. "He pretty much taught me all of organic chemistry in a night," she said.

She passed the class, and she had an epiphany. John pushed her like no one else could. She did the same for him. They were, as she put it, like two marathon runners "dragging each other across the finish line." John wasn't interfering with her schoolwork or her well-being. The way her parents had reacted to him was. "I realized, it's not because I'm in a relationship that I'm having a hard time," she said. "It's because I'm going through this experience with my parents, and I couldn't focus on anything at school."

Athira and John would continue to be each other's companion and goad. When I first interviewed them on Zoom during the pandemic, they'd been together six years. Their relationship was still underground. They sat shoulder to shoulder on their couch. The Venetian blinds were drawn over the window behind them, keeping out the glare of the spring afternoon. Athira's round, soft-cheeked face loomed close to the screen, with John in the background. His expression was intent and protective, a mustached and bearded 23-year-old version of the teen boy who'd always made sure she got home safely after their late-night playground dates.

They told me a lot had changed since their dramatic beginnings as a couple. After graduating from college, they moved in together in Baltimore to attend a master's program in biotechnology. Medical school, they hoped, would be next. They'd gradually won over John's parents. But whenever Athira thought about telling her own parents about John, all she could think was that they would cut off contact with her forever. She didn't want to have to choose between a life with John and the love of her parents.

It didn't make sense to me. They weren't teenagers anymore. They were a serious couple, in a prestigious graduate program. They wanted to get married. Their ambitions were clear. Their futures were promising. Their values and identities as Indian Catholics were compatible. "What's the problem, exactly?" I asked.

"When I was ready to be with John, they weren't ready to accept that their kid found someone without their being part of the process," Athira said. "At a later point in life, it would have been different."

"They just don't want to go back on their word of saying, 'Hey, you'll never be with that guy,'" John said. "If they set their mind to a belief, they don't want to change. I think all humans are kind of like that, but immigrant parents especially."

Hiding from Athira's parents had become a way of life, a chore. When Athira FaceTimed her parents, she had to warn John in advance so he would avoid being in view of her laptop camera. He had to stay quiet, like a little boy on a time-out. She didn't fight with them anymore, but she didn't feel close to them either. "They don't know the whole of the story, because in every story he's present," she said, tucking her long black hair behind her ears. "I can't lie to them, so I just don't say anything."

Psychologist and author Joshua Coleman has observed that, in the past half-century, personal growth and the search for happiness have taken precedence over loyalty to family. If parents get in the way of these priorities, then adult children increasingly sever ties; one study found that more than 1 out of 10 mothers between the ages of 65 and 75 were estranged from a child. For immigrant children raised on values of interdependence and family allegiance, cutting off contact with parents is unthinkable.[11]

Athira and John had grown up believing that a marriage isn't just between two people—it's also between two families. Without Athira's parents in the picture, their relationship, despite the depth and length of their commitment, was missing a vital brace. "I wonder what it would be like to be one of those kids who could just ask advice from their parents about their relationship," Athira said. "You can ask your friends, but you don't get the advice you would get from your parents. It's just not the same."

John looked at his knees. "It causes a lot of strain in the relationship," he said. "We just think, 'If only Athira's parents knew and they were okay with us, most of our fights wouldn't be there.' No matter what we fight about, it revolves around us having to hide things."

Athira closed her eyes. She leaned her head against her hand, her face falling half out of the frame of her laptop. "You would think as the years go by, I would feel less and less guilty," she said. "But I think it's had the opposite effect."

The plan was to confess that they were together after they got accepted into medical school. That would be the proof Athira's parents needed that she was thriving, not at the bottom of a well.

THE ROMEO-AND-JULIET EFFECT

In lighter moods, Athira and John joke about their "little Romeo-and-Juliet situation." They had all the trappings: edicts against seeing each other, sneaking around, feuding families. In the beginning, their parents' disapproval drove them closer together. "We wouldn't have gotten as serious in the relationship if they hadn't tried to stop us," John said.

A 1972 study on the impact of parental disapproval on committed couples pronounced such unions as amplified by the "Romeo and Juliet Effect." Couples with parents who interfered with the relationship experienced increased feelings of love and commitment. It was the kind of research finding that got a lot of traffic in the media because it confirms what we like to believe about love: External obstacles make it stronger. Recent attempts to replicate the original study, though, suggest otherwise. Couples facing parental disapproval reported *decreased* feelings of love and commitment. They trusted each other less and criticized each other more. In contrast, the more social support couples got from parents and friends, the more the couples thrived.[12] Romeo and Juliet may have fallen hard for each other, but their love didn't survive a week. Coping with family disapproval destroyed them.

Kathrine Bejanyan, an Armenian American psychotherapist who researches cross-cultural relationships, told me it's common for immigrant children to struggle to reconcile their family's traditional values with mainstream attitudes. They often can't be honest about their lives the way nonimmigrant peers can be. When she was coming of age in a tight-knit community of Armenian immigrants in suburban Los Angeles, the advice she got on handling conflicts with her parents often came from a Western perspective that didn't acknowledge her reality. "People would tell me, 'You should be open; you should be transparent.' I would love to have been those things, but there was too much at risk," Bejanyan said. "I didn't have someone to help me navigate the guilt of withholding information and figure out how to manage that in my own way."

In her practice, she allows that honesty is not always the best policy for young immigrants, however taxing it is to have to conceal aspects of their lives. She urges young people to empathize with where their parents are coming from. "They're not doing this to hurt you. They're just as constrained as you are," she tells them. "No one has control over the fact that this is what the culture says and this is what expectations are. You abide by them. Otherwise, there can be so much judgment and talking behind people's backs.

You can release some of the anger when you get that your parents are bound by the same sort of limits you are."

While some couples bond over facing the challenge together, others break under the strain. Partners who are the target of parental disapproval—the John position—may take the rejection personally. The partner in hiding—the Athira position—may become overwhelmed by the chronic anxiety of being discovered. When a young person has to choose between family and a partner, love doesn't always prevail. "The cognitive dissonance of being split in two can be too much for people," Bejanyan said. "They let go of the relationship because, if you hold on, you are disappointing so many people. It feels like a selfish act."

Athira and John's longevity was formidable. Their choices threatened their place in their immigrant community. Yet they also lived a radically different existence than most people their age, who considered flirting, having crushes, hooking up, Tindering, dating, falling in love, breaking up, and starting all over again the de rigueur roller-coaster ride of being young. Their relationship had a dogged, lonely quality, their dread about telling Athira's parents compounding over time.

After they finished graduate school, they returned to their respective Mount Prospect households. They got jobs as research scientists. The pandemic delayed their plans to apply to medical school, but they realized they couldn't wait much longer to tell Athira's parents about their relationship. She set a deadline for herself to tell them. When the day passed and I didn't hear from her, I worried.

A few weeks later, I checked in again. She hadn't told them yet.

Later in the summer, I reached out once more. Silence. Maybe she'd finally done the deed, I thought, and it hadn't gone well.

Finally, in mid-August, Athira emailed. "It took me a very long time to build up the courage to bring it up to them, but once I did it felt like a weight off my shoulders," she wrote. "Their positive response was overwhelming and brought tears to my eyes." I read Athira's carefully chosen words, then let out a whoop.

Two Continents, Two Generations, Two Cultures: Reconciling Different Expectations

In popular culture, the rebel relationship is framed as a hero's tale, a child torn between love and obligations to family and community. From *Fiddler on the Roof* to the cross-cultural rom-com *The Big Sick*, personal desire always triumphs. Young lovers awaken their parents to the superiority of romantic love over, as Tevye sings, "Tradition!" These narratives don't give much credence to a collectivist view of relationships. The irony of our reflexive embrace of freely chosen romance is that, statistically, arranged marriages fare about as well as, and in some ways better than, love matches. Researchers have found no significant difference in the levels of satisfaction, commitment, and love.[13] Arranged marriages are also less likely to end in divorce.[14] The main difference is how and when love develops. While feelings of being in love in marriages of choice peak early and then fade, love in arranged marriages grows over time.[15] Love is the result of, not the prerequisite for, a lasting companionship. One of the reasons is the social support arranged marriages receive. When conflicts arise, relatives step in as mediators, making partners more willing to work through difficult times.

When it was time for Athira's mother to wed in the early '90s, she knew she wanted an arranged marriage. Her father once told her she could choose her husband on her own, but the portrait he painted of the option was not very appealing. "If we arrange the marriage," her father said, "then we will be there throughout your life, because it was our choice." If she found a husband independently of her parents, her father cautioned, she would have to deal with any problems on her own, too.

Regi was already coping with plenty on her own. She was a nurse at a hospital in Oman, on the coast of the Persian Gulf. Her day-to-day existence was tedious and solitary. She endured the isolation for the sake of her family back home. Her father was in debt from a long hospitalization. To help pay it off, Regi joined a long tradition of Malayalam Christian women from Kerala who went into nursing, seeking economic opportunity and social mobility; Hindu and Muslim women, forbidden from physical contact with men, couldn't do the job. Hospitals in Europe, the Gulf countries, and the United States recruited the so-called brown angels of Kerala to cope with nursing shortages.[16]

Essentially, when Regi was around the age Athira was when she met John, Regi's life took on an urgency her daughter would never know. There was no room for distractions, including boys.

Now 53, Regi shared her story on an early winter afternoon, over a lunch of egg curry, fermented rice pancakes, and saag paneer she'd prepared and a Costco takeout salad of kale, mayonnaise, and toasted breadcrumbs. Athira's father was at work, which was for the best, Athira explained. My questions might poke at old wounds.

Athira and her mother had the same moon-shaped face and luxurious wavy black hair, which Athira wore loose and Regi pulled back in a ponytail. Their Labradoodle, Charlie, scampered underfoot. John sat at the head of the table, his presence in her home still relatively new. It had been just four months since their secret came out. Now their life together was finally moving forward, and quickly. They were not yet officially engaged, but they'd already set a wedding date with the priest.

Regi told me that, as Athira and her two younger siblings grew up in the United States, she realized that they were unlikely to agree to marry a near stranger as she had. But she and Saji did not want to budge on timing. "The main thing we were telling them and fighting with them all the time about was, 'Focus on your education first and get the job,'" Regi said. "'Your main aim is to stand on your own feet. When you are distracted, you won't be focusing on your studies. Once you complete your education, the rest of your whole life is free.'"

It was an awkward moment. Regi was resurrecting admonishments she'd used many times on Athira, even though John's presence in their dining room was proof things hadn't quite gone to plan.

"What was it like," I asked Regi, "when her oldest daughter didn't listen and started seeing John?"

"They won't agree," Regi said, glancing at Athira and John. "But in my thinking, they were distracted so much from their education."

Athira turned away from her mother and scrunched up her face. "No, I don't think so," she protested, giving her mother the side-eye.

"See, I said that they wouldn't agree!" Regi said.

"I think that my relationship was more of a support during that time," Athira said, a rising tightness in her voice. "The stress of the familial pressure was my distraction."

"I think you had different expectations," John offered quietly. "Your mom is saying she didn't have the luxury to be distracted. Am I right?" He looked toward Regi.

"That's true," she said.

"She also thinks the same thing for you," he told Athira. "That you shouldn't have the luxury of being distracted."

There was, they all delicately agreed, no way to go back in time. Regi allowed that her children were growing up in a different world. She had trained for her career knowing her family's well-being was at stake. Athira's life, Regi could see now, had much more flexibility. "They have more choices here," Regi said.

What hurt the most was the talk the couple's secretive beginnings generated in their community. "I was really upset with her," Regi said. "I should not hear about something from other people, like I don't know anything about my daughter and the public is telling me."

"We were scared," Athira said.

"If you had told me the truth," Regi said, "it would have been okay."

Athira didn't protest. She didn't want to say anything to bring back the years of her parents' fierce objections, punishments, and threats.

Immigrant parents—along with devoutly religious parents and others following strict codes of conduct—may enforce expectations with an authoritarian hand: Here are the rules, and you must follow them. This, Bejanyan told me, makes it hard for young people to feel heard and seen—and they may feel as if their parents don't care enough to listen.

She advises immigrant parents to emphasize that both they and their children share the challenge of living with collectivist values. "For parents, fear and panic cause this 'You must not do this, you are not allowed to do that' reaction rather than revealing the vulnerability underneath, which is 'I'm terrified for you, I'm scared for our family, I'm not sure I'm strong enough to cope with the judgment,'" she said. "Instead, you can acknowledge the challenge you're both under and talk about the cultural framework."

Bejanyan urges parents to open up about their own worries growing up under the pressure of community expectations. "That humanizes parents in their children's eyes. Rather than authoritarians that are making them do things, they start to see their parents as scared and uncertain and may have been pressured into doing things themselves. That tends to change the dynamic and brings about more open-heartedness."

Regi's fears about the impact of young love on her daughter's life did not come to pass. Both Athira and John got into medical school. Perhaps because of this, Athira's younger siblings were having a different coming of age. Her brother was openly seeing someone at college, and Regis was less strict with her sister, who was still in high school. Regi told me she learned from her oldest daughter that a little more freedom was okay, as long as her children told her what was going on.

"When there's hiding, there could be something wrong going on without you knowing, and that always worries you more," she said. "I told my younger ones, 'If you like someone, you have to tell me first.'"

Chapter 5

Queer

Desire and Identity in a Generation That Won't Think Straight

Before they became a couple, Chase and Sage were already close, the kind of close you read about with a piercing sense of envy in YA novels—that tell-each-other-everything, *The Fault in Our Stars* kind of close, without the doom of terminal illness. The summer before ninth grade, Chase would often rise at six, go for a run, and meet Sage at the high school track. They would lie face to face in the oval of grass, snuggling, as the morning warmed into day and joggers circled them in dogged routine. "We were really in tune with each other," Chase said. "We were already saying, 'I love you,' but just as friends."

In Lexington, their prim yet progressive Boston suburb, two teenage girls being affectionate in public could feel safe. That's how the world saw them then, and that was how they saw themselves. Chase then still identified as a girl, the gender he was assigned at birth, and a lesbian. Sage was bisexual. They were hurtling toward something big together, Chase sensed. When he finally asked her out, she was so happy she cried.

Chase started high school on a high. He excelled on the track team. He was ranked the 11th-fastest freshman girl in the country for the two-miler. His height—only five foot one—made him a kind of wonder. As he sped around the track, onlookers mused how he could pull ahead of girls with legs so much longer than his. He was outgoing, with an infectious giggle and close friends from track and his youth group at Hancock Church, a progressive congregation in a 19th-century stone building on the Lexington Battle Green, the town commons where the first shots of the Revolutionary War were fired.

And Chase had Sage. If they ignored the occasional "Can I watch?" jokes from clueless male classmates, the couple felt not only tolerated but also central at Lexington High, a #goals couple with widely hearted Instagram photos. They held hands and kissed unselfconsciously on the outdoor walkways of their California-style campus. As their peers flirted and hooked up and got together and broke up, their relationship lasted. "Younger friends would come out to me and be like, 'We're inspired by you two for living authentically and having a happy queer relationship and being public,'" Chase said.

Under the surface, his life was more complicated. He was struggling to give voice to a feeling that had whispered to him his whole life and was getting too loud to shove down: He was male. At the end of their freshman year, he told Sage, "I think I'm trans."

"I love you," she pledged. "Whatever happens, we'll figure it out."

Lexington is probably one of the better places on the planet to grow up queer. A Pride flag flew in front of Chase's church. One of Chase's best friends was coming out as trans, and most of his other friends identified as queer. Several of the country's top gender-affirming therapists and surgeons practiced in Boston, a short drive away.

Spending time with Chase as he detailed the story of his first love, I was struck by the ways that being a queer teen was becoming so *normal*, at least compared to when I was in high school in the 1980s in a Connecticut suburb not unlike Lexington. Then, queer was what you called boys who seemed girly, one of the gentler insults in a vast repertoire of homophobic slang. No one was out in my high school. I have a vivid memory of being on the school bus, watching the boy in the seat opposite mine pull up his window to talk to another boy before the bus pulled away from the curb. They were pale, shy kids, social outcasts. In that moment, the charge between them lit them up. It was the early '80s. I didn't know what I was seeing. I knew gayness existed but in an exotic, faraway, adult sense—not something real kids in my high school could be.

After I left to attend Oberlin College, then and still one of the most queer-friendly colleges in the country, the bus couple stayed on my mind, an emblem of the caution and invisibility of being a teenager attracted to people of the same gender. In adulthood, many in my generation would surge into the gay rights movement, galvanized by peers dying from AIDS as homophobia stalled the search for a cure. We were the first generation to, in a widespread way, come out as young adults to family, friends, and coworkers.

The movement wasn't as inclusive as it is now. Bisexuality was suspect, a way station for people who couldn't decide which team to play on and escaped into straight privilege whenever the going got tough. The stereotype haunted me when I came out as bi. My first girlfriend's lesbian friends warmly took me in, but I knew some cautioned each other not to date bi. Their rationale was that a bi woman will surely leave you for a man. After I moved a 12-hour drive away to take a job and the relationship faltered, I did exactly that, and I felt ashamed for conforming to stereotype.

Being trans was even more appallingly misunderstood and for much longer. When I was in graduate school, a feminist activist friend with an androgynous style scoffed at what she perceived as the exaggerated femininity of trans women. "They want to be women, but they don't want to be a woman like me," she said. While trans-exclusionary beliefs persist today, they're likely to face plenty of criticism, particularly from young people (just ask them why they're getting rid of the *Harry Potter* books they once cherished). What used to be known as gay liberation would evolve to include bi, trans, nonbinary, pansexual, polyamorous, asexual, and a range of other sexual orientations and gender identities.

These changes would accompany the rise of marriage equality and the triumph of the *Obergefell* ruling. We would watch our children come of age clamoring for inclusivity few of us could have dared imagine, much less pursue, when we were their age. Increasingly, young people expect full freedom to figure out who they are and whom they want to love, with the support of their schools, communities, peers, and parents.

THE QUEEREST GENERATION

Today's teens and emerging adults belong to the queerest generation in history, with more people identifying as queer than ever before. Nearly 20 percent of people 18–25 identify as LGBTQ, according to a Gallup poll.[1] The CDC estimates that about 1 in 4 high school students have a sexual orientation other than straight, up from 1 in 10 in 2016.[2]

By the time my daughter was a preteen, her peers were announcing their sexual orientation on Instagram. The typical script was a "I've been thinking about this a lot . . . " explanation, punctuated by a Pride flag emoji and sparking a long thread of congratulatory comments. All this was happening before most of her friends had started dating, leaving us parents to wonder, "How do they *know*?" It's a question I carried into reporting this book. Several of the young people I interviewed identified as bisexual or queer, even if they'd only dated the opposite sex. When I asked one of them to explain, she said simply, "That's just what I am."

For all the ways my generation advanced LGBTQ rights, sexual orientation was something you figured out by acting on an attraction too powerful to deny, because the world assumed you were straight, and it was so difficult to be anything but. Young people start from another place. They don't need proof of a same-gender relationship to determine their sexual orientation. The proof is how they feel.

Taking teens at their word is important. More is at stake in affirming where they're at than in finding out how sure they are about their identity or reminding them about all the elementary school crushes they had on the opposite sex. I'm struck repeatedly by how acutely sensitive teens are to parental judgments and doubt. Their main tactic for dealing with these reactions is to stop opening up about their lives, particularly when it comes to relationships. Teens who sense their parents disbelieve their sexual orientation may hide their crushes and relationships, either because they think their parents disapprove or—if they end up in straight partnerships—because they don't want to affirm parental doubts about their queerness. To that point, a hetero relationship shouldn't be seen as proof of heterosexuality. A bi or pansexual teen will still be bi or pan. Particularly confusing for parents, lesbian and gay teens may even date the opposite sex without revising their sexual orientation. For teens, sexual orientation can be just as much or more about identity than it is about specific relationships.

Parents, of course, can and should ask children how they realized what their sexual orientation was—but in an open, curious way, not by launching into a detective-style interrogation. The discussion should emphasize how their children feel about who they are. Along with the relief of understanding themselves better, young people, depending on their environment, might be contending with the excitement of finding queer community, fears about being bullied and ostracized, or both.

When I'm in a community like Lexington or on my college campus, being queer is so accepted that it's not a stretch to imagine that it would one day become the new default identity. Children would grow up with the assumption that they could be attracted to any gender, until or unless life experiences proved them likely to lean toward one. Elsewhere, though, this scenario seems far afield, as the conservative backlash against LGBTQ+ rights intensifies. But young people's openness about sexual orientation has a power that transcends state borders and reaches into reactionary households. As horrifying as it is that a gay boy in Florida can't talk about his sexual orientation in class, he'll know from his social media feed that queer teens elsewhere can thrive—and if he doesn't, then trusted adults should help him find safe online resources that show him.

Young people also see gender identity more expansively. Teenagers and adults younger than 30 are significantly more likely to identify as transgender or nonbinary than older adults.[3] In my college classes, students include their pronouns when they introduce themselves on the first day, whether they're trans; nonbinary; or cis, shorthand for *cisgender*, meaning they identify with the gender they were assigned at birth. The political uproar over gender-affirming medical care for minors is drowning out how matter-of-fact it's becoming for a child to start life with one gender identity and transition to another. At each school concert I attended in my daughter's middle school and high school years, one or two students would have new first names listed on the program, an indication they were socially transitioning to a different gender. The pop culture and social media young people grow up with is rife with celebratory representations of gender fluidity: Harry Styles and Jaden Smith wearing skirts, Janelle Monáe announcing she's "beyond the binary."[4] Demi Lovato, whose career started on the preschool hit *Barney and Friends*, careened from relationships with men to coming out as pansexual, then as a nonbinary "they," then as a "they" who is also okay with *she/her* pronouns.

Still, relatively affirming communities like Lexington are not the norm, and they tend to be in coastal, majority-white, privileged communities. As I explain, even in these places, it's plenty challenging to grow up queer. Gay, lesbian, bisexual, and questioning teens experience more mental distress and more violence than heterosexual teens. They are more likely to be bullied at school and online, have suicidal thoughts and behaviors, abuse drugs and alcohol, and experience sexual violence and coercion.[5] A survey by the Trevor Project, a suicide-prevention organization, revealed that more than a third of transgender and nonbinary teens had been physically threatened or harmed because of their gender identity, and half considered suicide in the past year. They contended with mounting worries about access to gender-affirming medical care, bathrooms, and sports teams.[6]

When your baseline existence is more trying, dating, with its mythic importance as a harbinger of hetero-teen normalcy, also may be fraught. To start, queer youth have fewer options. "Even in the best of circumstances where they're in very accepting environments, there are just fewer sexual and gender minorities around," said Michael Newcomb, the director of Northwestern University's THRIVE Center, which conducts research on sexual health and relationships in queer adolescents and young adults. "There are fewer opportunities to date, which means that you have fewer opportunities to learn relationship skills and go through those tumultuous teenage relationships that shape what you want out of future relationships."

Some ways queer young people start their dating lives are universal. They'll feel the same angst that straight teens do while waiting for the return text from a crush or figuring out how to communicate about emotions, needs, and desires. In other ways, their experiences will be different. Queer teens are more likely to look online for partners, reaching out to teens from the next town over or across the country.

Newcomb points out that, for gay and bisexual boys, online explorations are likely to be highly sexualized, setting up expectations they may not be ready for. "The Talk"—parent-child conversations about sex, rarely free of awkwardness even when everyone's straight—may be even more strained and less helpful, given that parents may not have experienced the kind of sex their child is having or interested in having; most school sex education curricula won't have much to offer, either.[7] He advises parents to consult queer-affirming sex education resources and encourage their child to speak with a trusted adult who shares their child's sexual orientation and gender identity.

The challenge of finding someone to date and dealing with the stigma of being queer may lead some teens to rush into the relative haven of an exclusive relationship. Even as an increasing number of teens nationally identify as sexual minorities, many in less-affirming communities will still contend with limited options. "There's this worry that you have to find the one person who's right for you immediately because there are so few of us available," Newcomb said. "You have to find someone now and lock it down."

A good romantic relationship can be a source of joy, a haven in a queer-phobic world. Newcomb's research shows lesbian and gay teens, particularly from racial minorities, are less stressed when they're in relationships, which help shield them from the impact of bullying and homophobia.[8] "When relationships are functioning well, they have so many positive benefits on people's health and well-being, particularly for sexual and gender minorities," he said. "For people who may lack the support that most people typically get from their families, a romantic partner can help people get on the track to general life satisfaction and health."

In Love and in Transition

When Chase's mother, Bettina, found out Chase and Sage were together, her first thought was, "This is starting too soon." Bettina described her own relationships as "completely messed up until I went into therapy in my early 30s." She wanted Chase and her younger son to wait until they were older to date. "But the horse was out of the barn," she said.

She and Chase's father, Mike, met with the new lesbian minister at church to make sure they struck the right balance between supporting the couple's sexual orientation and setting healthy boundaries. As best friends, Sage and Chase had been sleeping at each other's houses for months. Now that they were a couple, his parents decided that would have to stop.

Bettina and Mike were reassured by how calm Chase and Sage were together. Sage struck them as grounded and grown-up for her age. Mike, an automobile engineer with a shock of disheveled white hair and halting manner, called the relationship "constructive for both of them." He and Bettina quietly shared with Sage's parents the relief that no boys—no cis boys, they'd later qualify—were in the equation. "No one's going to get pregnant," Sage's father quipped, a line about lesbian couples I heard several times while reporting this book.

Whatever concerns Bettina and Mike had when Chase started dating would seem mild a year later, when Chase told them he was trans. They had so many questions: what the transition would mean for Chase psychologically and physically, how it would affect their younger son, and how and when Chase should come out as male to the community.

An issue that came up right away was track. If Chase transitioned to male during high school, he would have to race on the boys' team. Chase loved to run, and he loved to win. As a boy on the boys' team, he would no longer have a shot at winning. It wasn't a trivial matter. With all the public controversy about trans girls playing on girls' sports teams, few people acknowledge the flipside: the catch-22 of being a trans boy athlete. On boys' teams, you're at a competitive disadvantage. On girls' teams, you're suspect. Bettina told Chase, "If you move into transitioning but are still running as a girl, everybody's going to wonder if you're taking drugs because you're so fast, and that's just not a fair thing to do to your coaches or your teammates."

She and Mike urged him to choose: Transition and run as a boy, or delay and continue running as a girl. Chase decided to wait. He dutifully compartmentalized his life: elite runner for the next three years, then he'd come out as male. "I was like, 'This is something that's going to happen when I graduate, but I can't think about it now,'" he said.

Chase had a lot that a trans person in prior generations wouldn't have dared to expect: a supportive family and partner and an affirming community at school and church. But his existence was still constrained by a world that had no good way to enable the facets of his identity—trans and an athlete—to thrive at the same time. A lot was at stake—not only the thrill of being the fastest but also his educational future. Division III coaches were recruiting him, boosting his chances of getting into a good college.

Years later, when he was fully out as male, he would reflect on the ways his choice wasn't really a choice at all. I met him in Lexington a few months after his top surgery. He was a sophomore at a college he'd chosen because the coaches who recruited him as a female runner welcomed him on the men's team when he told them he was trans. Delaying the transition had been hard on him, he told me. While he had been relatively at peace with putting off gender-affirming medical care, he grew frustrated with his parents' warnings throughout high school against even the first steps of socially transitioning: using his new name and *he/him* pronouns. "You don't need to physically transition to be a valid person," he said. "I understand, it was like a fear-based thing, but that was really damaging."

Transition Is a Partner's Journey, Too
In those years, only Sage and his closest friends knew the truth. When they were alone together, Sage called him by his new name and used *he/him* pronouns. At school and in public, she used his birth name and pronouns. "I did a lot of code switching," she said. She carefully kept checking in with him about what kinds of touch and ways of communicating about sex were okay and what wasn't. With the help of her older brother, she bought him his first binder, a tight wrap of cloth to flatten his breasts.

When Bettina and Mike found out about the binder, they were taken aback. "I felt like he was getting advice that I would have wanted to be in on," Bettina said. "It felt like we were out of the loop and other people were much more in."

Chase was moving into what author Andrew Solomon calls a "horizontal identity," a trait in a child that is foreign to their parents. Vertical identities, such as race or religion, are passed down from parent to child and are more socially acceptable. Horizontal ones pose a challenge. They're often seen as flaws by the outside world, sending the children on a quest to find identity and community—an experience that can put distance between them and their parents.[9] Romantic relationships can be integral to this process. No matter how supportive parents are of trans identity, they're contending with the feelings, expectations, and memories tied up in the gender assigned to their child at birth— and likely limited knowledge of the tools and strategies of trans life. They may be in mourning for a privilege they never realized they had: of having a cisgender child who is safe in the world in the way a trans child is not. Their ability to support their child, however important, won't always compare to the affirmation of a teen partner and a community of peers.

In these ways, Chase's relationship with Sage was a sustaining force in his life, a realm where he didn't have to pretend to be what he wasn't. "From a very young age, I got the validation that, regardless of the fact I'm trans, I'm worthy of love, and someone could be attracted to me," he said. "That's something a lot of trans people don't have."

Sage, though, was quietly troubled over what his trans identity meant to her own sense of self. It had been hard enough to come out as queer in middle school. In the locker room, other girls looked at her like she was a predator and avoided changing near her. During those first months with Chase, she began to think she might be a lesbian, not bi, because she was too in love to imagine being with anyone else. She wondered, now that she was in a male-female relationship, what was she?

Early in their sophomore year, Sage pulled Chase aside in the hallway at school. She started crying. "I just wish you were a girl," she said.

Chase's first thought was for her well-being. "It's okay," Chase reassured her. "We'll figure this out."

But her confession struck at fears, common among trans teens, that living his truth would make him undesirable. Would he lose her? He had thought it ideal that Sage was bi, believing his gender wouldn't matter to her. Now it did, for reasons she stumbled to explain: Because he was now male, she felt less queer.

Chase never doubted Sage's love, but her words were shattering. "I don't think she meant it in a harmful way, but it's something that I think is going to stick with me forever," he said.

With its long cultural history, the specter of the unlovable trans person—once called transsexual—hangs heavily over young people in transition and their parents. Just a generation earlier, when Chase's parents were entering adulthood, the thriller *The Crying Game* was released, with a plot twist that viewers were urged to keep a secret from people who hadn't yet seen it: The hero's gorgeous female love interest turns out to be trans. During foreplay, he discovers her secret, strikes her, and rushes out of the room to vomit. The main character of *Boys Don't Cry*, based on the real-life story of trans man Brandon Teena, wins the heart of a Nebraska spinach-factory worker, only to be murdered in a violent hate crime. Often depictions of trans women relied on stereotypes: the ultra-femme, flamboyant, promiscuous mess, perhaps lovable as a quirky friend or a fling but not a contender for a real relationship. Trans men tended to get left out of the cultural narrative altogether.[10]

Today, pop culture, especially media geared toward teens, is shaking off this history. The ABC Family teen drama *The Fosters* features a relationship between Aaron, a trans male law student, and Callie, one of the main characters. The HBO show *Euphoria* centers the love story between Rue, a troubled teen grappling with addiction in the wake of her father's death, and Jules, a trans girl with her own dark past: Her mother tried to cure her gender dysphoria—the distress of having a gender identity that did not match her biological sex—by institutionalizing her, a traumatizing experience. The girls' emotional connection is compelling, and their conflicts over monogamy, sex, identity, and addiction give them even more credibility to young viewers. They are two teens undeniably in love and worthy of love, and it's complicated—and therefore eminently relatable. The relationship is iconic for both queer and straight teens, a sharp contrast to queer-coded Disney villains and the long history of LGBTQ+ characters on television and film who are deceptive, obsessed, evil, or die on-screen.[11]

Pop culture role models aside, the trans teens I've talked to tell me they face unique challenges in romantic relationships. Sam, who has identified as male since he was 13, said his love life has been complicated by a tricky form of bias: peers, straight and queer, who say they "won't date trans," insisting that this preference is a matter of sexual orientation, not transphobia. Trans teens who "pass"—a term that means others see you as the gender you identify as—have to figure out how and when to disclose to partners that they're trans. (I'll note here that many trans people have no interest in passing, rejecting the idea that you have to look and sound like cisgender people for your identity to be considered authentic.) Trans teens may struggle to express their desires about where they want to be touched and how and which words to use when talking about sex and body parts, particularly given that transgender perspectives are rarely incorporated into standard sex education curricula. Their sexual partners might not be understanding, especially in more casual encounters.

Robin, a trans woman in her early twenties who agonized for years about whether to start hormone treatments, told me that she avoided intimacy as a teen because of how emotionally consuming gender dysphoria was. "I was too preoccupied with the process to get physical with someone else," she said. Others may rush into sex to validate their gender identity. Trans teens are at heightened risk for relationship violence, sexual harassment, sexual assault, and fetishization. As with other queer and minority teens, being different and being the target of societal misunderstanding, discrimination, and hate are chronically stressful, affecting everything about their lives, including their relationships.[12] This makes regular conversations about consent, a subject I explore in-depth in the next chapter, particularly urgent. Parents, even if their gender identity is different from their child's, should not shy away from the subject. Cis adults can benefit from—and guide trans youth to—affirming online spaces, such as Scarleteen, a sex education resource founded by Heather Corinna, who is nonbinary.

In light of these challenges, the problems of cis partners of trans teens may seem less important. Cis partners have cis privilege. No one's telling them not to seek the medical care they need or grow their hair or lower their voice. They wake up every morning in a body with parts that match their sense of who they are. But they also undergo role confusion. They may need to reframe how they describe their sexuality and their connection to the queer community.[13] While there's little question that being trans is more socially marginalized than being the cis partner of a trans person, cis partners are also dealing with a lot.

From a historical perspective, queer identity was forged largely in contrast to the dualism of heterosexuality. Straight people contended with difference in relationships, the challenge of closeness with someone whose body and life experiences were different from their own. Gay and lesbian people could claim the benefits of loving someone who innately understood where they were coming from. The in-betweenness of trans and bi identities complicates this sense of solidarity.

Michael Newcomb's research finds that, while relationships help protect gay and lesbian teens against the stresses of growing up gay, bisexual and trans teens may not find love as sheltering. When bi teens date straight, they might find their queer identity invalidated; everyone assumes they're straight, and their partner may not understand what's it like to be a queer person. Relationships between trans teens and cis teens can leave partners feeling "even more isolated than they were before," Newcomb said. "Because perhaps they're going through a transition in the middle of being in a relationship, and their partner is not and has no idea what they're going through. So all of a sudden, this person who you were similar to, you're in so many ways becoming very different from."

As Chase and Sage contended with the challenge of love in transition, they only had each other to confide in. In their world of two, they ruminated over what was happening, growing even closer. Years later, when they were at colleges more than 1,000 miles apart and no longer a couple, they would both use the word *codependent* to describe their bond. Newcomb offered a broader perspective on what can happen in queer couples with strong communication and mutual support: For all ways the relationship enriches their lives, living in a world that still stigmatizes queer identities and relationships can mean that, when one partner suffers, the impact on the other is more profound.[14] "Because of the closeness of that relationship, you feel everything that your partner is going through," Newcomb said. "So in that case, stressors that are happening to your partner can start to impact the other individual, as well."

Parents might unwittingly be complicit in this bond, relieved that their child has a constant source of support from a peer who understands as a fellow member of the LGBTQ+ tribe. But peers should not shoulder too much of each other's burdens and caretaking needs. Trusted adults should be on guard against the potential for a queer couple to become what I've called overenmeshed, losing themselves in the relationship and letting other priorities and sources of support fall by the wayside.

Gradually, Sage grew more confident in her identity and less stressed about what was happening. She was in love with Chase. She was attracted to him. She knew none of this would change once he fully came out as trans. "I think after I got over the shock factor and all of the things that would change for me and for us in our relationship, I just had to think about how much I care about him and how this actually doesn't matter at all," Sage said. "There was just a point where I was not making it about me or my identity anymore."

The questions Chase and Sage grappled with—what one partner's gender transition means to who the other is—in some ways reflect their generation's growing investment in gender identity and sexual orientation. Superficially, this can come across as a preoccupation with labels. Some college newspapers stretch out the LGBTQ acronym to LGBTQQIAAP (lesbian, gay, bi, trans, queer, questioning, intersex, asexual, ally, and pansexual). The effort to particularize identity can strike older generations as jostling for authority and specialness, complicated by fluidity, which is the capacity for gender identity and sexual orientation to change or play out in unexpected ways. The teen who for years wore a binder and used *he/him* pronouns starts occasionally wearing glam femme clothing and going by *they/them*. The lesbian who's sleeping with a boy still identifies as a lesbian. When my niece came out as trans and a lesbian, some in my extended family confessed confusion: What was the point of becoming female if you still wanted to date girls? We had to talk about how attached we were to old scripts about what womanhood was for. It did not have to be for a relationship with a man. Gender identity and sexual orientation were separate matters. You could be assigned male at birth, attracted to females, *and* a trans female.

Certainly, there *is* power in asserting an identity and having others acknowledge it. In the end, though, why wouldn't we want to give young people that power? What queer youth are seeking is the kind of power we all want and deserve—the power of feeling heard and understood.

Gender Expansiveness: Moving beyond the Binary

Rachel Lynn Golden, a clinical psychologist and researcher who founded a New York City–based clinic that provides gender-affirming support, calls identity labels "like languages" for queer youth. "People are trying to underscore the dynamic nature of gender by saying, 'Use a different word for me,'" she told me when we met for breakfast on a late-winter morning. "Honoring somebody's wishes is a very practical thing you can do to make the world a more validating place for somebody."

The conflicts gender-expansive young people confront over "What does who you are mean to me?" aren't just about how a couple relates to one another, Golden told me. They're a reaction to a larger society that still views gender and sexual orientation on narrow terms: You're either male or female. Queer or straight. Cis or trans. "Trying to find a way to talk about gender in a very binary system is hard," she said "When somebody is starting to transition, that person's identity can feel misaligned with their relationship, probably because of the social constructs about identity. That's the true issue. You can't just love who you love. Having a relationship becomes wrapped up in 'What does this mean about me?'"

Compounding these issues are valid questions of desire and attraction. "As folks go through medical transition, sometimes those characteristics that people are attracted to change," she said. "If you're somebody who's growing a beard or their voice is changing or they're going through gender-affirming surgeries, I think there are ways in which folks sometimes feel like, are they still romantically and emotionally attracted to somebody, when they had envisioned themselves with a different partner having sex in different ways? And that is just all very complicated."

Given that, I asked her, is it transphobic not to want to be with someone once their gender changes?

Golden said it could be, then pointed out that the real issue lies with societal attitudes about gender. "We're so steeped in this culture that since birth conditions people about the right ways to love and the correct person to be with," she said. "That is the social pressure that limits the range of identities that we're allowed to care for and express. That shapes how relationships are formed and the ways people believe they can be intimate with each other. We don't yet have great ways of supporting people through relationships when things shift and they don't align with broader cultural demands."

She sees the ever-evolving discussion of identity labels as a sign that young people are at the vanguard of a societal transformation. The fluidity and variety of gender expressions and sexual orientations will one day, she hopes, lead us to see gender and attraction as phenomena with variations as "infinite as there are stars in the sky." This idea isn't new, she pointed out.

Indeed, evidence of gender expansiveness and same-gender relationships can be found throughout human history and across cultures: Priests in ancient Greece identified as female to perform goddess-worship rituals. Indigenous communities honored "two-spirit" people who were both male and female. Nonbinary hijra in South Asia took on special ritual roles.[15] The transition to an agrarian society meant, particularly in the West, a household-based economy that emphasized the economic self-sufficiency of the family unit and a patriarchal division of labor: Men owned the farm; women turned what was grown into the food, clothing, and other goods the family lived on; and their partnership produced more workers.[16] Christian European colonizers saw same-gender relationships and gender variance as sins and punished them violently. "We have this devastating history of the decimation of expansiveness," Golden said.

Yet as we finished our eggs and arepas in the nearly empty café, the frigid February air creeping in every time someone stopped by for takeout, the vision of a twinkling constellation of genders seemed increasingly remote. An increasing number of state legislatures and local governments were passing bans on gender-affirming medical care, dismantling discrimination protections, censoring school curricula and libraries, and forcing schools to notify parents if children want to change their name or pronouns. The political climate meant queer teens and their parents had to spend a lot of time and mental energy dealing with fundamental matters of survival: staying safe, staying sane, and getting the medical care they needed.

FIRST LOVE WHEN YOU'RE NOT OUT YET

Plenty of teens still aren't out at home, scared they'll be judged, rejected, or worse. Julian grew up in a family of Filipino immigrants in Glendale, a suburb north of Los Angeles. His parents were observant Catholics, and he couldn't bring himself to tell them he was gay.

In Julian's first year of high school, he developed a raging crush on Arrow, a boy with wild brunette curls and a chiseled jaw. Arrow was one of the first White boys Julian got to know; before, he'd gone to schools of mostly Asian, Black, and Brown kids. That mattered—"White supremacy at work," as Julian put it, making Arrow more desirable. Arrow had a girlfriend, and Julian knew he was one of many students, female and male, who wished they could take her place.

Then he did, in a way. Arrow and his girlfriend broke up. Julian knew Arrow wasn't doing well in his AP US history class, so he offered to help. Julian started spending afternoons at Arrow's house, a block away from school. Arrow confided in Julian that he had a sibling battling a heroin addiction and his mother was verbally and physically abusive. At night, they whiled away hours messaging back and forth. Julian treasured his status as a confidant. One day, Julian took a chance and kissed Arrow, and he kissed him back.

It was Julian's first kiss. Arrow would also be his first love and first sexual partner. No one at school or in their families knew what was happening. The secrecy was in some ways about being teenagers. The longer you don't reveal you're a couple, the longer your friendship can be cover for sex without parental rules. They were also sneaking around because Arrow didn't want anyone to know they were boys who liked boys.

The situation gave Arrow cover for refusing to acknowledge what was happening. They were doing everything people in a relationship do: spending time together, talking, listening to music, being vulnerable and affectionate, and having sex. Julian wanted them to be an official couple. Arrow would tell him that he could envision that one day, but he wasn't ready yet. "He never said we were in a relationship," Julian said. "I just wanted him to say we're boyfriends, but he never would."

The torment of being in an asymmetrical secret *something* with a boy he loved was amplified by isolation. No one else knew the reality of what he was going through. Young people don't always want to debrief their romantic disappointment with their parents, but choosing not to talk about a relationship is different from feeling like you *can't* talk about a relationship—and from the pain of knowing that no one considers the relationship valid but you.

I spoke with Julian after the relationship had been over for several years. He told me that he felt he'd missed out on what other teens went through in their first relationships—insight into what it took to be intimate with someone else. As a result, the beginning of his relationship with his current boyfriend was rocky. "I replicated the hot and cold of that first relationship," he admitted. "Some days, I would talk to my boyfriend often. Other days, I would leave him with radio silence. We got into a lot of fights early on because he was frustrated that I wasn't communicating."

When his boyfriend confessed that he was seeing a therapist to help cope with his distress over the relationship, Julian realized he wasn't the person he wanted to be. "I needed to be a better partner, and that took a lot of work," he said. He let his guard down, and the relationship lasted.

Though it's far more common for LGBTQ+ youth to come out to their parents than in prior generations, about a third are not out by their late teens and early twenties.[17] That means some of the normal rituals of first love—confessing a crush to your mom, introducing your partner to your parents—don't happen, leaving partners to figure things out on their own. While healthy romantic relationships can help shield queer teens from the stresses of being queer, partners shouldn't be expected to replace other sources of support from family, school, and society. For that matter, we shouldn't expect anything more out of queer teen relationships than straight teen relationships. Both are unlikely to last and very likely to entail a lot of trial and error, drama, and heartbreak. Throughout this book, I've emphasized how important it is for parents to show support for the ups and downs of adolescent children's romantic lives. It's even more crucial for queer young people, who walk through the world contending with threats and prejudice from a homophobic culture, a phenomenon known as the "minority stress model": When your daily reality is chronically hostile and you lack community support, your mental and physical health suffers.[18]

LETTING GO OF THE STRAIGHT STORY

When I told my mother in 1992 that I was bisexual, she was everything a queer daughter could hope for: supportive, interested, all in. I was grateful, but I wasn't all that worried in the first place. My mother is the kindest person I know and politically progressive. A few weeks after my confession, I checked in with her about her reaction. "I'm okay," she said. "I've been a little sad, though."

I asked her why. "It's just that all the things I'd always thought would happen for you—getting married, having children—now I just don't know that they'll happen," she said.

Thinking back to that conversation from the vantage point of 30 years, my mother's reaction reminds me of the concept of narrative fidelity: We get attached to preconceived notions of how a story will go, so much so that we may struggle when real life diverges from the script in our heads. The sonogram says you're having a boy, so cue up fantasies of fishing and baseball games. My mother raised a girl who, by all indications, was straight, with crushes on boys, then boyfriends. She assumed I'd move forward into a familiar future of marriage and parenthood. She wasn't wrong—that's what would eventually happen. But in my early 20s, I fell in love with a woman, throwing the future that we both had envisioned into question. While I reveled in the new possibilities of my life, my mother had to grieve at what seemed to be the loss of the narrative of my romantic future—what I call the "straight story," the standard heterosexual script she lived out and had little reason to expect that I wouldn't.

Kim, a mother and educator in eastern Massachusetts, raised her daughter, Hancie, in a more aware time. Kim in many ways was the dream parent for a kid who would grow up to be queer. Kim was a veteran of 1970s consciousness-raising feminist groups. She had frank talks with Hancie about sexuality, and their circle of close friends included a married lesbian couple. At first, Hancie seemed mainly into boys. She went through a couple of rounds of intense attractions to close male friends that ended the way many adolescent crushes do, with a short-lived attempt at a relationship that left her wanting more.

Hancie's first serious relationship was with a trans man she met while she was studying abroad in Amsterdam in a program focused on gender and sexuality. "It didn't surprise me," Kim said. "I thought, she just cares about who she cares about." When Kim and her husband met the couple in Amsterdam, Kim worried her husband would be uneasy, but the time went smoothly. Her husband loved beer and cycling, and so did his daughter and her boyfriend, so any initial awkwardness quickly dissipated.

Hancie's next relationship was with a woman. While Hancie had been matter-of-fact about revealing she was dating a trans man, telling her parents about her girlfriend was different. Hancie confided in her mother first, tentatively, telling her that the relationship was new but might get serious—while in fact it already was.

"Well, just remember, not all men are awful, and not all women are great," Kim said.

Hancie was taken aback at all the assumptions Kim was making: that Hancie was no longer attracted to men and that her relationship had anything to do with how she felt about men overall. In the days to come, Kim expressed concerns that Hancie would start dressing and acting differently. "As much as she doesn't want to admit that she had a vision for who I was going to be, she did," Hancie said. "You poured 21 years of your life into someone. You're going to have a vision for them in some way."

Hancie put off telling her father until her parents were on their way to her college graduation party, where she planned to introduce her girlfriend to them. She delivered the news over speakerphone while her parents were driving down the New Jersey Turnpike.

Kim watched the light drain from her husband's face. After the call, they had a huge fight. He hurled questions at her: Why hadn't their daughter told him sooner? Why hadn't Kim? How were they going to tell all their relatives, who were also on their way to the party? The news was hitting both of them much harder than Hancie's relationship with a trans man did, even though to the outside world that relationship was more socially rare.

Maybe, Hancie thought, her parents weren't bothered by her study-abroad romance because it was part of the newness and transience of travel, while she described her girlfriend as someone she might have a future with.

Hancie wasn't far off. "I'm not proud of this, but it went through my mind: 'Oh, my God, she's not going to have a man to protect her,'" Kim said. "It's like that kind of deep-seated thing that we're all confronting these days with racism—that feeling that, whoa, there's something way down in there I haven't addressed."

Kim thought back to her own upbringing. When she was in college and unsure about what major to pick, her father scoffed, "Why are you worried? You're just going to get married anyway." At the time, she was appalled. "But clearly that idea that I needed a man in my life was still stuck there," Kim said. The traditional male-female template for marriage and parenthood held more sway over her than she realized. She had to reconcile the clash between her ideals and her gut reaction. To be fair, Kim's fears about Hancie aren't entirely unfounded. Men still make more money than women, especially as they age, and heterosexual couples are still safer and have more privilege in the world than same-sex couples.[19] It isn't right, but it's real.

Kim and her husband pulled themselves together to meet Hancie's girlfriend. "Those fights never affected my experience of feeling loved by them," Hancie said.

Kim's reckoning brought me back to my conversation with Rachel Lynn Golden about gender expansiveness: that conflicts over queerness and queer identity are reactions to a binary way of thinking about sex and gender that increasingly fails to do justice to our lives and relationships. I hoped to see the day when her vision of gender possibilities, as infinite as the stars in the sky, would come to pass, freeing us all. In the meantime, parents who strive to be affirming to their queer children can acknowledge the ways parenting, like every meaningful human endeavor, is rooted in narratives of hope we harbor, often unwittingly, about our children's futures in life and love. It's okay to mourn the stories we have to let go of and to admit we may have gotten too attached to the gender of the characters—and to honor the fact that our children are much less likely to do the same.

CHAPTER 6

#MeToo Teens

Consent, Boundaries, and Dating Abuse

MUCH OF MY ADULT LIFE, I'VE BEEN INVOLVED IN THE MOVE-ment against sexual violence. For years, I carried a beeper one weekend a month as a volunteer for a victims' support organization. I've sat with rape survivors in police stations and hospital emergency rooms, helping them sort through the questions of whether to undergo a rape kit examination and file charges. As a journalist, I won a statewide award for my reporting on intimate partner violence. On campus, students who've endured sexual assaults and abusive relationships confide in me fears that they are ruined, that no one will want to date them, that they will never feel desire again. I have said, too many times, the words *It's not your fault*.

So from the time my daughter was very young, I emphasized that her body was her own. No one should touch her if she didn't want to be touched. I expected my experience would prepare me for her adolescence, when questions of consent and boundaries would become a lot more pressing and complex. But as I've emphasized throughout this book, true readiness comes not only from your awareness of a problem but also from reckoning with the messages and wounds from your past.

When my daughter was 13, she spent an evening on my iPad, messaging frantically with her friend, whom I'll call Dakota. Dakota had been hanging out with a close male friend and a few other boys. While everyone else played video games in the next room, Dakota's friend held her down and grabbed her breasts and genitals, even though she'd told him not to. She sent my daughter screenshots of messages from the boy, who begged her not to tell anyone. Dakota was worried she would get in trouble for being alone with a group of boys. After I read the message chain, I urged my daughter to encourage Dakota to tell her mother anyway.

"She told her," my daughter reported the following morning. "They went to the police and made a report."

"The *police*?" I said. Going to the police seemed like overreach for what had struck me as a misunderstanding the girl's parents could help her sort through.

It took weeks for me to see the situation for what it was: *This girl was sexually assaulted.* As a mother reading Dakota's distressed texts, my first reaction was denial: They were too young; it was too soon for what happened to be that big of a deal. I wanted to hold onto the innocence of my daughter's peer group. Both victim and perpetrator had played at my house, gotten rides in my car, and danced at my daughter's bat mitzvah. When I was a teenager, sexual assault was routinely excused with the explanation that, as my father would say, "boys can get out of control." I knew that I'd done the right thing in prompting my daughter to urge the girl to tell her mother. But I initially didn't take the account seriously enough, even though my daughter trusted me enough to tell me.

The case was scheduled for a family court hearing. My daughter and I submitted a long printout of the text exchange as evidence of what happened. She prepared to testify as a "prompt outcry" witness, a term for the first person the victim tells about a sex offense. I bought my daughter a high-necked black dress to wear to court. We met Dakota, her mother, and a group of supportive friends in the parking lot of the faded family court building in our local county seat. All the girls were also dressed modestly in black, following the same unspoken wardrobe rule of bleak propriety.

In the end, no one had to testify. The boy, wearing checked Vans and white jeans, admitted to several counts of forcible touching. At one point, his mother, a woman I'd had several pleasant chats with over the years, half rose from her seat, her hand up. She called out, "Wait!" as if to try to stop him, but he continued. To what extent did she believe that her son had done something wrong? Or was it a momentary impulse to rewind to the boy he'd been before that night and somehow prevent him from all of this?

The boy was sentenced to two years of juvenile parole. When I said goodbye to Dakota, I hugged her, looked into her reddened eyes, and said, "You are making a difference." Her bravery was an awakening, though I remained plagued by the thought: What if I'd been her mom and my first instinct had been to minimize what happened?

One of the biggest challenges for parents in responding to the reality of adolescent sexual assault is that we can't always readily see through our pasts—what happened to us, what we did, what we were told, what the world condoned—and what we want to believe about our children. This doesn't excuse anything. It only underscores that sometimes the work parents need to do can be deep and complicated before we can see our children's lives without blinders. I was an educated, aware parent and a woman who, in my professional life, investigated the reality of sexual assault without flinching. But I had also internalized messages from my upbringing. I needed to understand that my first instinct wouldn't always be the right one. I would have to check my reactions and question any urge to minimize news of sexual "drama" from the young people in my life. Simply put, I would have to respond as if it mattered.

Reenvisioning Consent and Boundaries

Long before the hashtag exploded on Twitter, the #MeToo movement began in response to the silence around young people's experiences of sexual violence. In 1997, African American activist Tarana Burke had no idea how to reply when a 13-year-old girl confided that she'd been abused. "I couldn't even say, 'Me too,'" Burke explained. The interaction would later inspire her to start a nonprofit to support victims of sexual harassment and assault and start using the expression on her MySpace page.[1]

The #MeToo hashtag went viral in October 2017 following news accounts of sexual assault allegations against film producer Harvey Weinstein. Though the focus of the Twitter storm was largely on adult perpetrators, girls quickly recognized the power plays of sexual harassment, bullying, and abuse in their own lives. "Yeah, this is pretty much our reality," high school student Maddy Eichenberg told the *New York Times*.[2]

What young people have to say, though, isn't just a junior version of the #MeToo outcry. They're part of a generation that's reworking old standards of sexual conduct. When I was in college, we chanted, "No means no," at Take Back the Night marches. The emphasis then was on stating what you didn't want to do. If the person you were with went ahead anyway, then that was sexual assault. Now, the standard increasingly is affirmative consent, the idea that each step of a sexual encounter should be a knowing, voluntary, and mutual decision. Partners should expect to give and get clear permission for each stage of a sexual encounter. After the US Department of Education in 2011 directed colleges to take sexual assault complaints more seriously, campuses implemented consent education programs to train students to recognize what affirmative consent is and how to practice it.

Yet only 11 states require consent education in public middle and high schools.[3] Learning about it in college is late in the game, and more than a third of high school graduates don't go to college.[4] Ideally, the process starts in early childhood, with the idea that kids should respect each other's boundaries and bodily autonomy. "Most schools are coming from a reactive place," said Elizabeth Greenblatt, a longtime sexuality educator who trains teachers. "Schools will address things if there's a problem, but there's not a lot of thought about how we can ingrain these ideas and make them an important part of who we are."

Teens, particularly girls, care a lot about consent and boundaries. They'll call out the gym teacher with roaming eyes, peers who try to use drugs and alcohol to lower the guard of people they want to hook up with, and even a movie character's failure to ask permission before kissing his (and it's usually his) beloved. My daughter criticizes situations and assumptions once considered unremarkable: a senior dating a freshman, a relationship between a boss and an employee, some degree of unwanted touch on a date as the nearly unavoidable price to pay for being a sexual being.

Pressure—asking more than once for sexual contact—is also suspect, as is any bid for intimacy from adults, particularly authority figures. In high school, I had a close friendship with one of my teachers, who was married and had a baby son. He used to tell me that I reminded him of an old girlfriend. When I told my daughter, she did not approve. "Mom, he was grooming you," she said flatly.

Because I'd felt out of place in high school, I had always treasured my relationship with the teacher. My daughter's words forced me to reconsider his attention in a way that made me sad. It was possible that my daughter was right, and I'd somehow dodged a bullet. It was also possible that I was right, and my teacher's intentions were platonic. Maybe my daughter and I were both right: The teacher was inappropriate *and* a source of support for me in a difficult time.

I envied my daughter's certainty, even as it unsettled me. It struck me as stemming from a generational pushback against an online world that normalized perpetual boundary breaches. Messages and alerts invade homework, sleep, in-person conversations, creating art, playing music, the joy of taking in the view at the top of a mountain (finally, cell reception!). These incursions can be casual, mean, interesting, crude (those dick pics and crotch shots), or genuinely urgent. The one thing they have in common is that they never stop interrupting young people's lives.

Media and social media remind teen girls of their vulnerability. My daughter and her friends all watched the Netflix docuseries on financier Jeffrey Epstein's sexual abuse of girls as young as 14. They closely followed the trial of sports physician Larry Nassar, with former teen gymnastic stars testifying about being molested, in several cases with their parents sitting only a few steps away in the examining room. Then there's porn. The vast majority of teens have watched porn online, often accidentally and at ever younger ages, shaping their views about sex.[5] Which is alarming, considering how porn routinely portrays sex acts that don't entail consent, emphasize male dominance and pleasure, and normalize ways of having sex that are likely to be painful or unpleasant for teen girls.

The fine-tuned consent radar many young people have doesn't mean the problem is solved. A slide deck on Instagram about the warning signs of a groomer or a TikTok feminist rewrite of Robin Thicke's misogynistic "Blurred Lines" into a manifesto for consent ("Just cuz you paid for dinner don't mean I owe you a favor.") won't be enough to help young people turn theory into practice.[6] Even if they insist they "know this stuff already," social media can't replace nuanced conversations with adults about the complexities of consent. Nor will social media give them sufficient understanding of the real attention, insight, confidence, and empathy required of both partners in a sexual encounter—and how hard it is to summon these qualities if alcohol and drugs are involved.

When you're new at handling desire, and even when you're not, it's incredibly difficult to know what you want. Especially if you're female. "We still don't have words for the receiving of touch we don't crave but commonly endure and even consent to because we don't feel entitled to resist it," writes author Melissa Febos in an article called "I Spent My Life Consenting to Touch I Didn't Want."[7] Peggy Orenstein emphasizes in her invaluable books about adolescent sexuality that teen girls tend to see their sexuality as a matter of how desired they are—what they look like, who wants them—as opposed to what *they* desire; this leaves them vulnerable to sexual encounters determined by what their partners want.[8] Boys, however, are socialized to prove their masculinity by "scoring." They get swept up in what Orenstein calls the "narcissism of male desire," prioritizing their own pleasure over a partner's feelings and desires.[9] This gender divide isn't absolute. Girls can be blind to their partners' needs and limits. Boys cope with peer pressure to seize every sexual opportunity, even when they aren't sure of what they want.

Sometimes young people's investment in boundaries and consent strikes adults as overreach, as when teens balk at the expectation to hug relatives and family friends with the explanation "my body, my choice." At my daughter's high school, a boy's request to cuddle with a girl he was seeing turned into a fast-spreading false rumor that he had sexually assaulted her, tarnishing his reputation. As Esther Perel pointed out to me, a narrow fixation on the minutiae of boundaries and consent can make us overly self-centered, blinding us to the interrelational aspects of human connection. "There's a person on the other side of a boundary, with their own feelings and humanity," she said.

This is rich terrain for family discussions. The word *boundary* is definite: a line in the sand, a fence, a crossing where guards stand sentry. In practice, the idea is often much fuzzier. We can encourage young people to talk about the challenging questions of how we should respond to each other when desires seem to clash. Is someone who keeps flirting when you don't flirt back being inappropriate? Is a partner who continues to express needs you can't satisfy overstepping bounds or merely being vulnerable and honest? What is the difference between trying to avoid hurting someone's feelings and appeasement? What do you do when you don't know what you want? Or when you're ambivalent, wanting something and not wanting something at the same time?

Moral absolutes about touch and desire can clash jarringly with the awkwardness, uncertainty, tensions, and misperceptions common to adolescent (and later) sexual experiences and romantic relationships. Tricia's son called her during his first year of college to tell her that he and his girlfriend were having tearful disagreements, some of them about their sex life. He kept checking in with her about what they did in bed, then days later she'd tell him she'd actually felt uncomfortable and unwilling. Tricia was terrified for her son, thinking about the media accounts she'd read of male students getting expelled for sexual assault. "It wasn't that I knew who was right or wrong," Tricia said. "I wanted to believe him, but I wasn't there, and I didn't want to make assumptions because he was my child." To her relief, the girlfriend ended the relationship without reporting her grievances. Tricia wasn't sure if she or anyone else could ever know the full truth of what happened—and not because she believed that either one of them was lying.

Perfect affirmative consent may not always be possible, as husband-and-wife legal scholars Jeannie Suk Gersen and Jacob Gersen discussed in a *New Yorker Radio Hour* feature on the new norms of affirmative consent on college campuses. "There's a lot of sex that's about that zone of not being sure, of being experimental, even doing something and having regret later. All of that is part of human sexuality," said Jeannie. Because of this, the goal of affirmative consent is often elusive. As Jacob put it, "We won't always know what we will or we won't like."[10]

We can, I believe, emphasize both interrelatedness and boundaries. Young people are capable of understanding that figuring out and expressing what they want and don't want is part of the responsibility of every kind of relationship—friendships, first dates, vaguely defined situationships, and committed relationships. Doing so is fundamental to our humanity. We can encourage the importance of turning down nonaggressive bids for touch without outrage or waging a smear campaign against the requestor—and help young people recognize the difference between expressing desire and being coercive.

Conversations about the subtleties of boundaries and consent take us beyond the basics of "The Talk," the rite-of-passage discussion about sex and what to do to prevent pregnancy and sexually transmitted infections (STIs). "The Talk" needs to be an ongoing process of regular, frank discussions about the gray areas of sexuality and consent. We should expect to be pushed to reevaluate our assumptions and biases. We may find ourselves revisiting mistakes we made in our youth and flashing back to harms we suffered. We can open ourselves up to the quest of fostering better understanding, for both teens and adults, of these challenging aspects of human sexuality. I don't think we have much of a choice. As Dakota's story shows, our children will confront these issues sooner than we think.

DATING ABUSE

From the time Kiki, a dating abuse survivor from Massachusetts, was little, she contended with powerful messages that "boys would act a certain way and girls would have to deal with it."

At age five, she burst into tears when a boy wouldn't stop poking her. She got into trouble for crying. No one blamed the boy.

At age 15, she went out for ice cream with a classmate. He casually suggested they stop by his house to say hello to his parents. The house was empty. He sexually assaulted her. It was her first sexual experience. She didn't tell anyone for the same reason Dakota hesitated to tell her mother: Kiki wasn't supposed to be alone with a boy.

Then, there was Tanner.

He was Kiki's counselor at the progressive New Hampshire camp at the center of her family's summers. Tanner—good-looking, popular, and the object of countless camper crushes—was nine years older. When she was 14 and he was 23, he flirted with her and, as they sat in the shadows of the campfire, secretly took her hand. Camper-counselor relationships were forbidden. Her parents, both teachers who worked at the camp to help afford to send Kiki and her siblings there, noticed the attention she was getting. When they confronted her, she insisted nothing was going on. "He's my counselor," she protested. "How could you think anything else?"

Tanner told her that he was in love with her, but they had to wait until she was 18 to "do anything about it." She went about her high school life: playing soccer, dating boys her age, all the while exchanging caring emails with him. Denise, Kiki's mother, and Fitz, her stepfather, were strict with their brood of seven: Kiki, from Denise's first marriage; the five children they had together; and an adopted son from Haiti. Her parents set firm curfews and brought the family to church on Sundays. Kiki didn't think they would approve of her correspondence with Tanner, so she kept it secret.

The summer after Kiki's 18th birthday, she and Tanner worked together as counselors and started a relationship. Her parents didn't like the age difference, but their daughter was an adult. They couldn't stop her. Besides, they liked Tanner. He was one of many camp folk who, during the school year, visited their home in Maynard, a Boston suburb, wanting to reconnect with the warmth, bustle, and acceptance of the camp community. Denise and Fitz always made room for visitors in the downstairs guest room, however precious the space in their modest four-bedroom 1950s Cape house.

After Kiki began college, she and Tanner kept the relationship going long-distance. He visited campus often. He would take her on moonlit motorcycle rides and spur-of-the-moment getaways. Sometimes he'd rent a hotel room; buy alcohol; and throw a party for her friends, underage first-year students who got carded out of local bars. She knew some of them whispered about her "pedophile boyfriend," but she told herself they didn't understand the exceptional love she and Tanner shared.

Tanner didn't like it when she worked on school projects with boys. Then he became more overtly possessive, showing up with little warning to insist she cancel her weekend plans so they could be alone together. She became increasingly isolated from her friends and campus social life. He cruelly put her down, wearing at her self-esteem. He encouraged her to keep up with his drinking until, as she described, "I couldn't move my body." Then he had sex with her in what she now recognizes was rape. In the summer, when they returned to their jobs at camp, he got jealous of male coworkers. One drunken evening, he pushed her off a low roof, humiliating her in front of their friends. A few counselors, worried about how he treated her and the near-constant smell of alcohol on his breath, urged her to leave him.

Tanner's persona still enchanted everyone else. He was great with the campers. No one knew how menacing he could be. At the evening campfires where years ago he'd taken her hand in his, he held her from behind and whispered to her about having sex with her later, even if she didn't want to. He told her he wanted to get her pregnant. She lived in terror of his cruelty, his assaults, and of having to bear his child. She also lived in terror of losing him.

After Kiki went back to college, Tanner's life fell apart. He was finally caught drinking at camp and got fired. After an argument with his mother, he had to move out of her house. Fitz and Denise, always given to helping friends in need, invited Tanner to stay in the guest room. Fitz would help Tanner get a job and start over. At first, Kiki encouraged the arrangement, then found that his presence in her childhood home made her feel trapped. Whenever she thought about confessing to her parents what he was doing to her, she froze. He was living with them in Maynard, with no place else to go. Even after he found his own place, he remained enmeshed in her family life.

After Kiki caught Tanner cheating on her, she summoned the strength to finally end the relationship. She provided her parents with little detail, making what happened sound like just another breakup. Tanner, meanwhile, could let himself be vulnerable with them. He was still struggling with his alcoholism, and they could see he missed their daughter terribly. One day, Kiki broke down and called Denise in a panic to tell her Tanner had unexpectedly shown up at her door.

"Talk to him," Denise urged. "I think he just wants closure."

"That's when I thought, 'I can't trust her because she's on Tanner's side with this,'" Kiki told me.

She cut off communication with Tanner and started the long journey of recovery on her own. Time and "a lot of therapy" helped her reinterpret Tanner's patient, clandestine courtship during her high school years as grooming: an adult building an intimate emotional connection to a child to gain power over her.

Kiki knew she couldn't fully live in her truth as a survivor until she told her parents. She wrote a long email about the relationship and waited to send it until she was about to board a plane to China, where she had a month-long teaching job. "I wanted them to have time to process it together," Kiki explained.

With their daughter half a world away, Fitz and Denise were devastated. Fitz chastised himself for inviting Tanner to stay with them, which he would later describe as "basically saving a rapist." Denise was overwhelmed with regret for unwittingly pressuring her daughter to appease Tanner. "Looking back, I'm horrified," Denise told me. "But I had no idea."

This wasn't supposed to happen, at least not according to commonly understood notions of what keeps young people safe: a middle-class upbringing (though barely so, given the strain of stretching two teachers' salaries to cover the needs of seven children) in a loving family living in a majority-White suburb with a low crime rate. Denise and Fitz supervised their children more than most parents did. The children were used to going to school and camp with either or both parents teaching in the same place.

Gauging the extent to which parents stand sentry over their children's lives—an increasingly impossible feat as children move from the teen years into early adulthood—misses the point. Adolescent dating abuse victims come from all kinds of families and circumstances. Love Is Respect, the youth-oriented arm of the National Domestic Violence Hotline, defines dating abuse as a pattern of behaviors, online or in person, aimed at having control over someone else. Dating abuse could involve physical harm; threats; sexual violence, pressure, or coercion; humiliation; monitoring; bullying; intimidation; isolation; stalking; and/or interfering with your ability to study, work, hold a job, or control your finances.

The problem is shockingly common. One in three teens will experience physical, sexual, or emotional abuse from someone they're in a relationship with before they become adults.[11] The rates of physical and sexual dating violence are higher for girls than for boys and higher for queer youth than for straight youth. Psychological violence—isolation, intimidation, aggression, humiliation, and other forms of emotional control—is the most common form of dating abuse, particularly as digital life amplifies and normalizes young people's capacity to surveil, bully, intimate, and threaten partners.[12]

BREAKING THE SILENCE

As Kiki related her story to me, I was struck by how mightily she'd held back from telling her parents and for how long. She explained that she feared that, if her parents knew, Tanner would end the relationship. She also felt uneasy sharing anything that had to do with sex with her parents. When she was in high school, her parents criticized her for wearing revealing clothing and for letting her boyfriend put his arm around her. Sex, her mother cautioned, was something Kiki should save for marriage. Even when she was in her late teens and 20s, her parents' initial reaction to her emerging sexuality took on its own life in her head, amplifying her sense of shame. Sex was something she was not supposed to be having, and any sign of her sexuality was supposed to be kept hidden. "It was hard to verbalize the sexual violence because I felt like I was talking about sex," she said.

I kept wanting to turn back time—to the vulnerable teen aglow with the thrill of being chosen by the older man everyone adored, to the college student tangled up in reasons not to share the brutal truth of her relationship—and urge her, "Tell your parents." The messages they sent about sex, their attachment to Tanner—surely none of this would have mattered if they had known about the abuse. I didn't fully understand Kiki's reluctance until I read a description by one of my students of the moment she finally told her mother about an abusive high school relationship: "My mother cried. She cried and she pleaded, 'Why didn't you tell me?' My mother couldn't understand that I couldn't have told her, because in the mess of my manipulated mind, she was my enemy."

Helen Friedman, a clinical psychologist who specializes in treating sexual trauma, explained that "abuse happens in secrecy and isolation." Abusers isolate victims to keep them under control. Difficult parent-child relationships make teens more vulnerable to this entrapment. "A harsh word from a parent to a teenager is experienced 10 times more intensely," Friedman said. "Young people don't trust adults to understand their feelings for their abuser. They think parents will judge them or force them to do something while they deal with their ambivalence."

In the wake of Kiki's email, her relationship with her mother began to change. They walked together in fundraisers for a rape crisis center in Boston and attended women's rights rallies. Denise was gratified by the renewed connection to her daughter. What she couldn't bring herself to do, though, was say the words that were rapidly taking over the social media feeds of women around the world: *Me too.*

Five years after Kiki pressed send on her tell-all email, I went to visit Denise and Fitz at their home in Maynard. Both were descended from Irish immigrants, with bright blue eyes, ruddy complexions, and an air of Old Country hardiness. We sat on Adirondack chairs overlooking their backyard, cluttered with the detritus of more than a quarter-century of raising kids: soccer goal nets, bicycles, two sailboats in disrepair for what Fitz estimated was at least a decade; they'd honeymooned in one of them.

It was a quiet time in their family life. Most of the kids were away at college or living on their own. Kiki had settled about an hour and a half's drive away on the North Shore, where she taught middle schoolers with learning disabilities. A few of their chickens pecked the grass around us, making a sound like a cross between a moan and a cat's meow, punctuated by clucking. "Look," Fitz said, pointing to a hawk perched high on a dead tree at the edge of their yard. "He could be after the chickens." He walked swiftly across the yard to shoo the hawk away.

Denise told me that she'd concealed from her daughter a disquieting similarity between their lives: Denise had also experienced intimate partner violence. In her first marriage, her husband made her stop working and playing hockey, a sport she loved. After Kiki was born, he began to physically abuse Denise. Her baby daughter in tow, Denise sought refuge with her parents, who reprimanded Denise for giving up on her marriage. Denise knew firsthand the despair of having parents who could not acknowledge what was happening to their daughter. "You don't want to do things to your kids that you didn't like that your parents did," Denise said. She didn't tell Kiki about the abuse out of fear that it would turn her against her father, who had partial custody.

But Kiki had known Denise's secret for years. When Kiki joined us for lunch on the back deck later that day, she said that Denise's mother, known to the family as Nana, disclosed that she'd suspected that Tanner had been abusive because she recognized the signs from Denise's first marriage. "She was worried about Tanner after your relationship with Dad," Kiki said.

Learning what happened to her mother at first gave Kiki a feeling of inevitability, that what she'd gone through with Tanner was somehow inherited. She also felt betrayed. Her mother, above all people, should have noticed the signs and understood. Then, Kiki's resolve surged: *This has to end*—in her life; in her sisters' futures; and, she hoped, in a society that was slowly beginning to reckon with its long history of blindness to intimate partner violence.

In front of my eyes, Denise and Kiki were finally acknowledging their shared experiences of abuse—and of not feeling seen at the height of the crisis. "I never wanted to be my mother," Denise said. "I remember how my parents didn't take my side. If I had known what was going on, I would have never taken Tanner's side. I would have never told you to talk to him for closure."

I asked Fitz, who'd been quiet, how he felt. He had a mild, not unkind scowl on his face. He said that he'd never felt comfortable with the "all in": love so consuming you can't see yourself outside of it. He was raised in a reserved family, where explicit expressions of love were rare. His high school girlfriend broke up with him because he never told her that he loved her. "It never even crossed my mind," he said.

As a high school teacher, he tended to feel teens weren't ready to deal with the complexities of their emotions. What happened with his stepdaughter—an "all in" kind of person, as he described—made him think he had to be more open to the emotional lives of young people. Learning the truth had sent Fitz reeling with guilt and "murderous anger" at Tanner, a man he'd tried to help. "It allowed me to see my limitations more clearly," he said.

Denise weighed in, offering that now the family discussed sex and relationships more frequently and openly. What happened, Denise said, "made us closer. It's opened things up."

Kiki agreed that Denise had undergone a huge shift in the way she talked about relationships. Kiki described herself as returning to the openness that was innate to her as a young girl, when she'd confide in her mother about her first feelings about boys. "For me, it went from feeling like I wanted to tell you every time I had a crush on someone to feeling like I couldn't tell you anything to the letter that told you everything," she said to her mother. "Now I can share everything because I have nothing to hide."

As I've interviewed parents for this book, I've heard versions of Denise's determination again and again: *I don't want my child to go through what I did.* We don't want them to inherit our troubles, our traumas, our pain. If they lead better lives and have better relationships, then maybe our own suffering will be redeemed. These feelings are even more acute when it comes to intimate partner violence. We have to reconcile these worries with a difficult reality. Though next-generation victimization is not inevitable, children who are exposed to intimate partner violence are at increased risk for experiencing abuse later.[13] We don't have to tell our children every detail of our pasts, but we can't let our pasts inhibit us from having the kinds of conversations that help our children cope with the dangers of the present.

More importantly, we live in a world that has not yet changed in the ways it should for our children to be free and safe from intimate partner violence. If our children are violated, the perpetrators—not our personal histories—are to blame, along with a society that doesn't do enough to prevent abuse and assault. Teen dating abuse and sexual violence are public health emergencies. When they go unaddressed, they can have long-term consequences, including depression, anxiety, alcohol and drug abuse, antisocial behavior, and suicidal thinking.[14] Disturbingly, people who've experienced dating abuse in adolescence are more likely to suffer it again as adults.[15]

INTIMATE PARTNER VIOLENCE IN UNEXPECTED PLACES: SAME-SEX COUPLES AND MALE VICTIMS

For Tori, a high school student in New Jersey, the trauma of being in an abusive relationship was compounded by the isolation of not being out as a lesbian to her parents. Without their knowledge, at 14 she got into a relationship with a tempestuous and emotionally needy girl. Her girlfriend would have rages that lasted until Tori calmed her by submitting to sex. When Tori tried to end the relationship, her girlfriend drove her down an isolated side road, locked the car doors, and told her they weren't going anywhere until Tori took her back. Tori's grades fell. She lost weight. She pulled out her hair, making bare patches on her eyebrows.

In Tori's online searches for guidance, everything she found was about straight couples in which the male was the abuser. "I didn't have a representation of a queer couple. It was hard to wrap my head around what was happening," Tori said.

Tori's experience of entrapment underscored how silence around sexuality, identity, and relationships can hinder young people in abusive situations from reaching out for help. "Discussing the abuse in the relationship would be tantamount to outing themselves," Friedman said. "Young people pick up on parental attitudes toward sex and sexual orientation, whether parents intend them to or not."

Females in same-sex relationships also contend with a long-standing mythology surrounding lesbian relationships: that they are naturally egalitarian and kinder, a utopian alternative to gendered power dynamics, free of the patriarchal scourge of abuse—a stereotype that Tori's girlfriend used to try to gaslight Tori. Her girlfriend recounted a former boyfriend who'd hit her. "I would never do that to you," she told Tori.

Gay youth contend with a different though equally misguided expectation. They're not supposed to have emotional lives at all, especially because they're not dating girls, one of the few contexts in which teen boys are allowed to be vulnerable. "We raise boys in this very patriarchal robot sensibility, to be tough men who don't think and feel," said Tony Enos, a public health educator in Philadelphia. "We teach them to turn off red flags and cues from their mind telling them they're sad or depressed or uncomfortable with something that isn't healthy."

Enos started his dating life with a series of relationships with abusive men, an experience he's spoken openly about in the workshops he's conducted for teens. "Representation matters," he said. "It really does help to see yourself in the thing that you need and to have that awareness. I wish I had known that there were resources for males in abusive relationships. Maybe I would have realized quicker that I was in one."

A sense of invisibility also affects straight boys who've experienced dating abuse. Research indicates that more girls than boys admit to being psychologically and physically abusive to partners. About 43 percent of boys say they've experienced dating abuse, compared to 51 percent of girls.[16] The point, though, is not so much to compare rates as to acknowledge that both boys and girls experience and perpetrate dating abuse. Boys may contend with stubborn misconceptions and stereotypes. Dating abuse, many people assume, entails a guy hurting a girl, not the other way around. Female aggressors are jokes, fodder for tawdry stalker movies and "crazy ex-girlfriend" comments (though the TV series of that name explores gender, mental illnesses, and romantic obsession with a lot of insight and wisdom). Many community resources—support groups, shelters, advocacy organizations—serve only women and girls.[17]

When DJ was in basic training for the army in Fort Hood, Texas, he dated a girl who became jealous and abusive when she drank. Later, she would bring him beer and apologize profusely. Then the next time she drank, she'd go through the same cycle again. On a getaway in Austin, she got drunk and became angry at him for looking at girls walking along Sixth Street, the hub of the city's live-music and bar scene. When he took her wrist to take her to their hotel room to sober up, she screamed, "Don't touch me!" A woman on the street berated him for grabbing his date.

"It was this whole scene where now it looks like I'm the abuser," he said. He backed away and hid until his date drove away. She then pursued him so aggressively that he had her banned from the army base. Even then, the harassment continued for years with barrages of text messages, emails, and phone calls, which didn't stop until long after he moved to another state.

Though research shows males who've been stalked and abused are less likely to seek help and less likely to be taken seriously when they report it, DJ said that wasn't the case for him.[18] Military security was quick to support his request to keep his girlfriend off base. Later, as a college student, a girl he dated briefly threatened to send her brothers to shoot him. The resident assistant in his dorm quickly helped him get a restraining order. "The next day, he knocked on my door and said, 'You know, we're here for you whatever you need,'" DJ said. "Everything ended up okay. But this can happen to anybody."

Young people who report abusive partners often are met with reactions that don't help: Where were you? What were you doing? What were you wearing? Why did you pick this person to date? Why did you stay? The response DJ received, in contrast, focused on providing support and taking action. He needed to be believed, and he was. He needed protection, and he got it. Granted, there were institutional concerns at stake—the safety of an army base and a college campus—and it should be said that neither the military nor higher education has a great track record of protecting women from abuse, assault, and stalking. But DJ's story shows how much prompt, no-nonsense problem solving matters.

"Emotional support is what we tend to think is most needed in the immediate aftermath, but what we've found in our research is that offering concrete, helpful things—I will get you the resources you want, I will help you get to the doctor, that kind of thing—is really quite important," said Anne P. DePrince, a psychology professor at the University of Denver who researches intimate partner violence.

Parents, she added, need to be careful not to let their own emotional reactions and sense of loss of control take center stage. "They should avoid things that sound like victim blaming, even if they're just trying to find out the details of what happened," she said. "Getting overwhelmed and angry on the part of the survivor is also not helpful but surprisingly common. It might be that a parent is just so heartbroken that this happened that their response becomes bigger and takes up all the oxygen in the room." Instead, she advised, stay focused on survivors and respond to their immediate reactions and needs, not your own.

THE FEELING AND THE FACT: COMMUNICATING WITH YOUR CHILD ABOUT RED FLAGS

Dating abuse prevention advocates urge young people and the adults in their lives to be alert for clues that a relationship may be becoming abusive, such as "love bombing," when a partner lavishes attention and gifts on you right away and expects your instant adoration in turn. That may be a tactic used to gain control. It feeds off idealized notions of love as a fated, instant, passionate, and all-encompassing connection. Young people love to mock love bombing. They may seem to see right through it when it happens to someone else. But they'll also scramble to justify a partner's 0-to-60 attention if they feel a strong, immediate connection. It's not that a strong, immediate connection is always suspect. It's how two people act on it and whether the relationship truly allows each person time and space to think and act for themselves.

Even online relationships can become suffocating. During the pandemic, a student told me that her girlfriend, who lived hundreds of miles away, became so controlling that she was afraid to go for a walk with her family, lest she couldn't immediately answer the girl's jealous texts. They had never met in person. Whether a relationship is in cyberspace or in person, parents should seize opportunities to help young people recognize the difference between healthy and unhealthy behavior. If a teen is perpetually distracted by a partner's bids for attention, then parents could open up a conversation about the possibility that the partner's expectations might be unhealthy. Parents can ask how often the partner acts that way and how it makes their child feel.[19]

Conflict-resolution skills are another key component to preventing dating abuse. "There's a lot around recognizing emotions and understanding your own emotional tendencies, so you can slow things down and choose a response that's healthier for you and your partner," DePrince said. "It's important to step back and think about what it means to be sensitive and assertive without being aggressive in relationships." Parents need to model these skills themselves. "When parents communicate through their actions that aggression is a way to solve problems, that aggression is part of what you do in relationships, then it tends to show up more in young people's relationships," she said.

Two themes in my interviews for this chapter weigh on me. The first is the calculation teens make when they've been harmed while they're breaking a household rule: No hanging out with boys unless other girls are there. Don't have sex before marriage. Don't sneak out past midnight. As I've described, young people often won't say what's happened to them because it happened when they were doing something they weren't supposed to.

Parents, of course, need to set household rules, a core tenet of authoritative parenting, which entails being nurturing and responsive yet setting firm limits. But they can also send the bottom-line message that their children's well-being matters more by saying, "Whatever you've been doing and wherever you are, I will help if you've been hurt or you're not safe."

The second theme has to do with how attached young people can get to a relationship, even when they're being mistreated. The first book my students read in my Love and Heartbreak seminar is bell hooks's *All about Love*, which emphatically states, "Love and abuse cannot coexist."[20] I can think of no better adage for young people and for all of us.

But by the time the 16 students in one recent section of the course read those words, at least 2 had been in high school relationships in which love and abuse did coexist. They had to reconcile her message with the reality of their past: that they stayed in relationships in part because they felt love, though the attachment was heightened by how badly the relationship destroyed their self-esteem, making them feel they deserved the abuse. Realizing that an abusive relationship is not love is a crucial stage in surviving one. But for parents and other concerned adults, wielding the bell hooks definition when a child feels in love may not work. Several parents—including one whose life's work was in intimate partner violence prevention—told me that they spotted signs early on that their child was in an abusive relationship, yet they still felt helpless. Their children were too attached and too afraid to lose the relationship, and they became defensive and secretive. No matter how hard they tried, the parents couldn't make the relationship end until the child was ready to end it.

Teen dating abuse prevention advocates point out that, even if young people aren't ready, they need to hear that their parents believe them and are concerned. Ultimatums or punishments aimed at keeping young people from their partner can backfire, leaving them feeling isolated or reluctant to share what's happening and strengthening feelings of loyalty to the relationship. Instead, parents can help their child sort through the "two Fs": the feeling and the fact. The feeling is "I love this person." The fact is "I'm not being treated correctly."[21] They can strategize with their child to come up with a safety plan, a process that acknowledges the danger of the situation. Several families use safe words, a phrase children can text or say over the phone, such as "Aunt Mary called," when they're feeling unsafe but don't want whomever they're with to know they're reaching out for help.

Simply having a plan in place can help young people gain perspective that they are in a situation that could become dangerous. When there's tension in the family, children may benefit from turning to other trusted adults, such as a coach or teacher, and getting support from intimate partner violence prevention advocates trained in helping adolescents. In addition to local community resources, the National Teen Dating Abuse Helpline (866-331-9474), which includes chat and text options, is one of several free and confidential services available.

IN THEIR SHOES: THE TEEN DATING ABUSE PREVENTION MOVEMENT

One Saturday afternoon in April, I watched a group of high school students at the Texas State Capitol gain a sense of what it's like to make choices in an abusive relationship. The 50 students had been selected by application to join the Teen Ambassadors of Hope, a program run by the Texas Advocacy Project (TAP), a nonprofit with the mission of ending domestic violence, dating abuse, sexual assault, and trafficking. They'd come to Austin to learn about healthy relationships, the warning signs of abuse, and the steps they could take to get victimized peers to sources of adult support.

I wanted to see the Teen Ambassadors of Hope in action because dating abuse prevention was not a thing when I was in high school. Anti–domestic violence activism, including teen dating abuse awareness, was still new and rare.[22] Now, 38 states mandate some form of dating abuse prevention in public schools—a significant figure, given that only 29 states require sex education. In addition, advocacy groups across the country offer youth-focused healthy relationship workshops, support groups for young survivors of dating abuse, and sexual violence prevention summer institutes, often with a focus on teaching teens how to become peer educators and activists themselves. Once the Teen Ambassadors of Hope completed the training in Austin, they would return to their hometowns, from Amarillo to Dallas to McAllen, to organize fundraisers and foster awareness of intimate partner violence, a problem that will affect one out of three Texans in their lifetime.[23]

Divided into groups of five, the students—mostly Latino and White, with a few Black and Asian teens—played In Their Shoes, an experiential learning game developed by the Washington State Coalition against Domestic Violence. The groups were assigned scenarios: a popular, wealthy White girl who becomes increasingly controlling with her Black boyfriend; a Japanese American lesbian whose long-distance girlfriend manipulates her from afar; a Mexican immigrant girl in a relationship with a boy who insults her limited ability to speak English. All were based on real-life teen relationships. The format of In Their Shoes is based on the Choose Your Own Adventure books. The student groups assume the role of the protagonist of their scenarios and make choices that shape the plots, using prompts from cards placed on tables around the room.

I shadowed a group with the story of Ashley, a high school girl dating Jimmy, an unemployed recent college graduate.

The students picked a card. Ashley, they learned, discovers a webcam under her pillow. Then her phone rings. She sees it's Jimmy.

"If you answer the phone, go to cell phone card number 3," a girl read out loud. "If you tell your parents, go to family card number 3."

"I don't really *want* to answer the phone," another girl chimed in.

"But we're supposed to be predicting what she would do, and she is head over heels for him," the cardholder pressed. "And he's manipulating her."

"Definitely pick up the phone," the only boy in the group said.

Ashley picks up. The group hurried across the room to get cell phone card number 3. The students learned that Jimmy snuck the webcam into Ashley's bedroom, and he wants her to set it up so he can watch her sleep. They picked another card, which told them that she calls her best friend for advice on what to do. The best friend gushes that Jimmy's request is the most romantic thing she's ever heard. She urges Ashley to get the webcam running.

As the group went from card to card, Ashley's life swiftly goes downhill. The webcam monitors her every move. Jimmy sneaks into her bedroom one night and pressures her into having sex for the first time. She gets pregnant. Her parents call her a filthy slut. She moves into Jimmy's bedroom at his parents' house. Jimmy pressures her to drop out of school. Finally, Ashley sneaks a phone call to the only trusted adult in her life, an aunt who lives in a city two hours away. The aunt rescues her. "You're already feeling better," the final card read. "Your aunt gets on the freeway driving east on a beautiful day."

The exercise was potent, taking the students into the pained intricacies of making decisions in a world of rapidly diminishing options and punishing consequences in a way that high-profile media stories of intimate partner violence can't do. I thought of Gabby Petito, the young Instagrammer murdered by her fiancé during a van trip across the country just days after she posted images of the couple laughing and kissing. Teens often first confront narratives of domestic violence through girls like her: straight, White girls who, until their deaths, seemed free, golden, revered, and winning the lottery of life. In the In Their Shoes scenarios, both victim and abuser are already vulnerable in the ways that American life can make young people vulnerable: parents who don't understand them, educational paths that dead end, poverty, marginalized identities.

As I walked out of the air-conditioned capitol into the warmth of the late-afternoon sun, I felt genuine relief that the students had deemed Ashley not quite head over heels enough to stay with Jimmy. They'd sent her off on a much healthier adventure.

I'd loved spending the day with teens committed to dating abuse prevention, who would go home to organize pickleball tournaments and other fundraisers and talk about the issue with their peers. When I was their age, the only thing I knew about what was then called "battered women" was from watching *The Burning Bed*, a 1984 TV movie starring former pinup model Farrah Fawcett as a woman who murders her demonically abusive husband. I hoped the Teen Ambassadors of Hope and other young healthy relationship advocates like them across the country would be able to make a difference.

But being in the shoes of Ashley in Texas was turning out to be fate with narrowing options. Shortly after my visit to Austin, the state's near-total ban on abortion went into effect. That meant Ashley would be more likely to see her pregnancy through—which would entail the lifelong responsibility of raising a child and an irrevocable link to her abuser.[24]

In other words, it would take a lot more than greater peer understanding and a supportive aunt to truly free her.

CHAPTER 7

The Most-Stressed Generation

Teen Relationships and Mental Health

THE SUMMER BEFORE HIS JUNIOR YEAR IN HIGH SCHOOL, AARON met Ellen at a punk show at a taco restaurant in Maine. He already knew a little about her, in the ambient way teens find out about each other on social media. She was a senior at an alternative school known for its emphasis on self-discovery and empathy and its flock of hippie kids. He'd admired her profile picture on Twitter, though it took him a beat to recognize her at the show, as she'd cut her long hair boyishly short. They struck up a conversation about music. She suggested he check out an album by Walter Mitty and His Makeshift Orchestra. He listened to it over and over, then sent her an exuberant text letting her know how much he liked it. The exchange took off over their shared enthusiasm for the burgeoning DIY music scene.

Aaron thought of himself as a late bloomer. He spent a lot of time playing video games and Legos, an obsession since early childhood. He described himself as someone with low self-esteem, tied into the bouts of depression and anxiety he'd been having since he was in middle school. Around girls he was attracted to, he felt confused and awkward. But on his first date with Ellen at a waterfront burger place, the connection they'd established over text held up. They met friends afterward at a nearby Starbucks.

Something in the burger he'd eaten roiled his stomach, and he dashed out to vomit down a sewer grate. Tourists veered around him with glances of disgust. "Like I had one too many last night, and I was like, 'Eff you, I'm 16,'" he said.

He returned to the Starbucks. "What's up, guys?" he said sheepishly. His friends knew the drill. With his many food allergies and jittery nerves, he threw up a lot. Ellen, to his surprise, still seemed interested in him. The gross-out rom-com scene of their beginnings became a running joke between them, their comic origin story: He threw up to get her to like him.

The relationship changed the way Aaron saw himself and the way he lived. He and Ellen spent hours creating mixtapes for each other with elaborate, handwritten liner notes. They hung out most days after school, and Ellen was allowed to sleep at Aaron's house on the weekends. They did random fun things, like baking cookies and hiking. After years of feeling alienated at his high school, he bonded with the kids he met through Ellen. He and Ellen even looked alike: tall and thin, with unruly curly brown hair. They would goof off in photos, one picking the other up like a groom carrying his bride across the threshold, then switching places. He stopped feeling like "this unlikeable person I'd pictured myself as," he said. "It made me so happy, the validation of, there's this cute older girl, and not only does she like me, but we mutually like each other, and I feel supported," he said.

He was aware his life was more privileged. Ellen's father ran a landscaping business, and her mother was a substitute teacher. His parents were professors at a well-endowed private college. He paid for everything when he and Ellen went out. Her home, though, was the more comfortable one. Tensions between Aaron and his mother, Darla, had been running high. The dynamic at Ellen's was a peaceful antidote to the fraught atmosphere at his house.

For a while, Aaron's relationship seemed to help Darla and Aaron get along. Darla adored Ellen. "She was a real powerhouse of a person, very smart, very ambitious, and fun to have around," she said. "Things were better because Aaron was happier, and when he was happier, I was happier."

For years, Darla had lived with her son's moodiness. When he climbed into the car after school, she never knew if he would crack a joke or burst into tears or rage at her. When he was with Ellen, Darla saw a different dimension of Aaron. She admired what the couple had together: how devoted they were to each other, without fights and disagreements. She was proud of how good her son was to his girlfriend.

Aaron's father, Jerry, also was pleased with the changes in his mercurial son. "To see the two of them together was pretty lovely," he told me. "He'd been in a certain mindset, and it was almost completely transformed, because now this other person is there, and they're learning from each other."

For Darla, the pleasure of witnessing her son's first love was occasionally tinged with regret. She'd never had anything like that when she was young. Her own first relationships were unhappy, nothing like what Aaron and Ellen shared. "This is terrible to say, but at times I was jealous of the relationship because it was so loving," Darla said. "They were very doting, very expressive, super intimate. I never had one like that, and I wished I had."

Aaron's closeness to Ellen's family also reminded Darla of what she lacked in her relationship with her son. "He would refuse to eat family dinner with us, but he would eat with her parents, which made me sad, but I was glad he was having family dinner somewhere," she said.

When Aaron clashed with his mother, Ellen comforted him. She was always there to hold him or answer his anxious late-night texts. "She was a person who had an outside perspective," Aaron said. "I'd never been open enough with anyone before and had someone who could validate me and tell me that it's okay that you don't feel okay."

Sometimes, though, his anxiety grew frightening, his anger turning inward. He would tell Ellen that he wanted to hurt himself. Sometimes he would tell her that he wanted to kill himself. She made him promise he wouldn't do either.

Then Darla got a call from Ellen's mother, who was increasingly worried about all that her daughter was shouldering. "You need to get Aaron to a therapist," she said. Darla was already looking for one.

The Age of Storm and Stress

In the hundreds of hours I've spent interviewing young people and their parents about relationships, I've been struck by how many of their stories intersected with mental health issues: bouts of anxiety and depression, addiction, suicidal thoughts, psychiatric hospitalizations. At times the world of adolescent love seemed divided into young people with serious mental health problems and partners who supported them. That's when I began to think of every teen love story as a mental health story.

Romantic experiences, from unrequited yearnings to the rise and fall of a first committed relationship, thrust young people into vivid and unprecedented experiences of passionate feeling, need, betrayal, jealousy, and rejection. They are new at this—and they are also relatively new *to themselves*, only beginning to gain an understanding of how they cope with emotions that test them. "These experiences are hard at any age but particularly at a time when beliefs about the importance of acceptance, identity, and social standing are heightened," said David E. Szwedo, a clinical psychologist and professor at James Madison University.

As G. Stanley Hall observed in his classic 1904 treatise *Adolescence*, throughout history and across cultures, puberty and the teenage years have been distinguished by the presence of anxiety and other "disturbances of the nervous system and of the mind." Though Hall is credited with defining adolescence as a distinct life stage, he was not the first to observe the distinctive emotional and behavioral qualities of this phase of life. Parents in ancient Greece gave offerings of fine cloth to the goddess Diana to cure their daughters' suicidal thinking. Medieval Arab physicians described the youthful tendency to succumb to religious melancholy.[1] "Books of nurture"—predecessors to modern-day parenting books—listed timidity, school refusal, and anxiety among the many emotional and behavioral issues. Adolescence, Hall pronounced, was a time of "storm and stress," a translation of the German *Sturm und Drang*, a genre of literature typified by Goethe's *The Sorrows of Young Werther*, the story of a young man who dies by suicide in the throes of a romantic obsession.[2] In her best-selling book *Coming of Age in Samoa*, anthropologist Margaret Mead, famously and controversially offers up the possibility that the anxious adolescent is the product of Western parenting values: If teen girls could thrive in a South Pacific island culture free of uptight sexual and gender norms, did adolescence have to be so hard?[3]

Contemporary understanding of the adolescent brain suggests that it might. The amygdala, the nucleus accumbens, and other brain regions involved in fear, emotional reactivity, and reward seeking mature faster than the prefrontal cortex, the area that helps us plan; exercise self-control; and sort through conflicting thoughts, future consequences, and other aspects of decision making. This developmental shift may make teens more vulnerable to anxiety and depression.[4] Certain kinds of stresses—academic; social media; competition with their peers; and, yes, romantic relationships—ramp up during adolescence, and teens become more aware of what's at stake in how well they cope with them.

Young people also have to contend with the expectations of educators and parents, who may emphasize academic and extracurricular achievement to an unhealthy degree. Teens will inevitably experience some degree of anxiety, a fundamental aspect of being human and an evolutionary adaptation meant to help us deal with danger. Anxiety keeps them on their guard walking through a dicey neighborhood alone for the first time. Worrying about a test will goad them to study for it. But to that point, adolescent anxiety may rise to an unhealthy degree because they perceive situations as more threatening than they actually are—that falling short of a perfect test score, for example, will mean they won't get into the right college and their prospects of future success will be forever damaged.[5]

Even if you are fortunate enough to be or have a relatively untroubled teen, you likely know of several others who are on prescription medication for depression and anxiety and some who've spent time in psychiatric units or addiction-treatment programs and plenty who feel constantly overwhelmed, unsure of how they'll get from one day to the next. Today's generation of adolescents increasingly is defined by stress and its toll on mental health. Generation Z is the most likely of all generations to report mental health problems and to seek help for them. More than 40 percent said that feeling sad or hopeless kept them from schoolwork or their regular activities for at least two weeks. Girls and LGBTQ+ youth are most at risk, with significantly higher rates of poor mental health and suicidal thinking.[6] Young people see anxiety and depression as the most pervasive problem facing their peers, worse than bullying, drug and alcohol addiction, and poverty.[7]

As a parent and a college professor, I'm often taken aback by the strength and pervasiveness of accommodations for mental health disorders. A friend of my daughter attends a high school that permits her to stay home for days at a time when she's anxious. From elite private colleges to state universities like my own, it's not uncommon for college students to approach professors on the first day of class to disclose a diagnosis and warn that they might have extra absences because of it. A manager at a suburban Banana Republic complains about turnover, her teen employees leaving not for better jobs with higher pay but to tend to their mental health. I've had plenty of conversations with parents who decry these trends as signs of a generation lacking resilience or who blame themselves for raising what author and

Psychology Today editor Hara Estroff Murano warned would become a "nation of wimps."[8]

I don't believe it's that simple. Consider what young people have been through. Karla Vermeulen, a psychology professor and colleague at SUNY New Paltz, calls emerging adults "Generation Disaster."[9] The oldest Gen-Zers were preschoolers when the Twin Towers collapsed, their parents trying to shield them from the dystopian images on the TV screen. However unimaginable the terrorist attacks of 9/11 were, the unimaginable just kept happening. My daughter, born in 2004, has for the most part lived a stable, middle-class existence in a small town. Yet her childhood was punctuated by unprecedented crises.

At five, my daughter shook her fists in anger when we told her about the Deepwater Horizon spill discharging thousands of gallons of oil daily into the Gulf of Mexico. Record-breaking hurricanes and tropical storms became normal events in the news and in our own community, where she's watched families drag waterlogged boxes and ruined furniture to the dump, roughed it through extended power outages, and toted canned goods and toiletries to donation drives. She was just two grades older than the youngest victims of the Sandy Hook massacre in my hometown of Newtown and a high school freshman during the Parkland school shooting and the youth-led wave of activism that followed. At her high school graduation, she grimly joked that she was glad not just for the degree but also for having made it out alive.

Before she even started high school, as I've mentioned, she was the main support for a friend who'd been sexually assaulted and prepared to testify on her behalf. The following fall, a cherished neighbor who used to babysit her died of an opioid overdose at age 20. Then came the pandemic; Black Lives Matter; January 6; and the Israel-Hamas War, which hit hard given our many Israeli relatives and the Arab and Jewish Israeli friends we made through a high school exchange program. Throughout it all, my daughter became increasingly aware that climate change was making the planet increasingly unlivable and democracy may not endure.

She witnessed too soon how being a girl, a student in a school, a neighbor, a community member, a person on the earth, a teen who wanted to be spending time with other teens were under threat. She's surrounded by peers who are actively coping with mental health disorders. "This generation has reason to be the most anxious, but they're also the most open about being anxious, which is good," she said. "We're in this together."

We've only just begun to measure the impact of these many, once-unimaginable series of events on the mental health of young people. All of this is compounded by the impact of growing up with smartphones and social media, which has been linked, particularly in girls, to depression and anxiety symptoms, along with self-harm, negative body image, suicidal thinking, loneliness, and poor sleep.[10] Young people of color are more likely to report their mental health is additionally strained by food insecurity, precarious housing, and debt, along with racial trauma suffered at school, from the police, and from news consumption.[11] A global survey of 10,000 young people aged 16–25 illustrated the depth of anxiety about climate change: More than half believed humanity was doomed, and two-thirds felt sad, afraid, and anxious. Nearly 40 percent said they hesitated to have children of their own, a figure that doesn't surprise me.[12] My daughter has been saying since middle school that she would never want to bring a child into *this*, and I've been having a lot of wistful conversations with my cohort of parents about the likelihood that we will never be grandparents. "We are living in end times," one of my students said. "I just can't see myself being a mother."

Saddled with the worries of multiple global crises and an unprecedented awareness of mental health, how does this most-stressed generation approach love? A cover article in the *Atlantic* on this generation's "sex recession" cited anxiety rates and other mental health concerns as one potential reason an increasing number of young people were less likely to date and waited longer to start having sex.[13] But the demographic trend doesn't capture the reality of adolescents who are taking their mental health woes into relationships. In speaking with Aaron and his parents, I was struck by the ways that being in a relationship gave him joy and, when he was down, provided solace. But his story also raises questions about the challenges mental health issues pose to first relationships—and the challenge relationships pose to mental health.

DATING AND DEPRESSION: AN UNDENIABLE LINK

While healthy, committed relationships in adulthood are associated with improved mental and physical health, for teenagers nearly everything about relationships—attraction, dating, sex—is linked with symptoms of depression, particularly for girls.[14] Studies spotlight connections between depression and dating, depression and sex, depression and flirting, and even depression and romantic *feelings*.[15] Breakups are a risk factor for a first bout with major depression in adolescence.[16] The research, I should underscore, does not mean that relationships cause depression—only that, during adolescence, there is an important and consistent correlation between symptoms of depression and experiences of dating and sex; the younger the teen, the stronger the connection.[17] Essentially, we first open our hearts to romantic connection at the same time we're becoming more susceptible to darker feelings.

"These things are colliding," said SUNY Stonybrook psychology professor Joanne Davila. Teens, she told me, are juggling a bewildering array of input: the desires and perceptions in their own heads; what peers are saying; ethnic, religious, or other cultural pressures; identity issues around sexual orientation or gender.

"Something's not going to go right," she said. "They're going to have breakups. They're going to have ambiguous situations. If they don't have the coping resources or the emotional regulation skills, they're really going to be in trouble. So many challenges come up that can both generate feelings of anxiety or depression, as well as interact with preexisting anxiety or depression."

Where does that leave an anxious or depressed teen? Young people may seek out relationships to shore up their self-esteem and feel better, only to find they're more sensitive to normal ups and downs and times when their partner can't soothe them. Their mental health may suffer as they confront the difference between what they thought their relationship would be like and the reality.

When he was 13, Brycen was hit by a series of life-changing losses. His uncle died suddenly of a heart attack. Just four months later, his grandfather died of cancer. Brycen's dad had never been a part of his life, and these two men were doting father figures. His first serious girlfriend cheated on him with his best friend, leaving him so distraught that his mother found him huddled in a closet, crying. "The cheating after the deaths was this moment in time when he's feeling like the pain was so excruciating that he just couldn't go on anymore," Christine, his mother, remembered.

Brycen, who is African American, also was becoming increasingly aware of the racism in his majority-White, upper-middle-class New Jersey community. No matter how much he excelled at school and on the track team, there would be friends who cracked bigoted jokes and parents who didn't want him to date their daughters. His next relationship, in high school, lifted his mood, even though he suspected his girlfriend's parents were among the wary. "Being in a relationship made me happy, and I couldn't feel the depression," he said.

One evening, a close female friend kissed Brycen. He hesitated, then kissed her back. The next day, he guiltily confessed what happened to his girlfriend. They broke up briefly, then reconciled. He continued to hook up with other girls on the sly. "If I was sad, which was most of the time, and I couldn't be around my girlfriend, I would go and find someone else," he said. "I had that craving, that itch, like I was in withdrawal." He hid what he was doing, playing the good boyfriend when he was with his girlfriend and the "single douchebag" when he wasn't. He eventually grew too miserable and exhausted to continue the relationship.

What he needed, Brycen realized in retrospect, were skills to manage his mental health: sitting with difficult feelings and being more open with trusted loved ones about when he was feeling down. "I was the person my friends talked to when they weren't feeling great, but I didn't really ever have a person like that myself," he said. "So I've had to build that skill of talking to people about my emotions."

He didn't date again until his senior year. He told his new girlfriend right away that he got depressed sometimes, and he inwardly resolved not to cheat on her. She was perceptive about noticing when he seemed down. "If I couldn't snap out of it, she would just sit there with me," he said. "She was never like, 'You have to be happy.' It was more like 'I want you to be happy, and I'll be here until you are' kind of approach." Relationships and sex, he realized, weren't medication. Sometimes he just had to give his moods space and time. He remained faithful throughout the relationship, which didn't end until they parted ways for college.

For some teens, relationship problems can lead to a more acute crisis: severe depression, self-harm, suicidal thinking, and suicide risk.[18] Even if the trigger seems trivial—the end of a short-lived flirtation, for example—what's going on inside can become an emergency. Suicidal thoughts or warning signs should never be written off as "relationship drama"; getting help is as urgent in this context as any other (the 988 Suicide and Crisis Lifeline can be reached by calling or texting 988).[19] Romantic issues are factors in a significant number of adolescents who attempt to commit suicide and do end their lives by suicide—in some cases impulsively and in some cases related to the suicidal thinking that can accompany clinical depression.[20]

Research shows that LGBTQ+ youth, who are already at significantly higher risk for depression, anxiety, and suicidal feelings, tend to have more relationship-related fears and anxieties than their straight peers. While being in a relationship can be an important affirmation of identity, linked to improved self-esteem and less internalized homophobia, dating is a game with higher stakes: It's harder to find partners and, in homophobic environments, riskier. Rejection and breakups can make a small community of trusted peers even smaller: If there are only four other queer kids at school and dating one of them doesn't go well, you've lost a significant fraction of your social life.

Sydney, at 14, was coping with chronic depression when Tanya, an older girl at her high school asked her out. Sydney told her a few times that she didn't want anything more than friendship, but Tanya persisted. "She started love bombing me harder," Sydney said. "I was very lonely, and I went with it. Then we just started acting like a couple."

Sydney hid the relationship from her family. The reasons were complicated: Sydney was embarrassed about Tanya; a lot of people at school considered her wild and didn't like her. Sydney's parents didn't know she was a lesbian. Whenever Sydney rejected something feminine—such as a girly dress choice—her mother would get upset, which Sydney took as a sign that coming out wouldn't be easy. Her parents already had enough to deal with. Sydney's severely disabled brother was acting out with increasingly challenging behaviors. Tanya's intensity was overwhelming, but it also lessened Sydney's isolation. "Someone's caring about me instead of the other way around," she said.

But Tanya's supportiveness could turn, in an instant, into hostility. Tanya was diagnosed with borderline personality disorder, a condition that, Sydney would learn, was related to the intensity of Tanya's attachment, her fear of abandonment, and her acute sensitivity. Conflicts would send Tanya dashing off to find someone else; once, on an off period with Sydney, Tanya got engaged. The on-again, off-again relationship lasted for three years, wearing at Sydney's mental health and self-esteem. Sydney didn't tell her parents until after it was over. They were startled to learn how vulnerable she was. "You're a feminist. You're so strong-willed. You don't bend to what someone else wants you to be," her mother said. "How did this happen?"

Sydney's story is one of the many examples of the interrelatedness of mental health, sexual orientation, and relationships. Her parents knew enough about her mental health issues to send her to a therapist. Yet until they learned about her sexual orientation and her hidden relationship, they had little understanding of what she was going through.

In an ideal world, Davila said, troubled young people would be better prepared for a relationship if they first took action to feel better about themselves and cope with heavy feelings. Parents play an important role in this process. Her research shows that teens who grow up without parental guidance in managing emotions and stress are more likely to experience symptoms of depression in early relationships.[21] In contrast, teens who have these skills will fare better.[22]

But overemphasizing readiness can backfire for people who fear they'll never feel whole. "The danger is that depression and anxiety will make people think that they are not good enough, not desirable enough, too needy for a relationship, and no one's going to like me the way I am, so I have to fix myself," Davila said. "That's going to get in the way and make them feel bad about themselves. I don't think it's black-and-white, like, 'I'm either ready for a relationship, or I'm not.'"

The better questions are, What am I ready for now? and What would be right for me, and what can I do? If young people are open to the input, then parents and other trusted adults can help them sort through these questions and understand that there may be a lot of trial and error as they proceed. The message to emphasize: If the relationship goes wrong, it doesn't reflect on your worth as a person.

Her advice reminds me of a memorable paper by a student in my Love and Heartbreak seminar called "A Scaredy Cat's Guide to Love." The author was diagnosed at an early age with ADHD and anxiety. "I don't handle change well, and it leads to panic attacks," she wrote. "I get overwhelmed easily and constantly worry. I constantly cancel plans at the last minute. Basically, I am a terrible candidate for a relationship." Yet she'd been in one for two years. She did not expect her boyfriend to save her or change her. At first, being honest with him about her needs was terrifying. She was convinced he would be put off by her diagnoses and her cautiousness—she wasn't the sort of person to throw herself into a romance. Instead, he dedicated himself to understanding her. "He accepted me for who I was, meltdowns and all," she said. More importantly, my student showed up to her first love with a hard-fought self-acceptance and the coping strategies she'd honed since childhood. If that is the product of a mental health–obsessed culture, I thought, bring it on.

Relationships as a Source of Support

When relationships are healthy and intimate, they have the capacity to bring light into the darkness of adolescent mental health woes. Relationships offer pleasure, adventure, *fun*—the delight of a close companion—all beneficial for mood, mental health, and physical well-being.

When times are hard, there is nothing wrong with seeking solace in a partner. First relationships are opportunities to learn to communicate needs, to figure out how to compromise when needs conflict, to explore the risks and opportunities of intimacy—all potentially beneficial to well-being and growth. Getting support is significant motivation for young people to be in a relationship in the first place. Developmentally, adolescents are in the process of gradually shifting their primary emotional support system from parent to peers. At 13, young people are still reaching out primarily to parents; at 18, it's friends, and by 21, it's romantic partners.[23] If teens have something to hide or parents who aren't emotionally available, they're more likely to seek peer support, though this also happens simply because what they want to talk about feels private or they feel their parents will be out of touch.[24]

Seeking solace in peers—their "tribe," as psychologist and author Lisa Damour put it—is part of the quest for autonomy, which entails, paradoxically, finding ways to cope with ongoing needs for emotional security.[25] Some degree of dependence on others is, in other words, a fundamental aspect of independence.[26] Having the skills to maintain healthy and satisfying relationships can reduce symptoms of anxiety and depression and improve decision making.[27] "Simply knowing that they have someone they can turn to may inspire more confidence to be independent," said Szwedo, who has researched the role of peer and romantic partner support seeking in adolescent development. "It may be important that teens know they have support they can fall back on if their efforts falter."

The problem comes when a romantic partner becomes the only other person on the lifeboat. No teen should shoulder the burden alone of another teen's breakdown. "That's not their job, and they don't have the capacity for that," Davila told me.

Aaron did start seeing a therapist, which gave him someone other than his girlfriend to talk to about his anxieties. He and Ellen stayed together for two years. Long after they broke up, Ellen told him how much of a strain his dark episodes had been on her. She'd wanted to take a break but worried she'd be responsible for making him worse. Her confession was a difficult awakening for Aaron. "I felt awful that the way I was acting could make another person want to distance themselves but also feel really afraid about what might happen," he said. "That's a huge regret, how selfish I was about my emotions."

NOT THE MAIN CHARACTER: THE EMOTIONAL LABOR OF CARE

Even if teens aren't supposed be the primary support for other teens' mental health problems, they often are. A Massachusetts high schooler told me about a family trip that he remembers little about because he felt tethered to his phone the whole time, feeling like he needed to respond immediately to every needy text from his girlfriend. A Texas teen stayed in his first relationship much longer than he wanted to because he felt responsible for helping his boyfriend manage his depression. An aspiring musician was thrilled to start dating a boy whose prowess on the guitar matched her own, only to watch him lose interest in practicing and medicate his anxiety with weed, a downward slide she tried mightily to halt.

Being needed in this way can seem like a marker of maturity and independence. It carries a certain clout. John Green's wildly popular young adult novels feature characters grappling with what it means to be supportive partners to peers suffering from mental health disorders and terminal diseases. The hit Netflix series *Thirteen Reasons Why* condemns the failure of high school students to prevent the suicide of a traumatized peer. Fictional teen caretakers embody the heroic ideals of this most-stressed generation: compassion, awareness, accommodation, the potential for one human being to elevate the life of another. Being a real teen caretaker, though, is not glamorous, your days caught up in the emotional labor of being the one who's always there, prepared to coax a beloved back from the edge.

I met Bethany in front of Surf Taco on Broad Street, a row of shops and restaurants in downtown Red Bank, New Jersey. It was one of the first warm days of early June, a year after she graduated from high school. She hiked up the spaghetti straps of her new-looking bright-green maxi dress and gazed out at the pedestrian mall, the outdoor tables filling up quickly for lunch. "This is what I wanted," she reminisced. High school in a town like this, where, after school, kids could hang out and be seen and get a cheap burrito with five different salsa options and talk and not feel the way she felt in Manasquan, a tiny beach town where everything was tidy and homogenized and you had to dodge strollers on the narrow sidewalk. Growing up there, she stood out as a girl passionate about music and art and a girl who wasn't White. Her mother is Korean American; her father, French.

Bethany was accepted by audition as a voice major at the Visual and Performing Arts Academy of Red Bank Regional, a large, more diverse public high school serving students from three towns on the Jersey Shore. VPA was created in the tradition of LaGuardia High School, the Manhattan public school the movie and TV series *Fame* was based on. The VPA kids were the kids everyone noticed. Bethany and her friends joked that going to Red Bank Regional often felt like being in a movie: Drama begets drama.

Bethany met Blake two months into her freshman year while they were waiting for the last after-school down-shore bus run. He was a junior. Even though she'd never had a boyfriend before, she thought she brought a certain savvy to the relationship. As she described it, "I'm a child of a very intense divorce." Her mother, Cathy, was an aspiring actress when she met her father, an attorney 10 years her senior. He was abusive and had bipolar disorder. When Bethany was a toddler, Cathy fled Paris and took her to New York, desperate to prevent Bethany's father from getting custody. After a rough stint as a broke single mother, Cathy remarried and became a successful interior designer.

Cathy had warned her daughter about power dynamics in relationships, the age disparity in her first marriage a cautionary tale. Bethany told Blake from the outset that she didn't want him playing the "I'm older/I'm wiser" card. "Intellectually we felt pretty on par, and he didn't seem like he was one of those guys that got into a relationship with a younger girl to feel bigger than someone," she said. "That's not what we were."

Blake impressed her with his grades and motivation. He was a star competitor on the school's engineering team. His ambition was in keeping with her own. She used the routine dead-air moments of high school—lunch, study hall, a class that petered out early—to duck into the practice rooms to rehearse. She was intent on absorbing everything she could about performing; an offhand comment by a teacher about the impact of citric acid on vocal folds caused her to swear off oranges. She added a second major in theater arts.

She and Blake were more independent and self-motivated than most of the kids she knew. They quickly became "like a little married couple," high school style. On weekends, they'd make dinner and watch movies. During the week they'd stay on a video call together while they did their homework. A word she used a lot, recalling that time, was *safe*. A lot of her friends were having their first sexual experiences in hookups and short-lived relationships they didn't feel secure in. Blake, who was her first sexual partner, cared about her and listened. He wasn't some "idiot kid who didn't know about consent," she said.

Her parents had a different take. Cathy liked him but also sensed something dark and unhealthy in him. Her husband put it more bluntly: "He looks like he could be a school shooter."

This hunch, though, gave them no real rationale to keep Bethany and Blake apart. Cathy remembers wanting to explain to parents whose kids hadn't yet gotten involved with anyone how helpless she felt: "I was like, 'Do they know that there's nothing you can do?' I mean, you can't say, 'Don't see that person,' and shut the door. They're going to see each other at school. They have phones. There's the internet. There's literally nothing I can do but be a safe place for her and let her know she doesn't have to hide anything from me." Her husband, who'd been clashing with Bethany since she entered puberty, distanced himself from the situation. Feeling very much on her own, Cathy did what she could to understand Blake. She went to his home to meet his father, treated Blake kindly, and sought inobtrusive ways to keep an eye on the couple.

The fall of Blake's senior year, deadlines loomed to apply to the colleges on his carefully crafted list. He worried his parents wouldn't be able to afford tuition, but instead of looking for scholarship money, he stalled and isolated himself. "He had some friends when we started dating, and one day I looked around, and he didn't have any," Bethany said. "I was kind of his only friend." His grades slipped. He stopped talking about college. He grew depressed. He confessed to Bethany that he thought about suicide.

Terrified, Bethany sent an anonymous tip into the Source, a mental health program at Red Bank Regional. That set in motion a chain of events that led to Blake being hospitalized in the local psychiatric ward. She wasn't allowed to speak with him until he got out a week later. He didn't seem much better. In the middle of class one day, he was so overcome with anxiety he fell out of his chair.

"You should just walk away," he told Bethany.

"I'm not going to walk away, because I think you're going to kill yourself," she said.

Before the end of the school year, Red Bank gave Blake notice: With all the days of school he'd missed, he wasn't eligible to graduate.

Bethany charged into the Source and screamed at the counselor. "Don't you understand what's going on? This kid needs help. That's your job."

As Cathy watched her daughter try to save Blake, she was frank: "I told her I hoped this wasn't going to be a theme with her," she said. "I didn't want her to become some sort of a rescuer. This could become a pattern, and many women have had that pattern."

The Blake she fell in love with wasn't coming back. He couldn't be much of a boyfriend, and she couldn't help him. She sensed that Blake was waiting, passive and sunk inside himself, for her to end the relationship, so eventually she did.

Blake managed to graduate. Bethany's star at school continued to rise. Her senior year, she landed the leading role in the spring play, and she was accepted into the theater program at the

New School in Manhattan. Blake drifted into a life of work and classes at the local community college, the boy she once loved becoming a "shadow of himself," she said. He dated several of her friends, "beautiful, awesome women" she would have thought to be way out of his league.

Perhaps he still had his charm, she mused, that same ability to convince girls that he was different, a boy who baked scones and flashed his keen intelligence. But there was something larger at play, she believed: The expectation is always for girls to fix the boys, the effort unsung, unrewarded, and draining. When I asked her to explain, she likened the dynamic to a play: "It just seems like girls, or at least the girls I know, they're not the main character. The guys are the main characters, and the girls are like a pit stop for the character development of these guys, sexually or emotionally or whatever. The girls get left behind. It happened to me, and it enrages me. Why aren't we ever the main character?"

THE TROUBLED PARTNER

The gender divide Bethany perceived is not absolute—I've spoken with plenty of males who've experienced the strain and responsibility of supporting a troubled partner. But in an era of reckoning about role disparities in marriages, parenting, and the workforce, it's worth recognizing that adolescent relationships may be one of the first times a girl confronts the invisible, unrecognized, and highly gendered work of emotional labor—the demanding work we do to manage the feelings of others and try to keep their lives on track, often to the detriment of our focus, productivity, and well-being.[28]

Not much is known about the impact of being a teen who becomes the main source of support to a peer with serious mental health issues. My digging led me to a doctoral dissertation by Margaret Klein Salamon, a Brooklyn psychologist and climate activist. Inspired by her own experiences as a teen with a serious boyfriend who became severely mentally ill, she researched women whose romantic partners had experienced psychotic episodes. Several in her small group of subjects were teenagers at the time.

The women confessed feelings of fear, confusion, loss, and social isolation. They described a complicated form of grief for partners who, though physically present, were psychologically absent. Sex became fraught and often nonconsensual. Wary of causing additional anguish or wounded pride, the women at times felt they couldn't reject their partners' advances. They experienced a form of survivor guilt. Their efforts to help were never enough. They stayed sane, while their partners didn't. They could leave the relationship for a normal life, while their partners remained mired in mental illness. The impact lasted for years after the relationships ended, leading the women to struggle with dating or avoid intimacy altogether. Klein Salamon argued that caring for a mentally ill partner isn't just a burden. It can become a form of trauma, an extreme stressor that overwhelms normal coping mechanisms and has an enduring psychological impact. The caretakers themselves may need care, particularly if they are teens—even if they don't seem to need it, because that's the MO of hypercapable young people striving for independence. "They may not want to talk about a partner's psychotic episode, but the number one most important thing *is* to talk about it," she said.[29]

Bethany and Cathy do talk about it. The experience of having a mentally ill partner is something, after all, that they've both experienced, part of the unique mother-daughter bond that began in the lean, scary days when Bethany was small, and they were in hiding from her manic father.

When I met with them together in the surf-themed Manasquan coffee shop where Bethany worked as a barista, Cathy confessed that, when her daughter and Blake first got together, she worried about the emotional legacy of her tumultuous first marriage. "I was very nervous," she said. "I wondered how she was going to be in a relationship. I wondered, 'Did I damage her? Did my marriage damage her? Is she going to be needy? Is she just going to want to run away? Or is she going to want to fix him?' And it was none of those things. It became apparent that, no, she can do this in a healthy way, arguably even healthier than I can do it."

Bethany interrupted her. "But it was a little bit of all of these things," she protested. "I was a little bit needy. A little bit avoidant. A little bit of a fixer."

Maybe, Cathy considered, the difference between her experience and her daughter's first love was about identifying what was happening. When dealing with her first husband, she didn't put a name to her role or consider what it meant. "I never let myself think about the position of a fixer and what it can do to you," Cathy said. "Bethany is only 19, but she can see it. She's more aware."

Bethany allowed that she might be the type of person who is good at helping peers through tough times. She's talked friends out of suicidal thoughts more times than she can count. She's wondered whether there is something inside her that's attracting distressed people or whether her generation is simply rife with people so messed up that anyone who can think straight ends up on support duty. Since Blake, Bethany has had a few short-term relationships, which she ended when her suitors started to seem too needy. "I don't want to be anyone's mommy," she said.

What she wants, she confessed, is a relationship in which she doesn't have to be so serious. By nature, she said, she's inclined to be the fun one. "I'm the ice cream in the affogato," she said. "I like the other guy to be the espresso."

I was a little embarrassed to admit that I didn't know exactly what an affogato was, so after our interview I found out. It's vanilla gelato with shot of hot espresso poured on top, not a surprising metaphor from a girl who grew up in a Jersey Shore community with a large population of descendants of Italian immigrants. As you eat an affogato, the espresso melts into the gelato, the contrasting tastes combining. Perhaps this was the message for Bethany and her most-stressed generation: the possibility of relationships that blurred the lines between bitter and sweet, between fun and serious, and between helping and being helped.

CHAPTER 8

It's Over

Breaking Up

BY NATURE SOFT-SPOKEN AND CAUTIOUS, MILES LET COLLEGE open him up. When he first arrived on his rural campus in Upstate New York, he was freaked out by how friendly everyone was. People smiled at him and wanted to know who he was. A cafeteria worker teased him about his stern expression. It was the face he had to wear at home, at St. Nicholas Houses, the Harlem projects where he grew up. Eventually, he let his face relax. He became a leader in the Black Student Union. He organized the spring fashion show. He was popular, though still a figure of quiet mystery with intent, almond-shaped eyes, his cornrows grazing his shoulders.

The fall of his sophomore year, he agreed to be one of the featured speakers at a retreat for African American students at a church off campus. In front of an audience of hundreds, he spoke about the alienation he felt as a child of the projects attending a majority-White campus. Loree approached him afterward to tell him that she related to his words. As one of the few Black kids in her town, she said, she'd experienced these feelings her entire life.

Their relationship built from that sense of shared experience, a union of two kids raised by single moms, along with curiosity about their differences. Saint Nick's, with its cramped Section 8 apartments and trash-strewn playground, was a world away from Loree's rural Hudson Valley community. Two months in, she told Miles she loved him.

"I shuddered away," he said. "I didn't want to believe I was in love."

Then he thought about how he felt when he was with her. Safe. Like he could be himself. Like he was good at this, at being her boyfriend and learning about her life. The fear passed. He told her he loved her, too. Their first Christmas together, they held each other and cried because what they had together was something neither of them had witnessed growing up: a loving couple, exchanging gifts. They wept for the aloneness of their mothers, the absence of their fathers, and their gratitude at having found each other. They daydreamed about the child they would have together, a daughter. He floated a name. Loree named a Sims character after her.

But Loree was anxious and mercurial. She would sleep through her classes one day and lash out at her friends the next. One morning Miles discovered her cutting the inside of her wrist. He convinced her to go to therapy, where she learned she had bipolar disorder. The diagnosis didn't scare him. Supporting her wasn't easy, but he was up for the work, ready to listen when she needed him and helping her remember to take her meds. He gave her one of his long-sleeved shirts to cover the scars on her wrist. "I never saw her mental illness like a flaw," he said. "I just saw it like, 'This is what this person has, and what can I do as her boyfriend to help her?'"

After more than a year together, Loree ended the relationship suddenly in a fit of jealousy over one of his female friends. She refused to discuss it. Miles called his mother, sounding so distraught that the next morning she drove to campus. She found him sobbing on the couch in an out-of-the-way residence hall lounge. His mother held him for a long time.

His girlfriend wouldn't answer his calls or texts, he said, and she'd blocked him on social media. "That's not her," he insisted. He was sure that she'd stopped taking her medication. He'd nursed her through past lapses. He insisted that, if she just got back on the meds, she would want him back. All she had to do was let him talk to her.

"We get it that you're upset and you're hurting," his mother said. "That's part of love. It will pass."

She recognized the impulse: Miles to the rescue. He'd been that way as long as she could remember. When he was a toddler in daycare, one of the teaching assistants told her that he'd given away his art supplies to a student who didn't have any. His mother asked what Miles did during art time. "He did without," the teaching assistant said. "They didn't share?" she pressed. No, the teaching assistant told her. He was okay with giving his supplies away and just sitting there. "He's very helpful," she said.

But as Miles reeled from the end of his first love, his mother knew the world would not see a kindhearted, self-sacrificing little boy. If he kept reaching out to Loree, the world would see a young Black man pursuing a girl who didn't want him. His mother made Miles promise not to go to his ex's dorm room or have any contact with her. "I don't care about the medication," his mother said. "You have it in your mind that she doesn't mean it, but if it's coming out of her mouth for you to leave her alone, if you go there, that's harassment." She imagined the campus police, expulsion, his college career over, or worse.

His mother had always been strict. When Miles was growing up, he had to be inside every night at seven, while his friends hung out late on the basketball court. He knew her rules mattered. He got good grades and went to college. The neighborhood kids without boundaries, he saw, turned aimless, sold drugs, or were incarcerated. The summer after the breakup, when he complained he was too depressed to go to his retail job, she refused to let him call out sick. Miles understood that his mother wanted him to hold his head up. He dragged himself to Athlete's Foot to hawk sneakers. But his mother's sternness couldn't shield him from what felt like an emotional purgatory, a sadness that went on and on.

Breakup Pain

Breakups hurt. I've listened to accounts from teens who, after the end of a relationship, couldn't eat, sleep, or focus. They paced. They wept. They lost weight. They fell behind on their schoolwork. They begged and bargained, claiming they'd be willing to stop being monogamous, lower their expectations, change, whatever it took to get the relationship back. They launched elaborate analyses of their ex's brokenness. They tried to anesthetize the feelings by playing video games and binge-watching old shows, years' worth of *Friends* or *Gilmore Girls* droning one episode after the other on their laptops over a few bleary days and nights. They believed their lives were ruined. They insisted they'd never do this—relationships—again. They shrank into a gloom they'd never known before and ghost-walked through their lives.

For parents witnessing these reactions, the immensity of teen breakup grief can stun. A mother and father told me that, after their son's girlfriend broke up with him, they rushed home from a dinner out. As they pulled into the driveway, they heard their son bellowing from behind his closed upstairs bedroom window, "I miss her already!" A mother drove her daughter home after her first relationship ended to find her daughter wouldn't get out of the car. How could she go inside, she sobbed, when the house was full of memories of her ex? How could she ever sleep at home again?

Even though most parents have been through breakups themselves, these displays of feeling can seem surreal. No one's died. No one's been diagnosed with a fatal disease or sent off to battle. No unstoppable evil has absconded with everything precious in life. My mother recently reminded me of the time I lay on her bedroom floor, crying and telling her I couldn't bear to be alive. "Which time?" I said wryly.

We laughed together because it happened 40 years ago, enough distance for me to mock myself. I did remember that time. I was 16, and my boyfriend had gone off to college and gotten himself a new girlfriend without telling me. But I would feel that bad several more times, the kind of bad no parent wants their child ever to feel. The excruciating nature of romantic rejection, a subject I've been writing about for years, remained so vivid to me that, nearly from the moment my daughter started seeing her first boyfriend, I worried about the moment it would end.

I saw the signs well in advance. My daughter's boyfriend had always been warm to my husband and me, and we enjoyed his presence in our home. Then his visits became less frequent. My daughter still saw him every afternoon at track practice, and I told myself maybe they were just going through a busy phase. Then, at a home meet, I saw him. He greeted me brightly, but he avoided my eyes, and I knew.

I would miss him, a feeling that many parents, I've found, experience after a breakup; sometimes they mourn the loss more than their children do. But when he broke up with my daughter, protective feelings overrode my wistfulness.

At first, my daughter seemed okay. She huddled with a friend, plowing their way through a plastic sack of drugstore candy. She did her homework. At bedtime, she finally let me in. She'd been turning away from my touch for months, but that night I lay down next to her and put my arms around her. We stayed that way for a long time, both of us unable to sleep.

Since then, I've heard versions of this story more times than I can count: parents holding weeping children for hours in residence halls or lying on a child's unmade bed surrounded by used Kleenex or sunken into the family sectional while shooing curious younger siblings out of the room. These hours are difficult because our children's pain pains us, and their pain seems without end.

I'm grateful my daughter accepted my soothing, a parent's original superpower. I said the same thing Miles's mother said and the same thing my mother said to me when my first relationship ended: This will pass.

But the process takes time. Heartbreak, as Florence Williams points out in her book of the same name, is a multistage process: rejection, grief, shame, and existential loneliness. Each takes its toll on mind and body, changing our brains and influencing our behavior. Feeling rejected raises blood pressure and levels of cortisol, the hormone that regulates the body in response to stress. Rejection is a blow to our self-esteem. It makes us feel we don't belong and that life has no meaning. We don't think as clearly or focus as well. We have less self-control, meaning that we're more likely to do things we'll regret later. We may be consumed by rage, jealousy, and desperation.[1] This onslaught makes us woeful strangers to ourselves, strangers we'd rather not get to know.

When I talk about breakups in my Love and Heartbreak seminar, I bring up a famous brain-scan study. Researchers at Stony Brook University used fMRI imaging to record changes in blood flow in the brains of 15 people—most of them college-aged—who had just gone through a breakup but were still in love. The idea behind brain-scan research is that the more blood flows to a certain part of the brain, delivering oxygen and glucose to cells, the harder that area is working. As the lovelorn subjects were shown photographs of their exes, the brain-scan images lit up, indicating the rush of blood to parts of the brain associated with deep attachment, passionate love, distress, and even physical pain. Several of the subjects wept and raged as the photos flashed in front of them. One illuminated area was particularly revealing: the nucleus accumbens, a central part of the brain's reward system, linked to craving, wanting, motivation, and addiction.[2] The abandoned lover is essentially in a state of withdrawal.

The study is handy, with an unbeatable immediacy and a clear takeaway. But it also plays straight into an illusion I've found that young people can harbor. Though they may want to couple up, they shouldn't let themselves "get addicted" to someone. If they feel they have, they're embarrassed. The adults in their lives may, in their own way, also buy into the idea that a young person should be able to readily shake off the loss of a close tie. This goes back to what I've discussed earlier as the tension between romanticizing first love and the belief that adolescence is a time to focus on individuation. Teens should be putting themselves first, not a relationship. In this light, a breakup comes across as a removal of an obstacle to independence, a restoration of the proper mission of adolescence.

There's no question that independence is important. It helps young people be healthier *in* relationships and more likely to be resilient when they end. But ideals of self-reliance also may lead young people suffering over breakups to feel like they've failed a test. The irony of this line of thinking is that their social media–soaked world is perfectly engineered to amplify these feelings. When we discuss the brain-scan study in class, I ask, "What about this experiment seems familiar?" I mime scrolling through a social media feed on a phone: "There's my ex, smiling on a mountaintop and living her best life! There's the boyfriend who cheated on me, out at the bar! Look, he sent me a Snap after two months of silence!"

The students get it. Social media exposure to photograph after photograph of a lost love is a lot like the setup of the study, often with a similarly dramatic response. "Basically, you put yourselves through hell whenever you check your phones after a breakup," I point out.

In the classroom and in my conversations with teens, I emphasize a paradigm that puts heartbreak and the idea of "love as addiction" in a broader context. The pain of rejection doesn't mean you've failed. It means you are part of the social world, a vast and elegant system, evolved to sustain humanity—not to incubate individuals who are best off existing in a bubble of one. Our very existence depends on our connections to one another. Being cast out of the fire circle in prehistoric times didn't make you independent in the way we now conceive the term. It put your life at risk because you wouldn't be able to survive alone. Our brains are wired to panic when we're ostracized because subconsciously we're grappling with this primal vulnerability.[3] It's what researchers call the "protest response," our brains taken over with figuring out ways to fix the broken attachment.

Getting dumped is particularly painful for many of the same reasons that romantic attraction is so compelling. A devoted mate comes with a host of benefits: a secure base to help you face life's opportunities and challenges, a portal to new perspectives and resources, the comfort of caring and being cared for, a buffer against loneliness and its associated health risks, and the prospect of passing on your genes to the next generation. Even if teens aren't consciously interested in sustaining the species or aren't having reproductive sex, the wiring of loss still functions. The intensity of the grief is a sign that, as anthropologist Helen Fisher calls it, "life's greatest prize" is lost.[4]

It's a prize that few teens will hold onto for very long. "It's pretty common for three or four breakups to occur during the teen years," Jennifer Connolly, a York University professor who studies adolescent relationships, told me. Most adolescent relationships are relatively brief, lasting 6 to 12 months.[5] Young people in committed relationships in Western societies have to contend with a paradox: a love that feels like it could last forever, alongside a near future in which that's highly unlikely to happen. A relationship that feels perfect at 15 may be on the rocks at 15½.

Teens are in a time of change, maturation, and exploration. They're new and often clumsy at balancing their increasing autonomy with the work of relatedness. While conflict-resolution skills are a factor in preventing adult breakups, they don't make teens more likely to stay together. The reason is that relationship goals are different in adolescence. Teens aren't as concerned with the long haul. Their priority is on the pleasure, attraction, and closeness they're enjoying *now*, not working out problems for the sake of the future.[6] When a relationship stops being fulfilling, they move on rather than make repairs. In this light, breaking up and being broken up with are inevitable, necessary skills. But this reality doesn't make breakups any easier to bear.

FROM VALIDATION TO REFLECTION

For many teens, breakups are their first significant experience of loss. Yet they often contend with messages that the feelings they're going through don't quite count. We tend to remind young people of their youth and opportunities and urge them to move on. If a relationship was short or took place mainly (or entirely) online, young people have even less permission to be thrown by the loss, even though a relationship of messaging and video calls for hours a day can be just as intense as a face-to-face relationship—or more, given the added charge of imagination and possibility. If you've been anticipating for months what it will be like to finally meet your beloved, then realizing that you never will is agonizing. Being told your relationship wasn't real in the first place doesn't help.

Adult efforts to minimize teen breakup pain contribute to a phenomenon known as disenfranchised grief. Breakup grief has many of the same qualities as bereavement—despair, anger, guilt, obsessive thinking, loss of control—without the socially recognized right *to* grieve. It's worse for queer youth, who may find a breakup puts them at odds with the small, tightly knit, vulnerable social circles that still characterize much of LGBTQ+ high school social life.[7] If they can't speak openly and safely about the split at home, their isolation increases.

Jasmine grew up in a multigenerational home of Pentecostal Christians from Puerto Rico. Knowing her family would disapprove, she tried to keep her first relationship with another girl a secret, passing her off as a close friend so all the time they spent hanging out together and sleeping at each other's houses would go unquestioned. When her mother, Fanny, found out, she snapped, "This is crazy. I didn't raise you to be gay." After the relationship ended, Jasmine suffered alone. She didn't dare come out to her grandmother, who had always been a confidant, and she couldn't unpack the breakup with her mother, who saw the relationship as a shameful phase. "Not being able to talk about such a big part of me stunk," she said. "I felt like they just didn't know who I was, and not talking about it felt like lying."

Her mother eventually softened and accepted Jasmine's sexuality without reservations. Jasmine's next big breakup, in college, was tough; her ex-girlfriend bullied Jasmine on Twitter and turned their friends against her. But this time, her mother was there for her. Fanny dropped everything to drive from Virginia to help her daughter move off campus. Jasmine was bereft, but she didn't feel as alone. "It was the act of her being there, coming from far away and supporting me," Jasmine said.

Disenfranchised grief also tends to be more trying for boys, who suffer just as much and just as long after a breakup as girls. But boys may not get as much support as girls, given entrenched social mores that discourage males from expressing sadness and strong emotions.[8] Nancy Darling, a psychology professor at Oberlin College, points out that romantic relationships tend to be the most supportive relationships teen boys have for expressing emotion, while teen girls often have richer networks of friends to confide in. "Boys fall in love faster, and they fall in love harder," Darling told me. "After a breakup, they've just lost what is probably their most intimate relationship."

After his breakup, Miles disappeared a lot, going to the tennis courts behind the campus gym in the middle of winter to be alone and cry. Friends feigned concern, only to turn whatever he told them into the latest tidbit of gossip. He began to feel that he'd made a mistake in letting himself become more trusting. He stopped talking to his mother about Loree because she kept telling him to move on. He didn't know how.

"It's like going to a basketball game and a basketball player is asking you, 'Where should I run?' And you just tell them to shoot," Miles said. He felt like he was still too far away from the basket. "I need to know stuff. Like how do I get over it? How do I get to that point? What should I have done? What are the next steps moving forward?"

When he went back home to Harlem, he confessed what happened with Loree to friends from high school. One offered him a blunt. Another, a boy still in high school, encouraged him to buy them liquor. They said he should find another girl. Not a girl he cared about, just a girl he could have sex with to help him forget. "I was like, no, that's not going to help me," he said.

Validating breakup grief starts with a simple step: acknowledging that breakups hurt and that young people going through them deserve to grieve, no matter how long the relationship lasted and however unlikely its future seemed. For some parents, this means giving their child the kind of support they never had. "I never felt like I could share what I was going through with my mom," Carol, a New Jersey mother, told me. "She would say I was pretending, that I was never really in love. I always felt alone." What Carol later realized was that her mother was still dealing with her own breakup pain. Carol's father divorced her mother after he fell in love with her best friend.

The grieving process creates an opportunity for young people to better understand the breakup and themselves. The brain-scan study showed increased activity in the forebrain area associated with responding to gains and losses. Rejection, then, may goad us to figure out what happened: what went wrong, whether we can fix it, and how to do better next time.[9]

Key to the process of recovery, researchers Grace Larson and David Sbarra found, is the restoration of "self-concept clarity." In a relationship, much of our identity is enmeshed with our partners. After it ends, we have to reconnect with who we are as independent people.[10]

This process can start with the way young people interpret their breakup. Young people—and the rest of us—tend to emphasize breakups as one partner's rejection of another. If you're the one who didn't want to break up, then you may see the breakup as a judgment on who you are. Stony Brook University psychology professor Joanne Davila's relationship workshop offers a powerful reframing. Breakups happen between people who couldn't or didn't want to meet each other's needs. Someone who breaks up with you *doesn't want what you have to offer.*

Whenever I present this concept to students, I feel the energy of the room shift as they take in the possibility that breakups don't have to be tribunals of the self. Relationships are reconceptualized as exchanges. When your partner turns down what you want to give them, the exchange no longer works. If you try to make it work through efforts to win the person back, then you're just getting more entangled in the same conundrum of unmet needs, making offerings that can't be received.

Stamford psychology professors Lauren Howe and Carol Dweck reviewed hundreds of personal narratives about the ends of relationships and distilled several themes. Some people saw breakups like a force of nature, something they had no control over. Some defined themselves by the rejection, seeing it as evidence of a personal flaw that doomed the relationship: They were too needy, too sensitive or insensitive, not attractive enough. Not surprisingly, the people who believed that a relationship ended because of their shortcomings had the most trouble recovering. The breakup wounded their sense of who they were, weighing on them for years and making them afraid to move on to new relationships. A third group saw the breakup as an opportunity for growth. They came to understand something new about what it takes to have a healthy relationship, such as the importance of good communication or their inability to control another person's feelings. In other words, they saw the story of the end of a relationship as a redemption narrative, in which bad leads to good, the outcome making what was difficult and painful ultimately worthwhile.[11] Redemption narratives don't absolve transgressions, such as infidelity or ghosting, but they also aren't fundamentally damning. They envision the self as having the capacity to change.

What can parents do to foster productive reflection in their children—the kind of talk that helps rebuild and potentially redeem the self in the wake of a breakup? The first steps are admittedly delicate ones, given teen sensitivity to invasions of privacy. "Just start out by saying, 'I'm sorry,' and simply asking them how they're doing," Darling said. "If you're quiet and don't grill them, hopefully they'll talk. If you grill them, they'll shut up." She advises allowing young people time and space to grieve while continuing to create opportunities for conversation. The idea is to be next to them, doing something dull, such as a car ride or household chores, which may lead them to feel like talking. They still might not say much. This in itself isn't reason to worry. Some may prefer confiding in peers or writing in a journal. Some may just need to take to their beds and hide. They may not seem to need you, but your presence is still meaningful, sending the message that their heartbreak is worthy of attention.

Don't try to get a young person to talk by bringing up your own romantic past. While many young people have told me that they appreciated learning about their parents' early relationships and how they ended, save this kind of disclosure for another time. The wake of a breakup is about the child, not the parent. Unless they ask, young people won't want to hear about how a parent rose from the ashes of a disastrous split when they're dealing with one themselves. "There are some parents for whom this is going to trigger bad memories of their own adolescent romantic history," said Laurence Steinberg, a Temple University psychology professor and author of several books about adolescent development. "How you felt when you were broken up with is probably not relevant to how your kid feels right now. Resist the temptation to say, 'This happened to me.'"

If and when young people do discuss their breakup, listen to how they tell the story. Are they casting the split in moral absolutes—that they were the victims of an evil, unfeeling ex? Are they saying the relationship ended because they aren't attractive or interesting enough? Black-and-white thinking can't validate the complexity of what's just happened or capitalize on the potential for growth. Northwestern University professor Alexandra Solomon preaches the power of fostering a "thick narrative" about the breakup: recounting the story of a relationship and its ending with nuance and detail. If teens say an ex "sucks," a classic adolescent plaint, Solomon advises that parents ask why. They can prompt teens toward a more comprehensive understanding of what happened with such statements as "It sounds like you were working hard to figure things out, and they just weren't able to respond."

Sudden or unexplained breakups leave teens with a gaping hole in their breakup story. When I brought this up with Solomon in one of our many conversations about love over the years, she acknowledged what a raw deal this is. Not getting an explanation leaves people at risk of interpreting the rejection as a sign of their lack of value. Parents can help young people turn this around by assuring them that they have every right to get a kind and respectful explanation for the end of a relationship. If they don't, it's a sign of the rejector's shortcomings, evidence of a lack of emotional maturity and an inability to be caring. This understanding can be incorporated into their breakup story. An ex's bad behavior becomes a challenge to be surmounted. Young people will be better off with someone who can talk about conflicts, an attribute they can consciously seek when they're ready to move on.

REGULATING STRONG EMOTIONS

Recovering from a breakup is rarely a neat process. It can circle in on itself, becoming endless and obsessive, past the point where thinking about what happened yields much insight. Teens may take to social media to vent, airing out grievances either overtly or with passive-aggressive statements. They may become hyper-vigilant about what exes are posting and whether it looks like they're getting involved with someone new. The breakup becomes a problem teens can't stop thinking or talking about. Young people may believe they're helping themselves by cathartically letting their feelings out. In fact, nonstop ruminating keeps young people focused on how bad they feel and may lead them to impulsively try to reconnect with an ex.

When this happens, young people will need to do the hard work of emotion regulation: exerting control over their state of mind and behaviors. Several experts told me that the first step should be (but often isn't) unfriending and unfollowing the ex on social media. This can feel extreme to teens. They believe it's mean or an admission of vulnerability, a failure to play it cool. Their reluctance should be met with questions: How does seeing what the other person is doing online make you feel? Do you want to move forward, or do you want to monitor the life of someone who no longer has much to offer you?

Distractions help young people catch a break from obsessive thinking. Physical exercise, baking, going out to a movie, even something as basic as taking shower or going outside for a few minutes may provide a few moments or hours when an ex is not top of mind. After a short (days, not weeks) initial period of mourning, teens should be expected to keep up with school commitments and activities. They should be encouraged to nurture other close social ties, spending time with friends in ways that don't always involve conversations about the ex. Teens are quite susceptible to corumination; past a certain point, a well-meaning friend's questions and indignation about the breakup may only inflame the hurt. If teens keep perseverating on what went wrong, encourage them to focus on specific, solvable problems, such as figuring out an after-school job schedule that avoids doing shifts with an ex or how to return a bag of belongings. This may help young people regain a sense of control over their lives.

Some young people will rush into the ultimate distraction—dating someone new. Conventional wisdom discourages the rebound relationship out of the belief that we need time to process a breakup before starting over. Parents may worry if a child gets involved again right away. Research by Lucia O'Sullivan, a psychology professor at the University of New Brunswick, suggests there may not be much reason for concern. Adolescents on the rebound still cope with plenty of unresolved feelings about the breakup, but their self-esteem and mental health are in good shape compared to people who stayed single after a split. "It's stressful for everyone to break up, but if they're in a new relationship, they do much better," she said. "The ones who hadn't bounced back into a relationship did the worst."

That said, the study was done on college students. Rebounding may not go as well with younger teens, who, as I've discussed, can be negatively affected by having too many partners too soon. At any age, jumping quickly into another relationship won't always be the right path. "There's still value to processing a relationship on your own, and there's still value to being single," O'Sullivan said.

There will be times when, no matter what young people do, postbreakup feelings seem endless and unbearable. Encourage teens to use a basic mindfulness technique from Davila's workshop: Sit with the feelings and breathe, accepting each emotion that arises without judgment. If they can, let the distress go and allow other, gentler thoughts and feelings to enter their minds. If that's impossible, they can simply accept that they can't make the emotions go away yet. Instead, they can tell themselves, "I can live with this for now. It's part of the healing process."

For some young people, breakups are inextricable from more entrenched mental health problems. About half of adolescents experiencing major depression for the first time reported they'd recently been through a breakup.[12] Relationship-related stalking and bullying are very real risks, particularly in an always-online world, where the temptation to fire off expressions of anger, frustration, or desire is always as close as a back pocket or a bedside table.[13] Breakups are the most common concern for adolescents seeking counseling. When a relationship is ending, teens are more likely to report concerns about self-harm, suicidal thoughts, and other serious mental health issues.[14]

Teens who already struggle with symptoms of depression tend to be more dependent in relationships and have fewer resources for coping with conflict, leading them to react with greater distress to breakups, with a longer, more complicated grieving process.[15] York University's Jennifer Connolly advises parents to watch the direction of teens' moods. Is the way they're talking about the breakup making them feel better or worse? Does their sense of hope increase over time? Or are they getting ever more exhausted and despairing? If young people are just as down and preoccupied with their ex four or five months postbreakup, then parents may need to consider getting them into counseling.

As I worked on this chapter, my daughter's junior year was coming to an end, the house buzzing with summer plans and prom preparations. Then, a friend told me her daughter was threatening to kill herself because her longtime boyfriend broke up with her days before prom. Two weeks later, in another state, a relative told me about a classmate who, in the wake of a breakup, drank heavily at a graduation party, texted her ex a harrowing final goodbye, and overdosed on antidepressants. Both girls, thankfully, are okay, but I was struck anew by the awful challenge of trying to assess just how fragile a heartbroken teen could be. When I cried on the floor to my mother that I couldn't bear to be alive, I was distraught, not suicidal, but another teen saying the same words might be far more vulnerable. Interpersonal losses, including breakups, peer rejection, and a friend's death, are a factor in 20 percent of youth suicides.[16] Mental health professionals warn that relationship status should be taken seriously when assessing suicide risk, with breakups a time to be particularly watchful for warning signs: increased drug or alcohol use, withdrawn behavior, giving away belongings, or talking about suicide.[17]

BREAKUP CRIMES: TEXTING AND GHOSTING

When Lily was 14, she started high school in a new school district. She made friends quickly, and one of them introduced her to Elijah. She consulted her friends about every aspect of the relationship. She worried about the fact that she and Elijah spent most of their time together hanging out after school and fooling around in the basement. Shouldn't they be going out to dinner sometimes? Her friends affirmed that Elijah wasn't being a good boyfriend. But she still cared a lot about him, and he was her first sexual partner.

On the six-month anniversary of the relationship, Lily was at her grandmother's house, texting with Elijah. She fished for some kind of recognition of the event: "Do we want to do anything today?" He didn't get the hint.

"Maybe we should call this off," she texted. "I'm not getting the same effort from you that I'm putting into this relationship."

"Okay," he wrote back.

Lily made a screenshot of the conversation and sent it to one of her friends. "He's not even fighting for you," the friend wrote. "She's right," Lily thought. "It's over."

Then she was hit by a wave of doubt. She tried to get Elijah to meet in person so they could talk about what happened, but he avoided her. As she shared the news of the breakup, she became increasingly self-conscious. "What I was feeling was complicated and emotional—what felt like adult feelings," she said. "By telling people I did it over text, it minimized the intensity of that moment. That I did it with characters sent from my grandmother's bathroom just felt embarrassing. It made it seem juvenile, not a real emotional moment."

Nearly 60 percent of teens say text breakups are the "least acceptable" way to end a relationship, though about a quarter of teens with romantic experience report they've done it.[18] The same friends that Lily had relied on to process what was happening in her relationship turned on her. Their loyalty reverted to Elijah, who was their friend long before she came to town. She overheard them talking disdainfully about how bad text breakups were, knowing they were taking digs at her. It didn't matter that much of her relationship with Elijah happened, like most of her social life, over text and social media. The breakup was a disaster. Lily started out wanting to draw a line with a boyfriend who wasn't treating her well, and somehow she'd become the villain.

I met Lily while working on a news article that would be published with the headline "Teens Are Terrible at Breaking Up."[19] It's true that teen breakups are often not pretty. Teens break up with each other over text. They break up with each other on the school bus. They make a TikTok announcing the end of their relationship before they tell their partner. They blurt out the news in front of other people. The moment of saying (as Steve Martin put it in a long-ago comedy skit) "I break with thee!" terrifies teenagers.

Young people also will break up by not breaking up at all. Digital life compounds people's reluctance to share bad news, known as the mum effect, and offers an escape hatch for rejectors to get out of the emotional labor of a breakup. Hence the practice of ghosting, the term for when a partner stops answering texts, DMs, Snapchats, and phone or video calls. The rejected person must, excruciatingly, infer through silence that a relationship is over. Teens are tuned in to the different implications of messaging platforms—one intimate, one immediate, one playful—and watching each one shut down is a unique form of teen torture.

I long thought of ghosting as inextricable from social media, dating apps, and smartphones. In my youth, when the household phone rang, you had to pick it up, not knowing whether the person on the line was your grandmother or the boyfriend you weren't into anymore. Then I talked to Charlie, a college student whose parents divorced when she was 13. "I had no model for what a relationship was supposed to look like," she said. "How did they compare to other relationships? Why weren't they happy? And how did that happen? It was confusing." The only relationship advice her father gave her was to "date a lot of people and avoid getting attached prematurely."

She called herself a "chronic ghoster" who routinely cuts off communication with people she's no longer interested in. "I don't feel like I'm equipped to have a conversation with somebody about the fact that I don't think this can go any further, so the easiest option is to just stop responding, which is terrible," she said. She knew ghosting was hurtful. One guy texted that she "sucks for doing this." Most said nothing.

Charlie's explanation is a version of a concern that I often hear: *I don't know how to do this any other way.* On one level, ghosting is a cop-out. When it's time to break up, you show up. You communicate that you want the relationship to end. But if you come of age in a home in which the central romantic relationship—your parents' marriage—ended without an explanation, silence as an MO for dealing with difficulties in your dating life seems a viable strategy. Technology may enable ghosting, but going dark in response to heavy emotional issues isn't new.

Being ghosted shrouds breakup grief in uncertainty. People are left wondering what they did to cause the silence, a question that can rapidly tilt into "What's wrong with me?" There's no closure, and the ambiguity of what happened "freezes the grief process," according to research by Leah LeFebvre, a University of Alabama communication studies professor.[20]

The irony of ghosting is that no one ever disappears completely. Even if you've forced yourself to stop expecting a DM from an ex or unfollowed the person, you'll see when they comment on someone else's post or do a TikTok all your friends are talking about. It's like a high school cafeteria you can never fully leave.

CHEATING

Young people hate cheating. They may acknowledge that fidelity isn't a given until and unless partners agree to be exclusive and monogamous. They may endure a ton of ambiguity in hookups and situationships. But young people are hard on people in committed relationships who fool around. They chastise cheaters and look down on peers who stay with people who've been unfaithful. It's the teen version of the contemporary grownup discourse about infidelity: Cheating is harmful and wrong, and people who stray are selfish and lack control. Ending the relationship is the best way for someone who's been cheated on to regain self-respect and what people tempted by others should do before they act on it.[21] Yet, adolescent infidelity is common. While around 70 percent of adolescents disapprove of it, an estimated 40 to 60 percent have been unfaithful in a relationship.[22]

Mateo, a high school student from Connecticut, never thought he'd be unfaithful. For a long time, the issue was purely theoretical. While all of his friends at boarding school were dating or hooking up, he remained solo, his efforts to court girls going nowhere. When he heard about a friend who clandestinely juggled a relationship at school with another at home, Mateo thought, "Man, why would he do such a thing?"

His junior year, he met Gina, who lived in Rhode Island, during a pickup frisbee game at a writers' conference, and they started dating long-distance. Over the summer, he took the bus to visit her on weekends. They explored her hometown together, a gritty riverfront city with cobblestone streets, cheap Middle Eastern food, and Old World Italian cafés. "There wasn't a single moment I spent with her that wasn't happy," he said.

Matteo's father, who'd never before talked to Mateo about relationships, took him for a drive in the family Volkswagen.

"He started telling me all these things, like some gate had been opened," Mateo said. His father told him there was a long legacy of men in their extended Peruvian family being unfaithful. His grandfather cheated. His uncle cheated. Mateo's father did, too, on a girlfriend, before he met Mateo's mother and they immigrated to the United States.

His father described the transgressions as part of a culture of machismo. He assured Mateo that he'd been faithful in his marriage, though once, on a trip back to Peru, an ex-girlfriend had come on to him. "I was halfway across the world. But I didn't do it," his father told him. "Not because I didn't want to, but because I didn't want your mother to find out." Even though Mateo wasn't used to his father speaking this personally, he recognized the theme: His father, who never finished college and came to Connecticut barely speaking a word of English, always tried to do what was best for his family.

Then Mateo went across the world himself, to China, on a government scholarship to learn the language and culture. He started seeing another girl on the trip. He justified the transgression as part of the once-in-a-lifetime experience he was having. "I thought, 'When is the next time I'm going to be in China? And if I can balance these things, if I can have my joy in China and have my joy in America, that's how I'm going to spend the time.'" And he did, telling himself that Gina would never have to know.

The guilt didn't hit until he returned. He had something he'd always wanted—a girl who loved him—and he had betrayed her. How could he keep seeing Gina without confessing everything and causing her pain? Other concerns tore at him. The long, expensive, next-to-impossible commute from his rural boarding school to see Gina. Senior year, which would be all about getting into college and his future. Ending the relationship seemed like the only way to end the guilt. So he did. "She has no idea about China," he said. "I don't think she ever will. Nobody knows except me."

First loves are first-draft responses to an important life question: What kind of a person will I be in relationships? As young people's sense of identity grows stronger, they value intimacy and loyalty more.[23] Yet they're also still exploring who they are. In the eternal human dance between loyalty—allegiance to loved ones and community—and autonomy, young people in Western society are brought up with the understanding that, as they enter adulthood, the freedom to pursue new opportunities—academic, professional, emotional, sexual—is fundamental to living their best lives. I'm not trying to justify teen cheating, which is, at heart, a broken promise with the capacity to cause great pain. But it's also true that staying committed to a partner at a time of growth, change, and identity formation won't always be easy and won't always be right.

The temptation of a fling illuminates this conundrum like little else. Several young people have told me that they cheated because the responsibilities of being in a relationship felt like too much to bear. Mateo realized early on in his relationship with Gina that their long-distance relationship would become constraining. When another girl on the other side of the planet wanted to be with him, staying loyal to Gina made less sense, given that the relationship had little potential to last.

After the breakup, though, Mateo felt sad and frustrated. He would ride his bike to a nearby lake, pluck flowers from the shore, throw them into the water, and think. "I said I would divorce myself from this, that I would keep it in China, across the ocean, and no ghosts would follow me," he said. "But they did." Did he know any better than his father, his grandfather, his uncle, his friend from high school? Had he learned nothing from them? "I want to be better than my father," Mateo said. "I want the lessons he tells me to actually live inside me. I don't just want to say that they do. I want to act as they do, as well."

Several young people described infidelity as a kind of trance. They give in to the allure of someone new. They're thinking yet not thinking of the consequences to come—that their partners, particularly given the tight and gossipy nature of teen social circles, will find out and end the relationship or that, like Mateo, they'll grapple alone with their secret, wondering what it says about who they are. Cheating seems to bring a kind of moral clarity to teen breakups. We know who's the perpetrator and who's the victim. But this binary also allows us to overlook the complexities of what faithfulness and infidelity mean in a life stage defined by transience and individual growth.

The Moral Dilemma of the Rejector

Even when infidelity isn't part of the picture, teens who leave someone who loves them can feel like the bad guy. There is no good way to break someone else's heart. They'll be judged no matter what they do.

Social psychologist Roy Baumeister points out that people who reject another person's devotion seem to be warding off the fundamental human urge to attach. We're supposed to want love. They turn away from it. They either hurt the other person by expressing that they're not interested or hurt the other person by avoiding doing so, perpetuating a deception. Baumeister calls this the "moral dilemma of the rejector."[24] Rejectors have no good option, no way not to be perceived as morally suspect, particularly in the minds of their peers, given the adolescent tendency to be judgmental.

The ability to turn down another's desire is fundamental to our autonomy. When it comes to touch and sex, we now grasp the idea that it's okay to reject someone else's advances. But it's a harder sell in a breakup, despite the obvious realities: Building a relationship is a reconnaissance dance, a process of two people getting to know each other. Implicit within this is that they get to keep deciding whether to continue. Even a relationship that was once fulfilling can become ungratifying, uncomfortable, hurtful, unhealthy, or not well suited to time and circumstances.

Teens need to be able to express—and accept—this reality. We need to encourage young people who intend to end a relationship to reflect on why so they can be clear about the reasons and express them with empathy and in person (unless that's not possible, as in a long-distance or online relationship). Ask if they'd like to do a role-play or brainstorm ideas for a script that avoids blaming, insults, and anger.

While some teens won't want the help, I've been amazed at how many teens are up for this kind of thing. Some even ask their parents to be nearby during the breakup—not, I should add, so parents can jump in and help (talk about helicopter parenting), but so young people sense an offstage presence reminding them of their commitment to stay true to themselves. If teens argue that they can express themselves better over text, then ask them to consider whether they'd want to be broken up with that way. Remind them of the ways texting can degenerate quickly, given how easy it is to impulsively press "Send" on an insensitive comment.

That said, an in-person breakup can also veer off course, so they should avoid dragging out the conversation. They should be in a place they can leave with ease, which may mean a parent or an older sibling is waiting around the corner to pick them up.

It might not be possible to avoid hurting someone else in a breakup, but it is possible to see ending a relationship as an ethical process, with choices that balance the needs of the self with our responsibilities toward others. "Breakups are a powerful source of ethical education, a way parents and other adults can talk to kids about the ways they're responsible for other people and the ways they should treat them with tenderness, courage, and care, even when it's hard," said Making Caring Common's Rick Weissbourd. And it will be hard. People who initiate breakups are rarely villains. They're likely carrying their own hurt, disappointment, and anger, which they must try to manage in a way that doesn't cause unnecessary harm. Insensitive breakups can create an enduring legacy, Weissbourd explained. People who are terribly hurt often reproduce that hurt with others.

He emphasized a fundamental principle for rejectors: "You don't abandon people." That means initiating a breakup in which the rejector explains why the relationship is ending, the person who's being rejected has a chance to get more information, and both can come away with the potential for learning from the loss.

A well-played breakup plays into the concept behind the "peak-end rule," developed by psychologists Barbara Fredrickson and Daniel Kahneman. Our memories of an experience are greatly influenced by how it ended.[25] A gracious breakup may seem an oxymoron, but I've been moved by young couples who've valiantly strived for a decent split, sending each other into the world with love, support, and wishes for better relationships to come. One former couple told me about their careful plan to end their four-year relationship. They still loved each other, but they knew they didn't want to stay together during college. They took a walk in the park where they had their first kiss, promised they wouldn't speak to each other for two weeks, and said their farewells.

Parting ways hurt, but in time the two forged a supportive friendship. They could look back on their breakup as a loving end to a relationship they both felt lucky to have had, an act that strived for generosity of spirit in a necessary loss.

Epilogue

How Much Does Your First Love Matter Later?

My first love changed my life.

I met David at a camp in Maine the summer I turned 14. We conducted a largely epistolary romance. I penned my letters from my Connecticut bedroom. He wrote from his apartment on Manhattan's Upper West Side, across the street from Zabar's, a food emporium that sold croissants, which in 1982 were too exotic for my local supermarket. I had never known anyone like him, someone my age with an intellectual curiosity that had nothing to do with getting high grades. While I was a creature of carpools—nothing in my rural town was within walking distance—he roamed New York on foot and by subway. He read classic works of philosophy and psychology. At the time, prompted by his obsession with the Police—the album *Synchronicity* had just come out—he was making his way through Arthur Koestler's *Ghost in the Machine*. He could toss off erudite phrases like *Freud would have a holiday with that one*.

We saw each other twice during the school year. The first time was over Christmas break. We planned to go skating in Rockefeller Center. We stopped by his empty apartment to pick up his skates, started kissing, and never made it to the rink. The second time, my parents took us to Greenwich Village to hear Paquito D'Rivera. My father was a huge jazz fan, and so was David. As I watched them hit it off, critiquing the show, I wondered why I had never before paid attention to the music my father liked. I resolved to start.

David's letters, handwritten in capital letters that seemed to dance across the page, thrilled me as much as they sent me into bouts of insecurity. My life seemed shallow in contrast, and I took inventory of all that was wrong with it: I talked on the phone too much and didn't read enough. I was too consumed with the expectations of others. I had become superficial. When I was younger, I had been more like David. I read constantly about anything that interested me and told any adult who would listen all about it. To keep up with David's sophistication, I decided, I had to revive the inquisitive girl I used to be and grow her up. The letter writing helped. I had time to craft prose fitting to the identity I aspired to: knowledgeable, caring, slyly flirtatious.

Reuniting at camp the following summer was not the joyful event I expected it to be. One of the first things David did was sit me down and confess that he had sex for the first time. It happened with a college girl at a party. His feelings for me hadn't changed, he assured me. He wasn't in love with the girl he'd slept with, the way he was with me. What he'd done was just what kids did in the city. "I was one of the last of my friends to have sex," he said. He had a preternaturally mature way of explaining things, like a guidance counselor delivering the news that you need to repeat algebra.

Though the news upset me, I accepted his explanation and tried to play it cool. He had the upper hand with the words *in the city*. Because everything in the city, in his world, was faster, more advanced. But the betrayals kept coming. As the summer progressed, he seemed to want to hang out with everyone at camp except me. When I pointed this out to him, he cited camp policy, which discouraged couples from spending too much time together. That stung. What good was young love that followed adult rules?

Near the end of the session, the whole camp slept outside in a field on a star-filled night. In the lax way of the 1980s, we were allowed to put down our sleeping bags next to whomever we wanted. In the middle of the night, with everyone else around us asleep, David and I wriggled together and reached into each other's sleeping bags, hoping no one would wake up and notice. It was my first experience of below-the-belt petting. "I wasn't expecting this," was the thought on repeat in my mind as what we did took on its own velocity, like rolling down a hill much steeper and longer than you thought.

The morning after, I sat with my sister and sobbed so hard I felt paralyzed. I didn't feel guilty. I didn't feel manipulated. I even initiated much of what happened. But I didn't feel at all in control, *yes* and *no* rivaling at every move, in a relationship that had become increasingly distressing. When he greeted me the next day with a knowing smile, I fled. The combination of unfamiliar desire and emotional lack overwhelmed me. I felt like I would never be whole again. Having sex for the first time, a year later with someone else, wasn't nearly as wrenching.

For many years after we broke up, David haunted my dreams. The plot lines changed, but the feeling of the dreams was always the same: My longing for him was about to be satisfied by sex or an ethereal reunion that would remove all uncertainty. Then everything would slip away. I would wake up bereft and shaken, then remind myself that I'd moved on.

Or had I? *Moving on* is a funny expression. We say it to urge people not to get mired in the past. We use a spatial metaphor—going from one point to the next—to suggest they can leave what happened behind, like a dodgy town on backroads you'll never drive again.

Here's the truth: David has been a part of me for more than 40 years. Our relationship was one of the most transformative events of my life.

I enter this epilogue knowing that first relationships matter immensely to young people. Why, for many of us, do they continue to matter throughout our lives?

The Indelible Story
Teen relationships are memorable because the love is memorable, and the adolescent brain makes it even more so. The arousal of romantic attraction sharpens focus, making lovers more likely to recall details related to their partner.[1] The neurotransmitters released when we experience strong feelings heighten memory, and the brain regions involved in intense emotions are more sensitive during adolescence. That's why people remember what happened in their teen years more than any other period of life.[2]

How the lessons of first love stick, though, is more complicated. I can't say, for example, that my relationship with David taught me how to avoid withholding men or be more secure in relationships. In fact, for a long time, it seemed the opposite. I felt stuck in a pattern of gravitating toward similar situations again and again. Had my relationship with David somehow cast a template for future attractions?

Our families of origin are the most important influence on our romantic relationships. Our parents provide our first model for what a romantic relationship is. How and whether they express affection to each other, how they communicate, how they manage conflict, whether they've been unfaithful to each other, and whether they're together or apart influence how we go about our relationships. Early family experiences also guide the development of the interpersonal skills that help future romantic relationships thrive. Children who grew up with clear communication and parenting that emphasizes consistency and reasoning are more likely in adult relationships to know how to advocate for their needs, give and get support, solve problems, and express love and affection. Above all, we're shaped by how our parents took care of us. Growing up with supportive, openly affectionate parents helps us gravitate toward warm, loving relationships in adulthood.[3] If we didn't have this, we may (but by no means are destined to) struggle with intimacy and have what psychologists call an "insecure attachment" pattern, characterized by fear and lack of trust in relationships.

The main takeaway of all of this is that we are drawn to what is most familiar from our early lives. Even when we think we've chosen someone different from our parents, we may find similarities emerging later, as if our unconscious minds recognized something our conscious minds couldn't. Particularly when we had it rough growing up. Freud called this phenomenon "repetition compulsion." "It's not that we want to get hurt again—it's that we want to master a situation in which we felt helpless as a child," writes therapist and author Lori Gottlieb. *"Maybe this time,* a part of you imagines, *I can go back and heal that wound from long ago by engaging with someone familiar—but new."*[4]

One of the reasons our earliest caretakers have such influence has to do with a phenomenon known as sexual imprinting: how young animals learn the characteristics of a desirable mate. Animals learn to associate certain rewards with certain conditions, which later affects their choice of a partner. One experiment, led by neuroscience researcher and psychologist Jim Pfaus, showed distressed baby rats that received a soothing touch in a lemon-scented environment would, in adolescence, prefer a lemon-scented sexual partner over an unscented one.[5] Our earliest soothers, whether they were amazing caretakers or highly flawed ones or somewhere in between, likely will have an indelible influence on our future mate choices.

Our first encounters with sexual pleasure also form associations that may guide future attractions. In a separate experiment, male rats that had their first sexual experiences with a Velcro jacket on refused to have sex once the jacket was taken off. The reward of the orgasm became linked with the conditions surrounding it. Once the jacket went back on, the rats copulated.

This suggests that our early experiences of sexual arousal and desire, masturbation, orgasm, and sexual intercourse are crucial in determining later preferences.[6] We associate sexual pleasure with the conditions in which it first occurred.

Pfaus compares the process to building a house—an erotic home base, if you will. "Your interactions with your parents are building blocks, and by adolescence, the building is built," Pfaus explained. "Then you have sexual experiences and relationships and romantic experiences. That won't change the way the building is constructed, but it's going to change the way the interior of the building is set up—whether it's a happy place or a depressed place or a place where you're always yearning for something that's unfulfilled. Those first experiences become a set archetype, a set way of thinking about relationships."

The idea that our first experiences with sex and pleasure matter so fundamentally to our future attractions can seem wistfully romantic if we had good first loves. The late psychologist Nancy Kalish researched "lost and found lovers"—former partners who later reunited, many of them each other's first love. She compared first love to learning a language. We learn to speak as babies to describe our world and our needs. If we learn a new language later, we rely on our first language, translating from our native tongue. "A first love—the person with whom we learn about love and actually create what love means—will be the standard at the beginning of any subsequent relationship, until we gain comfort with the new loved one," she wrote. The reunited high school sweethearts Kalish interviewed felt "uniquely blessed" to return to that first connection, that native tongue.

However tender this scenario, it ain't my rom-com. Given the vaguely defined, emotionally bereft, and confusing early experiences I've written about here, along with my own, I'm alarmed at the prospect that first experiences have so much bearing on future ones. These formative early associations, Pfaus told me, aren't destiny. He maintains that, while you can't change your original preferences, you can become more aware of the patterns you feel stuck in and gradually add new options. "You want to balance things you're already attracted to with some things you're less attracted to or types of people you never let yourself interact with before, and then you start to make a connection and imprint on something else," he said.

Anyone who's ever felt they've broken a cycle—a pull toward bad boys, for example, or woebegone souls who need saving—may recognize what Pfaus is talking about. I certainly did. It was how I felt as my relationship with my husband took root, and I realized that I could be in love without feeling perpetually insecure. The old pattern was still somehow a part of me, but to put it in clinical terms, I discovered I could also be attracted to a different set of conditions.

It's important to note here that what Pfaus observed in rat behavior has not been proven in research on humans and likely won't be, given the tricky ethics of messing with human sexual preferences. Even though Pfaus points out that, when it comes to sex, rat and human brains "work in some important similar ways," human relationships are far more complicated than lemon scents and Velcro jackets.[7]

Besides, the lab-controlled pleasure associations of rats don't begin to capture the existential impact of first love on the human animal. First love transforms your connection to time, the future becoming so electric with anticipation and possibility that it's hard to imagine the end of that love. Yet everything conspires against permanence: You make mistakes and cause pain. You're tantalized by other people. You have opportunities in other places, or your parents need to take the family elsewhere. You're too troubled, stressed, or busy. You want to be free, but the other wants to be close. You want to be close, but the other wants to be free. You feel too much. You feel too little. You feel the wrong things: more desire than love, more vulnerability than safety, more needy than caring, more preoccupied with status or the idea of love than the challenges of loving someone.

Most first loves are doomed to end. Because young people are in a time of transition, endings can feel like the relationship's been stolen away instead of fully played out. When you're young, you are supposed to prioritize where you're headed in life over everything else, even love. So even the most carefully planned breakups (and most aren't), timed elegantly around graduation day or a family move, can still end up feeling unresolved. You had something that had to end because you were too young to keep it going. Your heart is huge, but you can't put it first. The ruptured love story raises the question, What would have happened if you'd had more time, if you'd been more ready, more *grown?*

But perhaps this wound is also a unique blessing. As Jorge Luis Borges wrote, "Only what we lose belongs to us."[8]

MEMORIES THAT MAKE US

David wasn't a very good boyfriend. But he made a great muse.

I started reading again. I dropped my gossipy friends and made new ones who wanted to talk about ideas and books. I made, and mostly followed, schedules for practicing my violin and writing short stories. After I got my license, I started driving to New Haven to hang out with kids from other, more interesting towns. I could hum along to Mahler's Second Symphony and quote Susan Sontag. I'm sure I was occasionally insufferable. But I credit this shift in my life for turning me into a writer and an educator. I needed the discipline, the curiosity, and the high expectations of myself.

My first love had become what Connecticut College psychology professor Jefferson Singer calls a "self-defining memory," a story from my past that helped organize my understanding of myself. Certain memories keep their emotional potency because we associate them with our most significant desires. These memories clarify how we see ourselves and explain who we are to others. An event in our lives may become a self-defining memory not only because it was emotionally powerful but also because it connects with larger goals or unresolved conflicts.

Singer points out that self-defining memories take on an "iconic power in our mind," highlighting what we care about and shaping the themes of our life stories.[9] David was my first muse. There would be others. I could not have him, but I could become what I envied about him. Longing for him pushed me to become the person I wanted to be.

But there was another theme: My first love was also a cautionary tale I couldn't fully reckon with until I watched my daughter begin her love life and I felt as if I were reliving mine. On the surface, I was a mother intent on enforcing good policy for my 13-year-old. My husband and I agreed that she wasn't ready to be alone behind closed doors with her boyfriend. But when I think back to those days of rushing home from work to beat the school bus, as if it would deliver my daughter to her ruin if I couldn't get there on time, I realize something inside me was on overdrive. I was seized with a vigilance so primal it reminded me of when my daughter was a newborn, my brain and body geared completely toward feeding and protecting her. I wanted to prevent her from the shattering confusion I felt with David, the combination of unfamiliar desire and injured longing and being in something I couldn't control. I suspected my daughter sensed my panic, so I tried to explain what happened with David and the concerns I had about her. "That's not going to happen to me," she insisted.

"I don't see how you could know that," I said. I didn't press her about what she meant: She didn't intend to go far sexually? That she thought she felt more secure with her first love than I did with mine?

I would recognize similar reactions in other parents: *I don't want them to be treated poorly and feel like that's all they deserve. I don't want them getting too serious too soon, like I did. I don't want them to be cold or cruel.* In *The Emotional Lives of Teenagers*, Lisa

Damour observes that many parents find raising teens stirs up feelings about their own teenage years.[10] You have the gift of being able to empathize with your children's challenges because you've been there. But the guilt and anxiety over the prospect of history repeating itself can cloud your thinking. Perhaps I was trying to parent the girl I had been, not my own daughter. I wouldn't have changed the rules my husband and I set, but my reaction was a clarion call to listen to the feelings that arose, manage my distress, and see her relationship on its own terms.

My memories of David were now an even bigger part of the story of myself: as a romantic being; as a writer and a teacher; and now, too, as a parent. But after hearing so many stories from teens about what it's like to love and be loved and to cope with the stresses of coming of age, I began to think of David in another way: as a teen boy. He lived in New York City. He was sophisticated. But he was still a boy.

I pulled out our letters. I had years' worth, as we'd continued to correspond after our relationship ended. As I reread them, I saw anew the ways he was faltering. He started high school at one of the most competitive public high schools in New York. He dreamed of becoming an astronaut. But the school was an alienating place, large, crowded, academically demanding, and full of backstabbers. He wanted to transfer to another school. He described rising tensions with his mother. His father, who had remarried, promised that he would make room for David and his younger brother to move in, but there was always a reason that couldn't happen: The apartment didn't have enough room, but maybe the apartment next door would open up soon, so he and his brother could move there, a fantasy teen boy arrangement—independence and privacy, but with food and family a wall away.

David's last year of high school, his mother kicked him and his brother out. Even then, his father, who'd lost his job, didn't take them in. David and his brother squeezed into their grandmother's one-bedroom until David turned 18. Then they moved into a single-room occupancy hotel in a crime-ridden neighborhood. Forced to support himself and get his brother through high school, David worked in the glittery late-'80s Manhattan restaurant scene instead of going to college. By 19, he was managing a bistro with a fleet of aspiring models waiting tables. He gloated a bit about the models. I wasn't jealous. His change in fortune rattled me. This was not the life he was supposed to have. He should have been in college, talking about Sartre on a grassy quad.

It was a story of growing up too soon and epic parental selfishness. I wondered if his father had always been that way, making promises he would never keep, and if that's where David learned his strangely adult manner as the bearer of hard truths. At the same time, my own family life was also in a state of upheaval, albeit a far less brutal one. My father, the son of a Hungarian immigrant, had abandoned dentistry, the stable career his parents pushed him toward, to go into business. At first, his new career went well, but then for years, every venture he started failed. He grew depressed and angry, our family finances on increasingly shaky ground, his once-occasional rages happening more often. Both David and I had entered our teens assuming our place of privilege in the American meritocracy would hold and that our fathers, for all their flaws, would continue to provide for us as they always had. I was lucky. I could still go to college. Soon after I left, my father returned to dentistry.

First Love, the Poem

By the time I became a wife and a mother, I had fallen completely out of touch with David. Whenever I searched for him online, I got a long list of men with the same common last name who were not him. Then teen relationships became my life. I began this book during the first year of COVID, spending hours on Zoom interviewing people about their first loves. I could not help but think about mine. A wearying 6 months into the pandemic and nearly 40 years after David and I met, I thought to look for him on the camp Facebook page—of course!—and sent a friend request with the message "Yes, it's that Lisa Phillips. I hope you are well in this *tempus horribilis*."

We caught up over Messenger. It was nice, after all these years, to read his words again, albeit on a screen instead of a page of stationery. David told me he was divorced and living in Denver to manage a restaurant, just reopened after the shutdown.

"My latest book is about how first love is a life-changing rite of passage," I explained. I asked him if we could talk about what happened between us. He was game.

"How do you think our relationship changed you?" I wrote.

He answered me that night, in a message time-stamped 1:53 a.m., what I imagined to be post-restaurant-shift hours, plus our one-hour time-zone difference. He wrote that he still regretted hurting me, someone who had shown him "loving kindness and true connection." "The realization that I'd given too much value to physical intimacy and sacrificed that exploration with someone in a loving relationship for the empty fantasies being peddled to teenage men at the time, changed me. I regretted how I'd made you feel, and felt the loss of your sweet friendship," he wrote. "What you gave to me shaped what I would grow to desire in my relationships with women." We reminisced about writing letters, the afternoon of not ice skating, the evening listening to jazz. He apologized several times: "I'm just sorry that I hurt you and was such an idiot. Youth is wasted on the young. I had all I needed. If I'd known better, I would have never dreamed of letting you go."

For him, I realized, our love had been a different kind of self-defining memory: a pure and good connection he'd foolishly squandered. His regret may have been more poignant, I speculated, in the wake of the bitter, impure reality of a failed marriage and a virus-ridden world. It felt unreal, this notion of my younger self as a figure of unconditional love who'd slipped through his fingers. He never saw—and I never confessed—my consuming insecurities. A relationship I had come to see as fueled more by the idea of love than the satisfaction of real closeness lingered in his mind as an ideal, at least the kind of ideal you confess in bleary, predawn hours.

"You don't need to castigate yourself," I wrote. "We were figuring out who we were."

He brought up the night in the field.

"You got freaked out and ran away," he wrote. "I didn't understand. I knew you were conflicted, but I didn't understand why." He thought, he explained, that he had disgusted me: "You were scared, and that scared me."

"It wasn't disgust," I told him. "I think I didn't know what I was doing, yet I really wanted to do it. Yes and no can be simultaneous feelings."

I said more: how, after all the anticipation our letters and visits generated, how painful the summer at camp had been—"Because I wasn't getting what I wanted emotionally, I was really freaked out by what happened physically."

He understood. It was how he felt when he lost his virginity, he told me. The girl he had sex with hadn't heeded how conflicted he was: "I said I was a virgin, and she didn't care. I wasn't ready, and it led me to a dark, empty place."

The daunting self-possession I remembered all those years ago, when he told me that having sex was just a thing high school freshmen did in Manhattan, had been cover for a different reality, one he couldn't then express. As he tried to convince me that the sex didn't matter, he was also trying to convince himself. He had no language—I don't think many boys did then, and likely still too few boys do today—to say, "I was violated."

There we were, each other's first love, in late middle age reflecting on the meaning of our relationship. It's a story that intertwines with other ones. Our family stories. What it meant to grow up in the 1980s, when the glories of unsupervised childhoods could be poisoned by the sting of parental neglect. How

I saw myself as a girl, fortunate to have attracted a boy but not confident enough to stand by my own expectations for a relationship. How he saw himself as a boy, under pressure to have sex at his first opportunity, then left without a way to express how bad it felt. Back then, we called sexual debut "losing it," but he had no place to put his sense of loss.

"Thank you for your honesty and your willingness to delve into this past," David wrote. "I want, and have always wanted, your happiness."

I recognized what was happening in that cascade of gray message bubbles: We were experiencing the relief of feeling known and understood, a core tenet of emotional intimacy, something we'd tasted but hadn't had nearly enough of when we were teenagers.

Since then, we've stayed in touch, exchanging occasional "This made me think of you" messages. In a long video call, I read to him this account of our story. "I'm glad you've made something out of what we had," he said.

As 14-year-olds, we could never have imagined looking at each other's 55-year-old selves on laptop screens and talking about our long-ago love. Time had softened and wrinkled our faces, but a lot hadn't changed: his sly eyes, the warm timbre of his voice. I knew well from reporting the ways technology complicated and tested the lives of young people and their parents—indeed, *all* of our lives. But I was grateful for the ability to beam my first love into my grown-up life and gaze at him as an equal, the old doubts long gone.

When I interviewed Jefferson Singer about self-defining memories, I told him about my first love and how the meanings I've made from it have continued to evolve over the years: First, David was my muse. Then, our teen relationship became a cautionary tale for what I didn't want my daughter to go through. Finally, I saw us as two teens, trying to figure out how to love each other as their worlds tilted sideways. "I've had three stages of working through this," I said. "Three different ways of seeing my memories of the relationship."

Self-defining memories, Singer told me, are characterized by vividness and staying power. We return to them throughout our lives, mining them for new meanings. "Our memories are the lyric poems that we write in the course of our lifetimes, and those poems are subject to revision and reinterpretation, if we're open to that," he said. "A true sign of psychological growth and health is that we continue to look at those works that our memory creates and revisit them and react differently to them over time."

It was a beautiful idea: first love as a poem that continues to help us grow.

As I considered my renewed connection with David, I thought, "If only we could have communicated this way when we were teenagers." Of course, that wouldn't have been possible. We didn't then have 40 years of experience and perspective to bring to bear. But one of the gifts of writing this book has been glimpsing what *is* possible between young people. While there is plenty of hurt in these pages, there's also plenty of promise. I've encountered young people who are already working hard to do love better, who see love as a verb, an action, a skill to hone, an art to practice, a struggle worth having. They want to go beyond the "I want" of attraction and desire, beyond misguided romantic ideals, to pursue mutuality: the willingness to express what they want and need, hear the same from their partners, and seek resolution when their needs conflict. Nothing in this book will prevent the heartbreak of first crushes, relationships, and breakups. But with the support of the adults around them, maybe young people can come of age in a more love-literate world, where first romantic experiences, however flawed, are more likely to become memories that help them turn into the adults they want to be.

ACKNOWLEDGMENTS

I first thank the many young people and parents who talked to me and spent time with me for *First Love*. I am honored they shared my belief that their stories have the power to help others seeking to understand adolescent relationships.

I thank my editor, Christen Karniski, whose guidance made *First Love* possible. I also thank Sari Botton, who edited the Longreads essay that became the seed for this book, and my agent, Henry Dunow, who recognized the promise of my idea and helped me find a home for it.

I thank my employer, SUNY New Paltz, for supporting *First Love* with a sabbatical leave and a research and creative projects grant. I am grateful to Patricia Sullivan, the director of the Honors Program, for encouraging the creation of the Love and Heartbreak seminar. The class kept me in close touch with the new realities of adolescent relationships. Truly, my students taught me as much as I taught them.

Several enterprising young people helped me find interview sources for this book: Emily Fego and Seth Laxman, my SUNY New Paltz research assistants; Ericka Francois; Seth Johnson; Violet Monsour; Clara Mouw; Dynahlee Padilla-Vasquez; and Hannah Nishiura, my Oberlin College student intern. I thank Kay Boyes for her Gen-Z take on chapters and our fruitful office-hours conversations as she worked on her own writing project on young love. I thank Delilah Blue for the inspiration of her bravery.

I am grateful to ArteSumapaz for three weeks of writing time in the Colombian mountains and the stunning view of the twin volcanoes.

The Swim Ladies—Adah Frank, Elizabeth Lesser, Sunny Bates, Lisa Schnall, and Esther Perel—helped me incubate the concept for this book during our near-daily summer swims in 2020. Esther's insights and probing questions have had an indelible influence on these pages. Alexandra Solomon, Rick Weissbourd, and Rabbi Jonathan Kligler have also been guiding lights.

I thank Laney Salisbury and Bethany Saltman, who helped me shape years of musings into a book proposal, and Kenny Wapner, who provided crucial guidance. I thank the people who offered helpful thoughts on chapters: Jacquie Marino, Alisa Pearson, Lisa Coxson, Sherry Tagoe, Lori Catallozzi Brown, Elias Stuhr, and Rob Alexander and his students at Brock University. Hannah Copperman and Rachel Lynn Golden gave me critical advice on writing about gender expansiveness. Members of what my daughter calls the "Cool Moms book group"—Zahava Wilson, Alicia Mickles, Wendy Kagan, Julia Indiochova, Cari Pattison, and Erika deVries—read and discussed an early version of *First Love*, making the book feel real for the first time. Along with her feedback, Gretchen Primack was a wonderful sounding board for ideas.

I thank Debbie Dougan, my first "in-law," and KT Legnini, my second, both amazing and funny mothers I'm glad to have in my life.

I thank David Grant, my first love, for responding to this project with an open heart.

I thank my mother, Barbara Phillips, for reading chapters as they came out of the oven and for being, quite simply, the best mother in the world. I thank my sister, Kira Copperman, for her spot-on insights and for cheering me on at every stage of the process. My brother, Marc Phillips, has been a source of wisdom on the trials and tribulations of bringing up girls from the time my daughter was born. Arthur Phillips, my father, died while I was writing *First Love*. I still feel his faith in me, and I thank him for giving me my writer's soul.

I thank the members of my writers' group: Beverly D'Onofrio pushed me to find my voice as I made my way through the thicket of research. Teresa Giordano offered incisive feedback. Nina Shengold's impeccable editor eye gave the manuscript a necessary polish at the 11th hour. I've been talking to Robert Burke Warren about parenting since he was my daughter's preschool teacher, and his insights have had an important influence on this book; I credit him for the indispensable term *pseudo-marriage*. I thank Jana Martin for the walks, the talks, the wise notes, and above all for being my where-have-you-been-all-my-life dear friend.

I could not have written *First Love* without Rachel Somerstein, who was working on her own book at the same time. Our exchanges of feedback and moral support sustained me on this long journey.

I thank my husband, Bill Mead, who understands well how demanding the quest to create can be and gave me abundant space and love as I wrote.

I thank Clara Mead, my daughter. When she was born, a friend assuaged my worries about raising her with the words *Let her teach you*. This book stands as proof that she has.

Notes

Introduction

1. Florence Williams, *Heartbreak: A Personal and Scientific Journey* (New York: W. W. Norton, 2022), 42–55.

2. Erika Edwards, "CDC Says Teen Girls Are Caught in an Extreme Wave of Sadness and Violence," NBC News, February 13, 2023, https://www.nbcnews.com/health/health-news/teen-mental-health-cdc-girls-sadness-violence-rcna69964.

3. Office of Safe and Healthy Students, "Teen Dating in the United States: A Fact Sheet for Schools," US Department of Education, August 25, 2015, https://www2.ed.gov/about/offices/list/oese/oshs/teendating violence-factsheet.html#:~:text=Research%20shows%20that%20about%20one,have%20committed%20relationship%20violence%20themselves.&text=Nationwide%2C%2012%25%20of%209th%2D,they%20did%20not%20want%20to.

4. Jean M. Twenge and Heejung Park, "The Decline in Adult Activities among U.S. Adolescents, 1976–2016," *Child Development* 90, no. 2 (2019): 638–54, https://doi.org/10.1111/cdev.12930.

5. Mike Stobbe, "Pandemic Sent High School Sex to New Low, Survey Finds," AP News, April 27, 2023, https://apnews.com/article/teen-sex-survey-high-school-3d45d0441f531d1da9f5b44373becee4.

6. Craig McLean, "Generation Covid: 'I Have Forgotten How to Socialise,'" Face, March 22, 2022, https://theface.com/life/i-have-forgotten-how-to-socialise-lockdown-generation-covid.

7. Laurence Steinberg and Wendy Steinberg, *Crossing Paths: How Your Child's Adolescence Triggers Your Own Crisis* (New York: Simon & Shuster, 1994).

8. Jennifer Senior, "Why You Never Truly Leave High School." *New York*, January 18, 2013, https://nymag.com/news/features/high-school-2013-1/.

9. Richard Weissbourd, Trisha Ross Anderson, Alison Cashin, and Joe McIntyre, *The Talk: How Adults Can Promote Young People's Healthy Relationships and Prevent Misogyny and Sexual Harassment* (Cambridge, MA: Making Caring Common, May 2017), https://static1.squarespace.com/static/5b7c56e255b02c683659fe43/t/5bd51a0324a69425bd079b59/1540692500558/mcc_the_talk_final.pdf.

10. Susan Gregory Thomas, "All Apologies: Thank You for the 'Sorry,'" Huff-Post, updated October 22, 2011, https://www.huffpost.com/entry/all-apologies-thank-you-f_b_931718.

11. Kaitlyn Tiffany, "No One Knows Exactly What Social Media Is Doing to Teens," *Atlantic*, June 13, 2023, https://www.theatlantic.com/technology/archive/2023/06/social-media-teen-mental-health-crisis-research-limitations/674371/.

12. Zing Tsjeng, "Teens These Days Are Queer AF, New Study Says," Vice, March 10, 2016, https://www.vice.com/en/article/kb4dvz/teens-these-days-are-queer-af-new-study-says.

CHAPTER 1

1. Helen E. Fisher and Justin R. Garcia, "Slow Love: Courtship in the Digital Age," in *The New Psychology of Love*, ed. Karin Sternberg and Robert J. Sternberg, 208–22, 2nd ed. (Cambridge, UK: Cambridge University Press, 2018), https://doi.org/10.1017/9781108658225.011.

2. Amanda McArthur, "Why and How Do We Develop Crushes? An Expert Tells All," Sweety High, July 9, 2019, https://www.sweetyhigh.com/read/science-behind-crushes-helen-fisher-interview-070919.

3. Lucy L. Brown and Helen Fisher, "Love Is A Drive," *Anatomy of Love* (blog), February 1, 2013, https://theanatomyoflove.com/what-is-love/love-is-a-drive/.

4. Asurion, "Americans Check Their Phones 96 Times a Day," PR Newswire, November 21, 2019, https://www.prnewswire.com/news-releases/americans-check-their-phones-96-times-a-day-300962643.html.

5. Helen E. Fisher, Xiaomeng Xu, Arthur Aron, and Lucy L. Brown, "Intense, Passionate, Romantic Love: A Natural Addiction? How the Fields That Investigate Romance and Substance Abuse Can Inform Each Other," *Frontiers in Psychology* 7 (May 10, 2016): 687, https://doi.org/10.3389/fpsyg.2016.00687.

6. Lisa A. Phillips, "The Blistering Break-Up," *Psychology Today*, May 4, 2015, https://www.psychologytoday.com/us/articles/201505/the-blistering-break.

7. Elissa Strauss, "Why Your Kid's Crush Should Be Taken Seriously," CNN, March 26, 2022, https://www.cnn.com/2022/03/26/health/childhood-crushes-parenting-wellness/index.html.

8. Daniel J. Siegel, *Brainstorm: The Power and Purpose of the Teenage Brain* (New York: Jeremy P. Tarcher, 2014), 66–110.

9. Tracy R. Gleason, Sally A. Theran, and Emily M. Newberg, "Parasocial Interactions and Relationships in Early Adolescence," *Frontiers in Psychology* 8 (February 22, 2017): 255, https://doi.org/10.3389/fpsyg.2017.00255.

10. E. B. Hurlock and E. R. Klein, "Adolescent 'Crushes,'" *Child Development* 5, no. 1 (March 1934): 64.

11. Hurlock and Klein, "Adolescent 'Crushes,'" 63–64.

12. Susan Harter and William M. Bukowski, *The Construction of the Self: Developmental and Sociocultural Foundations*, 2nd ed. (New York: Guilford Press, 2015), 72–130.

13. Julie C. Bowker and Rebecca G. Etkin, "Evaluating the Psychological Concomitants of Other-Sex Crush Experiences during Early Adolescence," *Journal of Youth and Adolescence* 45, no. 5 (May 1, 2016): 846, https://doi.org/10.1007/s10964-016-0470-x.

14. Jennifer Connolly and Adele Goldberg, "Romantic Relationships in Adolescence: The Role of Friends and Peers in Their Emergence and Development," in *The Development of Romantic Relationships in Adolescence*, ed. Wyndol Furman, B. Bradford Brown, and Candice Feiring, 266–90, Cambridge Studies in Social and Emotional Development (New York: Cambridge University Press, 1999), 278, https://doi.org/10.1017/CBO9781316182185.012.

15. Ann C. Crouter, Alan Booth, and Chalandra M. Bryant, *Romance and Sex in Adolescence and Emerging Adulthood: Risks and Opportunities* (Mahwah, NJ: Taylor & Francis Group, 2005).

16. Bowker and Etkin, "Evaluating the Psychological Concomitants."

17. Judy Y. Chu, "A Relational Perspective on Adolescent Boys' Identity Development," in *Adolescent Boys: Exploring Diverse Cultures of Boyhood*, ed. Niobe Way and Judy Y. Chu, 78–104 (New York: New York University Press, 2004).

18. Connolly and Goldberg, "Romantic Relationships in Adolescence," 275.

19. Making Caring Common Project, "Our Mission," Harvard Graduate School of Education, accessed November 30, 2022, https://mcc.gse.harvard.edu/about/mission.

Chapter 2

1. Plato, "Plato's Other Half," *Lapham's Quarterly* 2, no. 1 (Winter 2009), https://www.laphamsquarterly.org/eros/platos-other-half.

2. Helen Harris, "Rethinking Heterosexual Relationships in Polynesia: A Case Study of Mangaia, Cook Island," in *Romantic Passion: A Universal Experience?* ed. William Jankowiak, 95–127 (New York: Columbia University Press, 1995).

3. Amanda Lenhart, Aaron Smith, and Monica Anderson, "Basics of Teen Romantic Relationships," chap. 1 in *Teens, Technology, and Romantic Relationships* (Washington, DC: Pew Research Center, October 1, 2015), https://www.pewresearch.org/internet/2015/10/01/basics-of-teen-romantic-relationships/.

4. Jean M. Twenge and Heejung Park, "The Decline in Adult Activities among U.S. Adolescents, 1976–2016," *Child Development* 90, no. 2 (March/April 2019): 638–54, https://doi.org/10.1111/cdev.12930.

5. Brooke Douglas and Pamela Orpinas, "Social Misfit or Normal Development? Students Who Do Not Date," *Journal of School Health* 89, no. 10 (October 2019): 783–90, https://doi.org/10.1111/josh.12818.

6. Joseph P. Allen, Rachel K. Narr, Jessica Kansky, and David E. Szwedo, "Adolescent Peer Relationship Qualities as Predictors of Long-Term Romantic Life Satisfaction," *Child Development* 91, no. 1 (January 2020): 327–40, https://doi.org/10.1111/cdev.13193.

7. Quoted in Society for Research in Child Development, "Teens' Same-Gender Friendships Key to Later Satisfaction in Romantic Relationships," ScienceDaily, January 24, 2019, https://www.sciencedaily.com/releases/2019/01/190124084924.htm.

8. Elizabeth Kivowitz, "Romance or Nomance? Adolescents Prefer to See Less Sex, More Friendships, Platonic Relationships on Screen," UCLA Newsroom, October 25, 2023, https://newsroom.ucla.edu/releases/adolescents-prefer-less-sex-more-friendships-on-screen.

9. Jean Twenge, "Why Today's Teens Are Taking Longer to Grow Up," CNN, updated September 25, 2017, https://www.cnn.com/2017/09/22/health/teens-grow-up-slower-partner/index.html.

10. Lisa Bonos and Emily Guskin, "It's Not Just You: New Data Shows More than Half of Young People in America Don't Have a Romantic Partner," *Washington Post*, March 21, 2019, https://www.washingtonpost.com/lifestyle/2019/03/21/its-not-just-you-new-data-shows-more-than-half-young-people-america-dont-have-romantic-partner/.

11. Office of the Surgeon General, *Our Epidemic of Loneliness and Isolation: The U.S. Surgeon General's Advisory on the Healing Effects of Social Connection and Community* (Washington, DC: Office of the Surgeon General, 2023), https://www.hhs.gov/sites/default/files/surgeon-general-social-connection-advisory.pdf.

12. Lisa Wade, *American Hookup: The New Culture of Sex on Campus* (New York: W. W. Norton, 2017).

13. Catherine A. Sanderson, Emily J. Keiter, Michael G. Miles, and Darren J. A. Yopyk, "The Association between Intimacy Goals and Plans for Initiating Dating Relationships," *Personal Relationships* 14, no. 2 (June 2007): 225–43, https://doi.org/10.1111/j.1475-6811.2007.00152.x.

14. Izz Scott LaMagdeleine, "What It Means When Your Teen Says They're Asexual and How to Support Them," Parents, updated September 19, 2022, https://www.parents.com/parenting/dynamics/lgbtq/what-it-means-when-your-teen-says-theyre-asexual-and-how-to-support-them/.

15. "Helen Fisher Explains Why Casual Sex Doesn't Exist," Big Think, April 23, 2012, video, 2:10, https://www.youtube.com/watch?v=6wT61wsgfk0.

16. Thorn and Benenson Strategy Group, *LGBTQ+ Youth Perspectives: How LGBTQ+ Youth Are Navigating Exploration and Risks of Sexual Exploitation Online* (Manhattan Beach, CA: Thorn, June 2023), https://info.thorn.org/hubfs/Research/Thorn_LGBTQ+YouthPerspectives_ExecutiveSummary_June2023.pdf.

17. Internet Matters, *Teens and Online Dating: Advice and Support for Parents*, accessed September 20, 2023, https://www.internetmatters.org/resources/online -dating-for-teens-parenting-advice/.

18. Wade, *American Hookup*.

19. Alexandra H. Solomon (dr.alexandra.solomon), "I have NOTHING but mad respect for those who are looking for love. Dating is courageous and messy and all of the things. I have a ton of empathy for people who," May 1, 2021, comment on Alexandra H. Solomon (dr.alexandra.solomon), "When you use a strategy to gain and keep someone's attention, you set yourself up for exhaustion and relational vigilance. You also, sadly, send yourself the," Instagram photo, May 1, 2021, https://www.instagram.com/p/COWBcQyjcI5/.

20. Anna Brown, "Most Americans Who Are 'Single and Looking' Say Dating Has Been Harder during the Pandemic," Pew Research Center, April 6, 2022, https://www.pewresearch.org/short-reads/2022/04/06/most-americans-who -are-single-and-looking-say-dating-has-been-harder-during-the-pandemic/.

21. Andrew Cherlin, "Marriage Has Become a Trophy," *Atlantic*, March 20, 2018, https://www.theatlantic.com/family/archive/2018/03/incredible -everlasting-institution-marriage/555320/.

CHAPTER 3

1. Erik H. Erikson, *Identity, Youth, and Crisis* (New York: W. W. Norton, 1968), 131–37.

2. Amanda Lenhart, Aaron Smith, Monica Anderson, "Basics of Teen Romantic Relationships," chap. 1 in *Teens, Technology, and Romantic Relationships* (Washington, DC: Pew Research Center, October 1, 2015), https://www .pewresearch.org/internet/2015/10/01/basics-of-teen-romantic-relationships/.

3. Arielle Kuperberg and Joseph E. Padgett, "The Role of Culture in Explaining College Students' Selection into Hookups, Dates, and Long-Term Romantic Relationships," *Journal of Social and Personal Relationships* 33, no. 8 (December 2016): 1070–96, https://doi.org/10.1177/0265407515616876.

4. W. Andrew Collins, "More than Myth: The Developmental Significance of Romantic Relationships during Adolescence," *Journal of Research on Adolescence* 13, no. 1 (March 2003): 1–24, https://doi.org/10.1111/1532-7795.1301001; Reed W. Larson, Gerald L. Clore, and Gretchen A. Wood, "The Emotions of Romantic Relationships: Do They Wreak Havoc on Adolescents?" in *The Development of Romantic Relationships in Adolescence*, ed. Wyndol Furman, B. Bradford Brown, and Candice Feiring, 19–49, Cambridge Studies in Social and Emotional Development (New York: Cambridge University Press, 1999), 33, https:// doi.org/10.1017/CBO9781316182185.003.

5. Inge Seiffge-Krenke and Schmuel Shulman, "Transformations in Heterosexual Romantic Relationships across the Transition into Adolescence," in *Relationship Pathways: From Adolescence to Young Adulthood*, ed. Brett Laursen and

W. Andrew Collins, 157–90 (Thousand Oaks, CA: Sage, 2012), 166, https://doi
.org/10.4135/9781452240565.n8.

6. Emily L. Loeb, Jessica Kansky, Rachel K. Narr, Caroline Fowler, and Joseph
P. Allen, "Romantic Relationship Churn in Early Adolescence Predicts Hostility, Abuse, and Avoidance in Relationships into Early Adulthood," *Journal of
Early Adolescence* 40, no. 8 (October 2020): 1195–225, https://doi.org/10.1177
/0272431619899477.

7. Jessica Kansky and Joseph P. Allen, "Long-Term Risks and Possible Benefits
Associated with Late Adolescent Romantic Relationship Quality," *Journal of
Youth and Adolescence* 47, no. 7 (July 2018): 1531–44, https://doi.org/10.1007/
s10964-018-0813-x.

8. David E. Szwedo, Joanna M. Chango, and Joseph P. Allen, "Adolescent
Romance and Depressive Symptoms: The Moderating Effects of Positive Coping and Perceived Friendship Competence," *Journal of Clinical Child and Adolescent Psychology* 44, no. 4 (2015): 538–50, https://doi.org/10.1080/15374416
.2014.881290.

9. Megan Price, Leanne Hides, Wendell Cockshaw, Aleksandra A. Staneva,
and Stoyan R. Stoyanov, "Young Love: Romantic Concerns and Associated
Mental Health Issues among Adolescent Help-Seekers," *Behavioral Sciences* 6,
no. 2 (June 2016): 9, https://doi.org/10.3390/bs6020009.

10. Elke D. Reissing, Heather L. Andruff, and Jocelyn J. Wentland, "Looking Back: The Experience of First Sexual Intercourse and Current Sexual
Adjustment in Young Heterosexual Adults," *Journal of Sex Research* 49, no. 1
(2012): 27–35, https://doi.org/10.1080/00224499.2010.538951.

11. Peggy Orenstein, *Girls & Sex: Navigating the Complicated New Landscape*
(New York: Harper, 2016).

12. Peggy Orenstein, *Boys & Sex: Young Men on Hookups, Love, Porn, Consent,
and Navigating the New Masculinity* (New York: Harper, 2020), 233–34.

13. Amy Schalet, "The Sleepover Question," *New York Times*, July 23, 2011,
https://www.nytimes.com/2011/07/24/opinion/sunday/24schalet.html.

14. Daniel J. Siegel, *Brainstorm: The Power and Purpose of the Teenage Brain*
(New York: Jeremy P. Tarcher, 2014), 241.

15. Elizabeth L. Paul, Amanda Poole, and Nancy Jakubowyc, "Intimacy
Development and Romantic Status: Implications for Adjustment to the College
Transition," *Journal of College Student Development* 39 (1998): 75–86.

16. Kendra Knight, "Emerging Adults' Discursive Construction of Work/
Partnership Boundary Strategies," *Western Journal of Communication* 86, no. 3
(2022): 379–99, https://doi.org/10.1080/10570314.2022.2060521.

17. Arthur Aron, Gary W. Lewandowski, Debra Mashek, and Elaine N. Aron,
"The Self-Expansion Model of Motivation and Cognition in Close Relationships," in *The Oxford Handbook of Close Relationships*, ed. Jeffry A. Simpson and
Lorne Campbell, 90–115 (Oxford, UK: Oxford University Press, 2013), https://
doi.org/10.1093/oxfordhb/9780195398694.013.0005.

Chapter 4

1. Loes Keijsers, Susan Branje, Skyler T. Hawk, Seth J. Schwartz, Tom Frijns, Hans M. Koot, Pol van Lier, and Wim Meeus, "Forbidden Friends as Forbidden Fruit: Parental Supervision of Friendships, Contact with Deviant Peers, and Adolescent Delinquency," *Child Development* 83, no. 2 (March/April 2012): 651–66, https://doi.org/10.1111/j.1467-8624.2011.01701.x; Nina S. Mounts, "Parental Management of Adolescent Peer Relationships: What Are Its Effects on Friend Selection?" in *Family and Peers: Linking Two Social Worlds*, ed. Kathryn A. Kerns, Josefina M. Contreras, and Angela M. Neal-Barnett, 169–93, Praeger Series in Applied Psychology (Westport, CT: Praeger, 2000).

2. Lisa M. Diamond and Sarah Lucas, "Sexual-Minority and Heterosexual Youths' Peer Relationships: Experiences, Expectations, and Implications for Well-Being," *Journal of Research on Adolescence* 14, no. 3 (September 2004): 313–40, https://doi.org/10.1111/j.1532-7795.2004.00077.x.

3. Marjory Roberts Gray and Laurence Steinberg, "Adolescent Romance and the Parent-Child Relationship: A Contextual Perspective," in *The Development of Romantic Relationships in Adolescence*, ed. Wyndol Furman, B. Bradford Brown, and Candice Feiring, 235–62, Cambridge Studies in Social and Emotional Development (New York: Cambridge University Press, 1999), https://doi.org/10.1017/CBO9781316182185.011.

4. Joanne Davila, Jonathan Mattanah, Vickie Bhatia, Jessica A. Latack, Brian A. Feinstein, Nicholas R. Eaton, Jennifer S. Daks et al., "Romantic Competence, Healthy Relationship Functioning, and Well-Being in Emerging Adults," *Personal Relationships* 24, no. 1 (March 2017): 162–84, https://doi.org/10.1111/pere.12175.

5. Judith G. Smetana and Pamela Asquith, "Adolescents' and Parents' Conceptions of Parental Authority and Personal Autonomy," *Child Development* 65, no. 4 (August 1994): 1147–62, https://doi.org/10.2307/1131311.

6. Jennifer M. Wyatt and Gustavo Carlo, "What Will My Parents Think? Relations among Adolescents' Expected Parental Reactions, Prosocial Moral Reasoning, and Prosocial and Antisocial Behaviors," *Journal of Adolescent Research* 17, no. 6 (November 2002): 646–66, https://doi.org/10.1177/074355802237468.

7. Eileen Wood, Charlene Y. Senn, Serge Desmarais, Laura Park, and Norine Verberg, "Sources of Information about Dating and Their Perceived Influence on Adolescents," *Journal of Adolescent Research* 17, no. 4 (July 2002): 401–17, https://doi.org/10.1177/07458402017004005.

8. Richard Weissbourd, Trisha Ross Anderson, Alison Cashin, and Joe McIntyre, *The Talk: How Adults Can Promote Young People's Healthy Relationships and Prevent Misogyny and Sexual Harassment* (Cambridge, MA: Making Caring Common, May 2017), https://mcc.gse.harvard.edu/reports/the-talk.

9. Davila et al., "Romantic Competence."

10. Kathrine Bejanyan, Tara C. Marshall, and Nelli Ferenczi, "Associations of Collectivism with Relationship Commitment, Passion, and Mate

Preferences: Opposing Roles of Parental Influence and Family Allocentrism," *PLOS ONE* 10, no. 2 (February 26, 2015): e0117374, https://doi.org/10.1371/journal.pone.0117374.

11. Joshua Coleman, "A Shift in American Family Values Is Fueling Estrangement," *Atlantic*, January 10, 2021, https://www.theatlantic.com/family/archive/2021/01/why-parents-and-kids-get-estranged/617612/.

12. H. Colleen Sinclair, Kristina B. Hood, and Brittany L. Wright, "Revisiting the Romeo and Juliet Effect (Driscoll, Davis, & Lipetz, 1972): Reexamining the Links between Social Network Opinions and Romantic Relationship Outcomes," *Social Psychology* 45, no. 3 (May 2014): 170–78, https://doi.org/10.1027/1864-9335/a000181.

13. Ekua Hagan, "Arranged vs. Love-Based Marriages in the U.S.—How Different Are They?" *Psychology Today*, August 1, 2012, https://www.psychologytoday.com/us/blog/the-science-love/201208/arranged-vs-love-based-marriages-in-the-us-how-different-are-they.

14. Dhwani Vora, "Why Arranged Marriages Are Considered Better than Love Marriages in Indian Society," *Times of India*, March 17, 2021, https://timesofindia.indiatimes.com/life-style/relationships/love-sex/why-arranged-marriages-are-considered-better-than-love-marriages-in-indian-society/articleshow/81549410.cms.

15. Robert Epstein, Mayuri Pandit, and Mansi Thakar, "How Love Emerges in Arranged Marriages: Two Cross-Cultural Studies," *Journal of Comparative Family Studies* 44, no. 3 (May–June 2013): 341–60, https://doi.org/10.3138/jcfs.44.3.341.

16. Disney Tom, "Malayali Brown Angels Heal the World: How Nurses Are Kerala's Biggest Export," *Times of India*, September 2, 2022, https://timesofindia.com/time-special/life/malayali-brown-angels-heal-the-world-how-nurses-are-keralas-biggest-export/articleshow/108401900.cms.

CHAPTER 5

1. Jeffrey M. Jones, "U.S. LGBT Identification Steady at 7.2%," Gallup, February 22, 2023, https://news.gallup.com/poll/470708/lgbt-identification-steady.aspx.

2. Centers for Disease Control and Prevention: "2021 Number and Percentage of Students, by Sexual Identity," updated April 27, 2023, https://www.cdc.gov/healthyyouth/data/yrbs/supplemental-mmwr/students_by_sexual_identity.htm.

3. Anna Brown, "About 5% of Young Adults in the U.S. Say Their Gender Is Different from Their Sex Assigned at Birth," Pew Research Center, June 7, 2022, https://www.pewresearch.org/short-reads/2022/06/07/about-5-of-young-adults-in-the-u-s-say-their-gender-is-different-from-their-sex-assigned-at-birth/; Jody L. Herman, Andrew R. Flores, and Kathryn K. O'Neill, *How Many Adults and Youth Identify as Transgender in the United States?* (Los Angeles: Williams

Institute, June 2022), https://williamsinstitute.law.ucla.edu/publications/trans -adults-united-states/.

4. Tomás Mier, "Janelle Monáe Shares Non-Binary Identification: 'So Much Bigger than He or She,'" *Rolling Stone*, April 21, 2022, https://www.rollingstone .com/music/music-news/janelle-monae-shares-non-binary-1341131/.

5. NCHHSTP Newsroom, "CDC Report Shows Concerning Increases in Sadness and Exposure to Violence among Teen Girls and LGBQ+ Youth," Centers for Disease Control and Prevention, updated March 9, 2023, https://www .cdc.gov/nchhstp/newsroom/fact-sheets/healthy-youth/sadness-and-violence -among-teen-girls-and-LGBQ-youth-factsheet.html.

6. The Trevor Project, "2022 National Survey on LGBTQ Youth Mental Health," accessed February 28, 2023, https://www.thetrevorproject.org/survey -2022/.

7. David Oliver, "Let's Talk about (Queer) Sex: The Importance of LGBTQ-Inclusive Sex Education in Schools," *USA Today*, updated August 8, 2022, https://www.usatoday.com/story/life/health-wellness/2021/08/05/sex -education-importance-lgbtq-inclusivity-schools/8046137002/.

8. Sarah W. Whitton, Christina Dyar, Michael E. Newcomb, and Brian Mustanski, "Romantic Involvement: A Protective Factor for Psychological Health in Racially-Diverse Young Sexual Minorities," *Journal of Abnormal Psychology* 127, no. 3 (April 2018): 265–75, https://doi.org/10.1037/abn0000332.

9. Andrew Solomon, *Far from the Tree: Parents, Children and the Search for Identity*, 1st Scribner hardcover ed (New York: Scribner, 2012), 1–48.

10. Charlotte Alter, "Trans Men Confirm All Your Worst Fears About Sexism," *Time*, May 16, 2016, https://time.com/transgender-men-sexism/.

11. *The Celluloid Closet*, directed by Rob Epstein and Jeffrey Friedman (New York: HBO, 1995).

12. Adrian C. Araya, Rebecca Warwick, Daniel Shumer, and Ellen Selkie, "Romantic Relationships in Transgender Adolescents: A Qualitative Study," *Pediatrics* 147, no. 2 (February 2021): e2020007906, https://doi.org/10.1542/ peds.2020-007906.

13. Barry L. Motter and Lia Softas-Nall, "Experiences of Transgender Couples Navigating One Partner's Transition: Love Is Gender Blind," *Family Journal* 29, no. 1 (January 2021): 60–71, https://doi.org/10.1177/1066480720978537.

14. Michael E. Newcomb, "Romantic Relationships and Sexual Minority Health: A Review and Description of the Dyadic Health Model," *Clinical Psychology Review* 82 (December 2020): 101924, https://doi.org/10.1016/j.cpr .2020.101924.

15. Erin Blakemore, "How Historians Are Documenting the Lives of Transgender People," *National Geographic*, June 24, 2022, https://www .nationalgeographic.com/history/article/how-historians-are-documenting-lives -of-transgender-people.

16. John D'Emilio, "Capitalism and Gay Identity," in *The Lesbian and Gay Studies Reader*, ed. Henry Abelove, Michèle Aina Barale, and David M. Halperin, 467–76 (New York: Routledge, 1993).

17. Sabra L. Katz-Wise, Margaret Rosario, and Michael Tsappis, "Lesbian, Gay, Bisexual, and Transgender Youth and Family Acceptance," *Pediatric Clinics of North America* 63, no. 6 (December 2016): 1011–25, https://doi.org/10.1016/j.pcl.2016.07.005.

18. Michael L. Hendricks and Rylan J. Testa, "A Conceptual Framework for Clinical Work with Transgender and Gender Nonconforming Clients: An Adaptation of the Minority Stress Model," *Professional Psychology: Research and Practice* 43, no. 5 (October 2012): 460–67, https://doi.org/10.1037/a0029597.

19. Carolina Aragão, "Gender Pay Gap in U.S. Hasn't Changed Much in Two Decades," Pew Research Center, March 1, 2023, https://www.pewresearch.org/short-reads/2023/03/01/gender-pay-gap-facts/.

CHAPTER 6

1. Sandra E. Garcia, "The Woman Who Created #MeToo Long before Hashtags," *New York Times*, October 20, 2017, https://www.nytimes.com/2017/10/20/us/me-too-movement-tarana-burke.html.

2. Wendy Lu, "What #MeToo Means to Teenagers," *New York Times*, April 19, 2018, https://www.nytimes.com/2018/04/19/well/family/metoo-me-too-teenagers-teens-adolescents-high-school.html.

3. SIECUS: Sex Ed for Social Change, *Sex Ed State Law and Policy Chart: SIECUS State Profiles* (Washington, DC, July 2022), https://siecus.org/wp-content/uploads/2023/12/2022-Sex-Ed-State-Law-and-Policy-Chart.pdf.

4. National Center for Education Statistics, "Immediate Transition to College," accessed February 19, 2024, https://nces.ed.gov/fastfacts/display.asp?id=51.

5. Michael B. Robb and Supreet Mann, *Teens and Pornography* (San Francisco: Common Sense Media, 2023), https://www.commonsensemedia.org/sites/default/files/research/report/2022-teens-and-pornography-final-web.pdf.

6. Devon Cole (devoncolemusic), "This song had to be rectified #fyp #blurredlines #robinthicke #consent #lyricsoftheday," TikTok video, September 18, 2021, https://www.tiktok.com/@devoncolemusic/video/7009364370962582790?lang=en.

7. Melissa Febos, "I Spent My Life Consenting to Touch I Didn't Want," *New York Times Magazine*, March 31, 2021, https://www.nytimes.com/2021/03/31/magazine/consent.html.

8. Peggy Orenstein, *Girls & Sex: Navigating the Complicated New Landscape* (New York: Harper, 2016), 7–73.

9. Peggy Orenstein, *Boys & Sex: Young Men on Hookups, Love, Porn, Consent, and Navigating the New Masculinity* (New York: Harper, 2020), 175–76.

10. Quoted in Sara Nics, "The New Norms of Affirmative Consent," *New Yorker Radio Hour*, August 30, 2019, https://www.wnycstudios.org/podcasts/ tnyradiohour/segments/new-norms-affirmative-consent.

11. Love Is Respect, "Teen Dating Violence Awareness Month," February 2024, https://www.loveisrespect.org/get-involved/tdvam.

12. Office of Juvenile Justice and Delinquency Prevention, "Teen Dating Violence: Literature Review: A Product of the Model Programs Guide," updated January 2022, https://ojjdp.ojp.gov/model-programs-guide/literature-reviews/ Teen-Dating-Violence.

13. C. Nadine Wathen and Harriet L. MacMillan, "Children's Exposure to Intimate Partner Violence: Impacts and Interventions," *Paediatrics and Child Health* 18, no. 8 (October 2013): 419–22.

14. Centers for Disease Control and Prevention, "About Teen Dating Violence," February 8, 2024, https://www.cdc.gov/violenceprevention/ intimatepartnerviolence/teendatingviolence/fastfact.html.

15. Hannah Doucette, Charlene Collibee, and Christie J. Rizzo, "A Review of Parent- and Family-Based Prevention Efforts for Adolescent Dating Violence," *Aggression and Violent Behavior* 58 (May–June 2021): 101548, https://doi.org/10 .1016/j.avb.2021.101548.

16. Michele L. Ybarra, Dorothy L. Espelage, Jennifer Langhinrichsen-Rohling, Josephine D. Korchmaros, and Danah Boyd, "Lifetime Prevalence Rates and Overlap of Physical, Psychological, and Sexual Dating Abuse Perpetration and Victimization in a National Sample of Youth," *Archives of Sexual Behavior* 45, no. 5 (July 2016): 1083–99, https://doi.org/10.1007/s10508-016-0748-9.

17. Love Is Respect, "Guys Can Be Victims, Too," accessed June 13, 2023, https://www.loveisrespect.org/resources/guys-can-be-victims-too/.

18. Mayo Clinic Staff, "Domestic Violence against Men: Recognize Patterns, Seek Help," Mayo Clinic, January 13, 2024, https://www.mayoclinic.org/healthy -lifestyle/adult-health/in-depth/domestic-violence-against-men/art-20045149.

19. Angela Lee, interview by author, June 21, 2023.

20. bell hooks, *All about Love: New Visions* (New York: HarperCollins, 2000), 6.

21. Lee, interview.

22. Peace over Violence, "Barrie Levy," September 22, 2022, https://www .peaceoverviolence.org/updates-impact/where-are-they-now-barrie-levy.

23. Texas Advocacy Project, "Statistics," accessed May 16, 2024, https://www .texasadvocacyproject.org/statistics.

24. Eleanor Klibanoff, "Hispanic and Teen Fertility Rates Increase after Abortion Restrictions," *Texas Tribune*, January 26, 2024, https://www.texastribune.org /2024/01/26/texas-abortion-fertility-rate-increase/.

Chapter 7

1. G. Stanley Hall, *Adolescence: Its Psychology and Its Relations to Physiology, Anthropology, Sociology, Sex, Crime, Religion and Education*, vol. 1 (New York: D. Appleton, 1904), 264–65.

2. Hall, *Adolescence*, 1:266–67.

3. Margaret Mead, *Coming of Age in Samoa: A Psychological Study of Primitive Youth for Western Civilization* (New York: Perennial Classics, 2001).

4. Agata Boxe, "The Teen Brain, in Flux, Vulnerable to Mental Health Disorders," BrainFacts.org, June 15, 2020, https://www.brainfacts.org:443/diseases-and-disorders/mental-health/2020/the-teen-brain-in-flux-vulnerable-to-mental-health-disorders-061220.

5. Janet Hibbs and Anthony Rostain, *The Stressed Years of Their Lives: Helping Your Kid Survive and Thrive during Their College Years* (New York: St. Martin's Press, 2019), 150–51.

6. Erika Edwards, "CDC Says Teen Girls Are Caught in an Extreme Wave of Sadness and Violence," NBC News, February 13, 2023, https://www.nbcnews.com/health/health-news/teen-mental-health-cdc-girls-sadness-violence-rcna69964.

7. Juliana Menasce and Nikki Graf, "Most U.S. Teens See Anxiety and Depression as a Major Problem among Their Peers," Pew Research Center, February 20, 2019, https://www.pewresearch.org/social-trends/2019/02/20/most-u-s-teens-see-anxiety-and-depression-as-a-major-problem-among-their-peers/.

8. Hara Estroff Marano, *Nation of Wimps: The High Cost of Invasive Parenting* (New York: Crown, 2008).

9. Karla Vermeulen, *Generation Disaster: Coming of Age Post-9/11* (New York: Oxford University Press, 2021).

10. Jonathan Haidt, "The Dangerous Experiment on Teen Girls," *Atlantic*, November 21, 2021, https://www.theatlantic.com/ideas/archive/2021/11/facebooks-dangerous-experiment-teen-girls/620767/.

11. The Annie E. Casey Foundation, "Generation Z and Mental Health Issues," updated May 12, 2024, https://www.aecf.org/blog/generation-z-and-mental-health; Alfiee Breland-Noble and the AAKOMA Project, *State of Mental Health for Youth of Color 2022*, (Arlington, VA: AAKOMA Project, April 2023), https://aakomaproject.org/wp-content/uploads/2023/04/SOMHYOC-FullReport.pdf.

12. Elizabeth Marks, Caroline Hickman, Panu Pihkala, Susan Clayton, Eric R. Lewandowski, Elouise E. Mayall, Britt Wray, Catriona Mellor, and Lise van Susteren, "Young People's Voices on Climate Anxiety, Government Betrayal and Moral Injury: A Global Phenomenon," SSRN Scholarly Paper (Rochester, NY: Social Science Research Network, September 7, 2021), https://doi.org/10.2139/ssrn.3918955.

13. Kate Julian, "Why Are Young People Having So Little Sex?" *Atlantic*, December 2018, https://www.theatlantic.com/magazine/archive/2018/12/the-sex-recession/573949/.

14. Scott Braithwaite and Julianne Holt-Lunstad, "Romantic Relationships and Mental Health," *Current Opinion in Psychology* 13 (February 2017): 120–25, https://doi.org/10.1016/j.copsyc.2016.04.001; Joanne Davila, "Depressive Symptoms and Adolescent Romance: Theory, Research, and Implications," *Child Development Perspectives* 2, no. 1 (April 2008): 26–31, https://doi.org/10.1111/j.1750-8606.2008.00037.x.

15. Davila, "Depressive Symptoms."

16. Scott M. Monroe, Paul Rohde, John R. Seeley, and Peter M. Lewisohn, "Life Events and Depression in Adolescence: Relationship Loss as a Prospective Risk Factor for First Onset of Major Depressive Disorder," *Journal of Abnormal Psychology* 108, no. 4 (November 1999): 606–14, https://doi.org/10.1037//0021-843x.108.4.606.

17. David E. Szwedo, Joanna M. Chango, and Joseph P. Allen, "Adolescent Romance and Depressive Symptoms: The Moderating Effects of Positive Coping and Perceived Friendship Competence," *Journal of Clinical Child and Adolescent Psychology* 44, no. 4 (2015): 538–50, https://doi.org/10.1080/15374416.2014.881290.

18. Megan Price, Leanne Hides, Wendell Cockshaw, Aleksandra A. Staneva, and Stoyan R. Stoyanov, "Young Love: Romantic Concerns and Associated Mental Health Issues among Adolescent Help-Seekers," *Behavioral Sciences* 6, no. 2 (June 2016): 9, https://doi.org/10.3390/bs6020009.

19. If you or someone you know is having thoughts of suicide, call or text 988 to reach the 988 Suicide and Crisis Lifeline, or go to Speaking of Suicide at https://speakingofsuicide.com/resources/ for a list of additional resources.

20. Steven Schlozman, "The Trauma Felt in Teen Breakups," Clay Center for Young Healthy Minds, February 12, 2020, https://www.mghclaycenter.org/parenting-concerns/the-trauma-of-teenage-breakups/.

21. Sara J. Steinberg and Joanne Davila, "Romantic Functioning and Depressive Symptoms among Early Adolescent Girls: The Moderating Role of Parental Emotional Availability," *Journal of Clinical Child & Adolescent Psychology* 37, no. 2 (2008): 350–62, https://doi.org/10.1080/15374410801955847.

22. Szwedo, Chango, and Allen, "Adolescent Romance."

23. Szwedo, Chango, and Allen, "Adolescent Romance," 957.

24. Kei M. Nomaguchi, "Gender, Family Structure, and Adolescents' Primary Confidants," *Journal of Marriage and Family* 70, no. 5 (2008): 1213–27, https://doi.org/10.1111/j.1741-3737.2008.00561.x; Szwedo, Chango, and Allen, "Adolescent Romance," 957.

25. Lisa Damour, *Untangled: Guiding Teenage Girls through the Seven Transitions into Adulthood* (New York: Ballantine Books, 2017).

26. David E. Szwedo, Elenda T. Hessel, Emily L. Loeb, Christopher A. Hafen, and Joseph P. Allen, "Adolescent Support Seeking as a Path to Adult Functional Independence," *Developmental Psychology* 53, no. 5 (May 2017): 949–61, https://doi.org/10.1037/dev0000277.

27. Shmuel Shulman, Joanne Davila, and Lital Shachar-Shapira, "Assessing Romantic Competence among Older Adolescents," *Journal of Adolescence* 34, no. 3 (June 2011): 397–406, https://doi.org/10.1016/j.adolescence.2010.08.002.

28. Gemma Hartley, *Fed Up: Emotional Labor, Women, and the Way Forward* (New York: HarperCollins, 2020), 13.

29. Margaret E. Klein, "The Trauma of a Romantic Partner's Psychotic Episode: An Emerging Clinical Picture" (PhD diss., Adelphi University, September 2014).

CHAPTER 8

1. Florence Williams, *Heartbreak: A Personal and Scientific Journey* (New York: W. W. Norton, 2022), 76–79.

2. Lucy L. Brown and Helen Fisher, "The Rejected Brain," *Anatomy of Love* (blog), February 25, 2013, https://theanatomyoflove.com/the-results/the-rejected-brain/; Helen E. Fisher, Lucy L. Brown, Arthur Aron, Greg Strong, and Debra Mashek, "Reward, Addiction, and Emotion Regulation Systems Associated with Rejection in Love," *Journal of Neurophysiology* 104, no. 1 (July 2010): 51–60, https://doi.org/10.1152/jn.00784.2009.

3. Lisa A. Phillips, "The Blistering Break-Up," *Psychology Today*, May 4, 2015, https://www.psychologytoday.com/us/articles/201505/the-blistering-break.

4. Helen Fisher, "The Brain in Love," TED, February 2008, video, 15:36, https://www.ted.com/talks/helen_fisher_the_brain_in_love/transcript.

5. W. Andrew Collins, Deborah P. Welsh, and Wyndol Furman, "Adolescent Romantic Relationships," *Annual Review of Psychology* 60 (January 2009): 631–52, https://doi.org/10.1146/annurev.psych.60.110707.163459.

6. Thao Ha, Geertjan Overbeek, Anna Lichtwarck-Aschoff, and Rutger C. M. E. Engels, "Do Conflict Resolution and Recovery Predict the Survival of Adolescents' Romantic Relationships?" *PLOS ONE* 8, no. 4 (April 2013): e61871, https://doi.org/10.1371/journal.pone.0061871.

7. Ritch C. Savin-Williams and Lisa M. Diamond, "Sexual Identity Trajectories among Sexual-Minority Youths: Gender Comparisons," *Archives of Sexual Behavior* 29, no. 6 (December 2000): 607–27, https://doi.org/10.1023/A:1002058505138.

8. Rostyslaw W. Robak and Steven P. Weitzman, "The Nature of Grief: Loss of Love Relationships in Young Adulthood," *Journal of Personal and Interpersonal Loss* 3, no. 2 (April 1998): 205–16, https://doi.org/10.1080/10811449808414442.

9. Phillips, "Blistering Break-Up."

10. Grace M. Larson and David A. Sbarra, "Participating in Research on Romantic Breakups Promotes Emotional Recovery via Changes in Self-Concept

Clarity," *Social Psychological and Personality Science* 6, no. 4 (May 2015): 399–406, https://doi.org/10.1177/1948550614563085.

11. Lauren C. Howe and Carol S. Dweck, "Changes in Self-Definition Impede Recovery from Rejection," *Personality and Social Psychology Bulletin* 42, no. 1 (January 2016): 54–71, https://doi.org/10.1177/0146167215612743.

12. Scott M. Monroe, Paul Rohde, John R. Seeley, and Peter M. Lewinsohn, "Life Events and Depression in Adolescence: Relationship Loss as a Prospective Risk Factor for First Onset of Major Depressive Disorder," *Journal of Abnormal Psychology* 108, no. 4 (November 1999): 606–14, https://doi.org/10.1037/0021 -843X.108.4.606.

13. Emily F. Rothman, Eva Bahrami, Nnenna Okeke, and Elizabeth Mumford, "Prevalence of and Risk Markers for Dating Abuse–Related Stalking and Harassment Victimization and Perpetration in a Nationally Representative Sample of U.S. Adolescents," *Youth and Society* 53, no. 6 (September 2021): 955–78, https://doi.org/10.1177/0044118X20921631.

14. Megan Price, Leanne Hides, Wendell Cockshaw, Aleksandra A. Staneva, and Stoyan R. Stoyanov, "Young Love: Romantic Concerns and Associated Mental Health Issues among Adolescent Help-Seekers," *Behavioral Sciences* 6, no. 2 (June 2016): 9, https://doi.org/10.3390/bs6020009.

15. Shmuel Shulman et al., "Adolescent Depressive Symptoms and Breakup Distress During Early Emerging Adulthood: Associations With the Quality of Romantic Interactions," *Emerging Adulthood* 5, no. 4 (August 1, 2017): 251–58, https://doi.org/10.1177/2167696817698900.

16. Johan Bilsen, "Suicide and Youth: Risk Factors," *Frontiers in Psychiatry* 9 (October 30, 2018), https://doi.org/10.3389/fpsyt.2018.00540.

17. If you or someone you know is having thoughts of suicide, call or text 988 to reach the 988 Suicide and Crisis Lifeline, or go to Speaking of Suicide at https://speakingofsuicide.com/resources for a list of additional resources.

18. Amanda Lenhart, Aaron Smith, and Monica Anderson, "After the Relationship: Technology and Breakups," chap. 5 in *Teens, Technology and Romantic Relationships* (Washington, DC: Pew Research Center, October 1, 2015), https: //www.pewresearch.org/internet/2015/10/01/after-the-relationship-technology -and-breakups/.

19. Lisa A. Phillips, "Teens Are Terrible at Breaking Up. Here Are Six Ways Parents Can Help Them Improve," *Washington Post*, April 15, 2021, https://www .washingtonpost.com/lifestyle/2021/04/15/teens-are-terrible-breaking-up-here -are-6-ways-parents-can-help-them-improve/.

20. Leah E. LeFebvre, Mike Allen, Ryan D. Rasner, Shelby Garstad, Aleksander Wilms, and Callie Parrish, "Ghosting in Emerging Adults' Romantic Relationships: The Digital Dissolution Disappearance Strategy," *Imagination, Cognition and Personality* 39, no. 2 (December 2019): 125–50, https://doi.org/10 .1177/0276236618820519.

21. Esther Perel, *The State of Affairs: Rethinking Infidelity* (New York: Harper, 2017), 11.
22. Ana M. Beltrán-Morillas, Laura Villanueva-Moya, M. Dolores Sánchez-Hernández, María Alonso-Ferres, Marta Garrido-Macías, and Francisca Expósito, "Infidelity in the Adolescence Stage: The Roles of Negative Affect, Hostility, and Psychological Well-Being," *International Journal of Environmental Research and Public Health* 20, no. 5 (March 1, 2023): 4114, https://doi.org/10.3390/ijerph20054114.
23. Beltrán-Morillas et al., "Infidelity in the Adolescent Stage."
24. Roy F. Baumeister and Sara R. Wotman, *Breaking Hearts: The Two Sides of Unrequited Love* (New York: Guilford Press, 1992), 105–8.
25. Lexie Kane, "The Peak-End Rule: How Impressions Become Memories," Nielsen Norman Group, December 30, 2018, https://www.nngroup.com/articles/peak-end-rule/.

Epilogue

1. Sandra J. E. Langeslag, Jamie R. Olivier, Martine E. Köhlen, Ilse M. Nijs, and Jan W. Van Strien, "Increased Attention and Memory for Beloved-Related Information during Infatuation: Behavioral and Electrophysiological Data," *Social Cognitive and Affective Neuroscience* 10, no. 1 (January 2015): 136–44, https://doi.org/10.1093/scan/nsu034.
2. Laurence Steinberg, *Age of Opportunity: Lessons from the New Science of Adolescence* (Boston: Houghton Mifflin Harcourt, 2014), 21.
3. Mengya Xia, Gregory M. Fosco, Melissa A. Lippold, and Mark E. Feinberg, "A Developmental Perspective on Young Adult Romantic Relationships: Examining Family and Individual Factors in Adolescence," *Journal of Youth and Adolescence* 47, no. 7 (July 2018): 1499–516, https://doi.org/10.1007/s10964-018-0815-8.
4. Lori Gottlieb, "Dear Therapist: I Still Obsess about My Ex from a Decade Ago," *Atlantic*, May 23, 2018, https://www.theatlantic.com/family/archive/2018/05/dear-therapist-get-over-ex/560966/.
5. James G. Pfaus, Tod E. Kippin, Genaro A. Coria-Avila, Hélène Gelez, Veronica M. Afonso, Nafissa Ismail, and Mayte Parada, "Who, What, Where, When (and Maybe Even Why)? How the Experience of Sexual Reward Connects Sexual Desire, Preference, and Performance," *Archives of Sexual Behavior* 41, no. 1 (February 2012): 31–62, https://doi.org/10.1007/s10508-012-9935-5.
6. Pfaus et al., "Who, What, Where, When."
7. Quoted by Yowei Shaw, "A Very Offensive Rom-Com," April 5, 2019, season 5, episode 5, in *Invisibilia*, produced by Yowei Shaw, podcast, MP3 audio, 1:01:02, https://www.npr.org/programs/invisibilia/710046991/a-very-offensive-rom-com.
8. Cristina Nehring, *A Vindication of Love: Reclaiming Romance for the Twenty-First Century* (New York: Harper, 2009), 193.

9. Jefferson A. Singer, *Memories That Matter: How to Use Self-Defining Memories to Understand & Change Your Life* (Oakland, CA: New Harbinger, 2005), 26.

10. Lisa Damour, *The Emotional Lives of Teenagers: Raising Connected, Capable, and Compassionate Adolescents* (New York: Ballantine Books, 2023).

Select Bibliography and Resources

The Ace and Aro Advocacy Project. "Identity Terminology." 2020. https://taaap. org/learn/identity-terminology/.

Brown, Emma. *How to Raise a Boy: Classrooms, Locker Rooms, Bedrooms, and the Hidden Struggles of American Boyhood*. New York: One Signal, 2021.

Brown, Lucy L., and Helen Fisher. *The Anatomy of Love: Know Thy Brain, Know Thy Self, Know Thy Partner* (blog). Accessed May 14, 2024. https:// theanatomyoflove.com/.

The Center for Parent & Teen Communication. Accessed May 15, 2024. https:// parentandteen.com/.

Centers for Disease Control and Prevention. *Youth Risk Behavior Survey: Data Summary and Trends Report*. Washington, DC: Centers for Disease Control and Prevention, 2021. https://www.cdc.gov/healthyyouth/data/yrbs/ pdf/YRBS_Data-Summary-Trends_Report2023_508.pdf.

Common Sense Media. "Teens and Pornography." January 10, 2023. https:// www.commonsensemedia.org/research/teens-and-pornography.

Corinna, Heather. *S.E.X.: The All-You-Need-to-Know Sexuality Guide to Get You through Your Teens and Twenties*. 2nd edition. New York: DaCapo Press/Perseus Books, 2016.

Damour, Lisa. *The Emotional Lives of Teenagers: Raising Connected, Capable, and Compassionate Adolescents*. New York: Ballantine Books, 2023.

———. *Untangled: Guiding Teenage Girls through the Seven Transitions into Adulthood*. New York: Ballantine Books, 2017.

Davila, Joanne, and Kaycee Lashman. *The Thinking Girl's Guide to the Right Guy: How Knowing Yourself Can Help You Navigate Dating, Hookups, and Love*. New York: Guilford Press, 2016.

Erikson, Erik H. *Identity, Youth, and Crisis*. New York: W. W. Norton, 1968.

Fisher, Helen. *Why We Love: The Nature and Chemistry of Romantic Love*. New York: Holt Paperbacks, 2005.

Furman, Wyndol, B. Bradford Brown, and Candice Feiring, eds. *The Development of Romantic Relationships in Adolescence*. Cambridge Studies in Social and Emotional Development. New York: Cambridge University Press, 1999.

Hall, G. Stanley. *Adolescence: Its Psychology and Its Relations to Physiology, Anthropology, Sociology, Sex, Crime, Religion and Education.* 2 vols. New York: D. Appleton, 1904.

Hibbs, Janet, and Anthony Rostain. *The Stressed Years of Their Lives: Helping Your Kid Survive and Thrive during Their College Years.* New York: St. Martin's Press, 2019.

hooks, bell. *All about Love: New Visions.* New York: HarperCollins, 2000.

Institute for Sexual and Gender Minority Health and Wellbeing, Northwestern University. Accessed May 14, 2024. https://isgmh.northwestern.edu/.

Jensen, Frances E., and Amy Ellis Nutt. *The Teenage Brain: A Neuroscientist's Survival Guide to Raising Adolescents and Young Adults.* New York: HarperCollins, 2015.

Laursen, Brett, and W. Andrew Collins, eds. *Relationship Pathways: From Adolescence to Young Adulthood.* Thousand Oaks, CA: Sage, 2008.

Love Is Respect. Accessed May 14, 2024. https://www.loveisrespect.org/.

Orenstein, Peggy. *Boys & Sex: Young Men on Hookups, Love, Porn, Consent, and Navigating the New Masculinity.* New York: Harper, 2020.

———. *Girls & Sex: Navigating the Complicated New Landscape.* New York: Harper, 2016.

Perel, Esther. *The State of Affairs: Rethinking Infidelity.* New York: Harper, 2017.

Pew Research Center. "Teens and Youth." Accessed May 14, 2024. https://www.pewresearch.org/topic/generations-age/age/teens-youth/.

Phillips, Lisa A. *Unrequited: The Thinking Woman's Guide to Romantic Obsession.* New York: Harper Paperbacks, 2016.

Relationship Development Center, Stony Brook University. Accessed May 14, 2024. https://you.stonybrook.edu/davilalab/.

Scarleteen. Accessed May 14, 2024. https://www.scarleteen.com/.

Schalet, Amy T. *Not under My Roof: Parents, Teens, and the Culture of Sex.* Chicago: University of Chicago Press, 2011.

Siegel, Daniel J. *Brainstorm: The Power and Purpose of the Teenage Brain.* New York: Jeremy P. Tarcher, 2014.

Singer, Jefferson A. *Memories That Matter: How to Use Self-Defining Memories to Understand & Change Your Life.* Oakland, CA: New Harbinger, 2005.

Solomon, Alexandra H. *Loving Bravely: 20 Lessons of Self-Discovery to Help You Get the Love You Want.* Oakland, CA: Harbinger Publications, 2017.

Solomon, Andrew. *Far from the Tree: Parents, Children and the Search for Identity.* New York: Scribner, 2012.

Steinberg, Laurence. *Age of Opportunity: Lessons from the New Science of Adolescence.* Boston: Houghton Mifflin Harcourt, 2014.

———. *You and Your Adult Child: How to Grow Together in Challenging Times.* New York: Simon & Schuster, 2023.

Steinberg, Laurence, and Wendy Steinberg. *Crossing Paths: How Your Child's Adolescence Triggers Your Own Crisis.* New York: Simon & Schuster, 1994.

Sternberg, Karin, and Robert J. Sternberg, eds. *The New Psychology of Love.* 2nd edition. Cambridge, UK: Cambridge University Press, 2018.

The Trevor Project. Accessed May 14, 2024. https://www.thetrevorproject.org/.

Twenge, Jean M. *iGen: Why Today's Super-Connected Kids Are Growing Up Less Rebellious, More Tolerant, Less Happy—and Completely Unprepared for Adulthood—and What That Means for the Rest of Us.* New York: Atria Books, 2017.

UCLA School of Law Williams Institute. "Transgender People." Accessed May 14, 2024. https://williamsinstitute.law.ucla.edu/subpopulations/transgender-people/.

Vermeulen, Karla. *Generation Disaster: Coming of Age Post-9/11.* New York: Oxford University Press, 2021.

Vernacchio, Al, and Brooke Lea Foster. *For Goodness Sex: Changing the Way We Talk to Teens about Sexuality, Values, and Health.* New York: Harper, 2014.

Wade, Lisa. *American Hookup: The New Culture of Sex on Campus.* New York: W. W. Norton, 2017.

Warner, Judith. *And Then They Stopped Talking to Me: Making Sense of Middle School.* Penguin New York: Crown, 2021.

Way, Niobe, and Judy Y. Chu, eds. *Adolescent Boys: Exploring Diverse Cultures of Boyhood.* New York: New York University Press, 2004.

Weissbourd, Richard, Trisha Ross Anderson, Alison Cashin, and Joe McIntyre. *The Talk: How Adults Can Promote Young People's Healthy Relationships and Prevent Misogyny and Sexual Harassment.* Cambridge, MA: Making Caring Common, May 2017. https://mcc.gse.harvard.edu/reports/the-talk.

Williams, Florence. *Heartbreak: A Personal and Scientific Journey.* New York: W. W. Norton, 2022.

Zaloom, Shafia. *Sex, Teens, and Everything in Between: The New and Necessary Conversations Today's Teenagers Need to Have about Consent, Sexual Harassment, Healthy Relationships, Love, and More.* Napierville, IL: Sourcebooks, 2019.

Index

About the Author

Lisa A. Phillips has written about mental health and relationships for the *New York Times*, the *Washington Post*, *Psychology Today*, *Cosmopolitan*, Salon, Longreads, and other outlets. She teaches journalism and Love and Heartbreak, a popular seminar about romantic relationships, at the State University of New York at New Paltz. She is the author of two previous books: *Unrequited: The Thinking Woman's Guide to Romantic Obsession* and *Public Radio: Behind the Voices*.